Salem Possessed

The Social Origins of Witchcraft

Paul Boyer and **Stephen Nissenbaum**

Harvard University Press
Cambridge, Massachusetts
and London, England

Frontispiece: Part of the Salem Village Church Covenant, with signatures, 1689. Reproduced from Charles B. Rice, *Proceedings at the Celebration of the Two Hundredth Anniversary of the First Parish at Salem Village* (Boston, 1874). Courtesy of the First Church (Congregational), Danvers.

© Copyright 1974 by the President and Fellows of Harvard College
All rights reserved
Third printing, 1975
Library of Congress Catalog Card Number 73-84399
ISBN 0-674-78525-8
Printed in the United States of America

1977

Salem Possessed

We resolve uprightly to study what is our duty, & to make it our greif, & reckon it our shame, whereinsoever we find our selves to come short in the discharge of it, & for par--don thereof ~~to betake~~ humbly to betake our selves to the Blood of the Everlasting Covenant.

And that we may keep this Covenant, & all the branches of it inviolable for ever, being sensible that we can do nothing of our selves,

We humbly implore the help & grace of our Mediator may be sufficient for us: Beseeching That whilst we are working out our own salvation, with fear & trembling, He would gratiously work in us both to will, & to do. And that he being the Great Shepherd of our souls would lead us into the paths of Righteousness, for his own Names sake. And at length receive us all into the Inheritance of the saints in Light.

1.	Samuel Parris · Pastor.	The Women which embodyed
2.	Nathaneell Ingersoll	with us are by their severall
3.	John putnam	Names as followeth Viz
4.	Bray wilkins · 79	1. Eliz: (wife to Sam:) Parris
5.	Joshua Rea:	2. Rebek (wife to John) Putman.
6.	Nathaniel Ingersoll	3. Anna (wife to Bray) Wilkins.
7.	peter Clayes	4. Sarah (wife to Joshuah) Rea.
8.	Thomas putnam	5. Hannah (wife to Jnº (junr.) Putman.
9.		6. Sarah (wife to Benjª.) Putman
10.	John Putnam junr	7. Sarah Putman.
11.	Edward Putnam	8. Deliverance Walcott
12.	Jonathan putnam	9. Peiry (wife to william) Way.
13.	Benjamin putnam	10. mary (wife to Sam:) Abbie.
14.	Ezekiel Cheever	
	Henry Wilkins	
15.	Benjª wilkins	
16.	william way	
17.	Peter Prescott	

Illi quorū nominibus hoc signum præfigitur
+ è vivis cesserunt.

For
Max Willner
W. H. Boyer
Grandfathers

Contents

Maps

Charts

Genealogies

Preface

This book, too, has its history. It began in the autumn of 1969, when the two of us introduced at the University of Massachusetts in Amherst a course, "New Approaches to the Study of History," designed to give undergraduate students the opportunity to explore a single event in depth through the careful and extended use of primary sources. As our first unit of study we chose a topic which had been used successfully for this teaching purpose by Stephen Nissenbaum and others at the University of Wisconsin: Salem witchcraft.

We began our teaching with the usual body of sources which scholars have combed over the years: the depositions submitted at the trials and the spate of publications, both narrative and polemical, which the trials provoked. But what had started purely as an interest in experimental teaching soon assumed a scholarly dimension, as we became aware of an immense body of unexplored documentation about Salem Village, the community in which the witchcraft outbreak first erupted. For example, in the archives of the First Church of Danvers, Massachusetts (the direct descendant of the "witchcraft" parish of 1692), we found extensive records for both Salem Village and its church from the founding of each in 1672 and 1689 respectively—records which included community votes, tax assessments, and lists of local officials. Here, we soon realized, lay buried far more information about the civil and ecclesiastical history of the Village and its inhabitants than was to be found in any existing historical account of the background of Salem witchcraft. These data, in turn, were illuminated for us by a large sheaf of petitions—the residue of decades of Village conflict—which provided almost a roll-call breakdown of divisions within the community. Some of these petitions, with their lists of signers, we found transcribed in the church records, others in the Massachusetts Archives at the State House in Boston. Further enriching these community records was an even larger body of family materials—wills, deeds, estate inventories, lawsuit testimony—in the Essex County courthouse. A previously ignored manuscript volume of sermons by the Reverend Samuel Parris, the Village minister from 1689 to 1696, which had come into the possession of the Connecticut Historical Society in Hartford, proved to be an intensely personal commentary on the community's problems— and Parris's own.

All in all, we realized that here was probably as large a body of first-hand documentation as existed for any seventeenth-century community in British America. Our first impulse was simply to try to bring some of these materials together in a form more accessible to our students and to scholars in general—an impulse which resulted in our jointly edited book, *Salem-Village Witchcraft: A Documentary Record of Local Conflict in Colonial New England*, published in 1972 by Wadsworth Publishing Company of Belmont, California.

But our pleasure at the richness of all this local and personal documentation was exceeded by our surprise at how casually and rarely any of these materials had been tapped by historians. Only one writer, we found, had made any direct use of them, and that more than a century ago. In 1867, Charles W. Upham, a Salem minister, mayor, and U.S. Congressman, who had steeped himself in the inner history of Salem Village, published *Salem Witchcraft*, a two-volume study which, by dealing with many of the sources we had found, began the difficult job of deciphering that inner history.

Even Upham's analysis, however, impressive as it is, remains incomplete and ultimately unsatisfactory. Like most nineteenth-century local historians, Upham idealized the sturdy colonial yeomen who figure in his narrative, dwelling almost affectionately on their petty disputes but often drawing back from confronting the larger patterns implicit in these disputes or from analyzing them in serious political terms. Ever sensitive to the colorful vignette or the quaint detail, he often left out or obscured more significant matters. For example, while lavishing careful attention upon a protracted but ultimately peripheral land dispute between the Nurse family and the eccentric son of a former colonial governor, he barely hinted at the far more crucial rivalry between the two principal families of Salem Village, the Putnams and the Porters. Similarly, he relegated to a small-type supplement his account of the efforts of Samuel Parris's opponents to force the minister from his pulpit, and he neglected (perhaps deliberately) to include the two key petitions which reveal the names of the antagonists and the full scope of the factional battle they were waging.

Of the modern historians of Salem witchcraft, the few who have discussed the pre- or post-1692 situations at all have continued to rely uncritically on Upham's imperfect narrative and analysis. They have ignored not only the manuscript records but also those sources which over the years did find their way into print, including the Salem Village parish records and the Essex County probate and court records for most of the seventeenth century. So far as we can tell, Charles Upham has been the only historian of Salem witchcraft to have read through any of these sources, published or unpublished. Even Marion L. Starkey's engaging 1949 narrative of the witchcraft trials, *The Devil in Massachusetts* (which despite its occasional imaginative embellishments remains the best researched and certainly the most dramatic account of the events of 1692) draws exclusively—and superficially at that—upon Upham for its "background" sections.

Why is it that twentieth-century historians of Salem witchcraft have not bothered to explore the history of Salem Village, or the lives of the men, women, and children who peopled it, apart from that fleeting moment when the community achieved lasting notoriety? In the first place, there have always been other contexts, seemingly more significant, into which the witchcraft outbreak could easily be placed without going beyond the events and documents of 1692: the history of the occult, the psychopathology of adolescence, the excesses of repressive Puritanism, the periodic recrudescence of mass hysteria and collective persecution in Western society. (*The Devil in Massachusetts*, for instance, was consciously written in the shadow of the Nazi holocaust, while Arthur Miller's 1953 play about Salem witchcraft, *The Crucible*, was of course a parable about McCarthyism.)

But beyond this, it is only recently that historians (ourselves among them) have begun more fully to realize how much information the study of "ordinary" people living in "ordinary" communities can bring to the most fundamental historical questions. For too long, such studies were patronizingly dismissed as fit only for antiquarians and genealogists whiling away their declining years amidst the comforting reminders of a fading ancestral heritage.

Today, all this is changing. Employing many different methodologies and exploring many different problems and time periods, historians have begun to discover the richness of the ordinary. This is particularly true in the area of American colonial studies, where a cornucopia of fascinating books—all published within the last dozen years—have shown how the day-by-day lives and problems of people in early New England towns can illuminate precisely those matters which have traditionally been the concern of historians: the essential character of a culture and the dynamics of social change.

As we thought about these matters, it became increasingly clear to us that except for a brief moment, the inhabitants of Salem Village were "ordinary" people, too, living out their lives in an obscure seventeenth-century farming village. Had it not been for 1692, they would most probably have been overlooked by "serious" historians. But—as we have also come to see—it is precisely *because* they were so unexceptional that their lives (and, for that matter, the trauma which overwhelmed them in 1692) are invested with real historical significance. When "Salem witchcraft," like some exotic cut flower, is plucked from the soil which nurtured it —or, to change the image, when the roles assigned to the actors of 1692 are shaped by a script not of their own making—then this terrible event cannot rise above the level of gripping melodrama. It is only as we come to sense how deeply the witchcraft outbreak was rooted in the prosaic, everyday lives of obscure and inarticulate men and women, and how profoundly those lives were being shaped by powerful forces of historical change, that the melodrama begins to take on the harsher contours of tragedy.

We have not explored the larger history of Salem Village merely as a means of understanding the witch trials more fully, nor have we treated the witch trials merely as an additional source for chronicling the ups and downs of a single village's history. Rather, we have tried to use the interaction of the two—the "ordinary" history and the extraordinary moment—to understand the epoch which produced them both. We have, in other words, exploited the focal events of 1692 somewhat as a stranger might make use of a lightning flash in the night: better to observe the contours of the landscape which it chances to illuminate.

As that historical landscape emerged, we discovered some surprising features. All our reading about the events of 1692 had prepared us to view the witch-hunters as a dominant and ruthless group that had taken the offensive against a set of weak and powerless outcasts. What we actually found, as the trials fell into a longer historical perspective, was something quite different: the witch-hunters may have been on the offensive in 1692, but it was a fleeting offensive—counter-offensive, really—in the midst of a general and sustained retreat. Reading about the witchcraft trials without being aware of their pre- and post-history, as we came to realize, was somewhat like reading about the "Battle of the Bulge" of late 1944 without knowing that it was a desperate German counter-thrust in the face of a sweeping Allied advance—an advance which had begun half a year earlier and which would end a few months later in total German defeat. Similarly, the men and women who have gone down in history as the witch-hunters of 1692 were already in retreat by that time, and though it was a matter of years rather than months, they, too, would soon be defeated.

To trace in detail the stages by which we arrived at our present view of late-seventeenth-century society would require an essay at least as long as this entire preface. That essay would surely include the names of Bernard Bailyn, who as our teacher and as the author of *The New England Merchants in the Seventeenth Century* (1955) introduced us to the social and economic roots of conflict in colonial New England, and of Michael Walzer, whose seminal essay "Puritanism as a Revolutionary Ideology" (*History and Theory*, 1963) illuminated for us some of the psychological dimensions of that conflict. And such a foray into intellectual autobiography would also have to include the experience of living through the 1960's; the decade of Watts and of Vietnam helped us realize that the sometimes violent roles men play in "history" are not necessarily a measure of their personal decency or lack of it. These perceptions deepened our sense of the ambiguities inherent in the events we were studying, as we watched Salem Villagers for whom we had developed real sympathy driven to instigate the deaths of their own neighbors.

A word about our collaboration. In the fullest sense, this book represents an equally shared labor. From the original outline (scribbled on a lunch bag one afternoon in September 1970) on through the long process of writing, revising—and revising again

—we have worked together. There remain no chapters, no paragraphs, hardly a sentence even, that one or the other of us would be able to claim as his "property." We would like to consider the book the product of an exploration into the possibilities of cooperative scholarship, an attempt to reduce somewhat the intellectual and emotional toll so often exacted by solitary academic labor. *Salem Possessed* would probably never have been written except as a collaboration; in any case, we believe it to be a better book than either of us could have produced alone.

Our debts, however, extend far beyond what we owe to each other, for friends and colleagues have played a valuable and valued role at every stage: Jack Wilson provided us with our first public forum, a Smith College Humanities Seminar in November 1970, and he has remained a constant source of clarity and good will; John Demos initiated the train of events which led to the publication of our book in its present form, and he has encouraged us at several points along the way; Max Hall, as editor for the social sciences at Harvard University Press, sought us out after a colloquium at the Essex Institute in Salem in the summer of 1971 and, within a mile of Gallows Hill, invited us to submit our as yet unfinished manuscript for consideration by the Press. His confidence, support, and assistance have been forthcoming ever since, and we hope, for his sake as well as our own, that they have not been misplaced.

Several fellow laborers in the field of early American social history have read our entire manuscript and offered extremely helpful critiques: Nell Baum, Richard Bushman, and John Demos. Other colleagues have provided important suggestions on the basis of shorter versions or oral presentations: David Allmendinger, Paul Faler, David H. Fisher, Stanley Katz, Leonard Richards, David N. Smith, and Maris Vinovskis. Kai T. Erikson and Michael Zuckerman commented helpfully on a Salem witchcraft paper we presented at the annual meeting of the Organization of American Historians in April 1972. Hugh Bell and Robert J. Wilson shared specific research findings with us. We never did get to read Richard Gildrie's doctoral dissertation on Salem Town in the pre-1670 period, but in conversation he has confirmed several of our conclusions. Ann Boyer and Judy Nissenbaum brought a skeptical and sympathetic eye to their reading of the manuscript; on questions of style and structure, they were often our court of last resort. Our graduate-student colleagues in the "New Approaches" course sustained an environment of informed interest in the book which proved most favorable to our productive efforts. Two of them, Kate Douglas Torrey and Patricia Tracy, rendered invaluable assistance in checking the accuracy of our citations, maps, and statistical data. We have mined the research projects of several of our undergraduate students in the same course; their work is acknowledged at appropriate points in the text.

We should also like to thank the Connecticut Historical Society for permitting us to use the manuscript sermon book of Samuel Parris; the Reverend Edward H. Glennie and the Prudential Board of the First Church of Danvers for allowing us to use the Salem Village church records; Leo Flaherty, curator of the Massachusetts Archives, and his wife; the staff of the Essex Institute in Salem; our typist Mrs. Eleanor Starzyk; our gracious editor Joan Ryan; and the University of Massachusetts Research Council for a grant which helped us bring the manuscript to completion.

Finally, a word about our policy in quoting seventeenth-century sources: for manuscripts, we have modernized spelling, punctuation, and capitalization to make the prose more accessible to modern readers. For printed sources, we have generally modernized capitalization while retaining the original punctuation and spelling.

Paul Boyer and Stephen Nissenbaum

Salem Village in the Seventeenth Century: A Chronology

1626	Founding of the town of Salem.
1630's	Settlement begins in the "Salem Farms" region of the town.
1653	Thomas Putnam, Jr., born to Lieutenant Thomas and Ann Holyoke Putnam.
1669	Joseph Putnam born to Lieutenant Thomas and Mary Veren Putnam.
1672	"Salem Farms" becomes the separate parish of Salem Village; James Bayley hired as its first preacher.
1679	Bayley resigns amidst criticism by some Salem Villagers.
1680	George Burroughs hired as the new Village preacher.
1683	Burroughs leaves Salem Village.
1684	Deodat Lawson hired to succeed Burroughs as preacher.
1686	Death of Lieutenant Thomas Putnam; a challenge to his will fails.
1686-87	Futile effort to ordain Lawson and form a Village church.
1688	Deodat Lawson leaves the Village; Samuel Parris arrives.
1689	April: Governor Edmund Andros overthrown in a *coup* at Boston. November: Formation of the Salem Village church and ordination of Samuel Parris as its minister.
1690	Marriage of Joseph Putnam to Elizabeth Porter.
1691	October: Opponents of Parris win control of the Salem Village parish Committee.
1692	January to May: Witchcraft afflictions, accusations, arrests. June to September: Witchcraft trials and executions.
1693	Parris's supporters and his opponents jockey for position.
1694	March: The pro-Parris group regains control of the parish Committee.
1695	April: An ecclesiastical council, meeting at Salem Village under the leadership of the Reverend Increase Mather, hints that Parris should resign; eighty-four of Parris's Village opponents petition the council members to take a stronger stand; death of Mary Veren Putnam. May: The council members recommend more forcibly that Parris resign; 105 of Parris's Village backers sign a petition in his behalf.

June: The Salem Village church endorses Parris, who agrees to stay on; Thomas Putnam, Jr., unsuccessfully challenges Mary Veren Putnam's will.

1696   July: Resignation of Samuel Parris.

1697   Parris leaves the Village; Joseph Green replaces him.

1699   Deaths of Thomas Putnam, Jr., and his wife.

1752   Salem Village becomes the independent town of Danvers.

Salem Possessed

The city of heaven, provided for the saints,
is well-walled and well-gated and well-guarded,
so that no devils, nor their instruments,
shall enter therein.

The Reverend Samuel Parris
September 1692

Abbreviations Used in the Notes

EIHC
   Essex Institute Historical Collections, Essex Institute, Salem.

EQC
   Records and Files of the Quarterly Courts of Essex County, Massachusetts, 1636–1683, 8 vols. Salem, 1911–1921.

County Court Records
   Manuscript volumes of unpublished county court records, Essex County Courthouse, Salem.

PR
   The Probate Records of Essex County, Massachusetts, 1635–1681, 3 vols. Salem, 1916–1920.

Essex Prob.
   Unpublished probate records, Essex County Registry of Probate, Courthouse, Salem.

Essex Deeds
   Registry of Deeds, Essex County Courthouse, Salem.

Mass. Arch.
   The Massachusetts State Archives, State House, Boston.

Sermon Book
   Samuel Parris, Manuscript volume of sermons preached in Salem Village, 1689–1695. Connecticut Historical Society, Hartford.

Village Records
   "A Book of Record of the Several Publique Transactions of the Inhabitants of Salem Village, Vulgarly Called the Farms." Bound with Volume One of the Salem Village Church Records in the library of the First Church, Danvers, Mass., and reprinted in the *Historical Collections of the Danvers Historical Society*, XIII (1925); XIV (1926); and XVI (1928).

Church Records
   The records of the Salem Village Church, 1689–1696, as kept by the Reverend Samuel Parris, comprising Volume One of the church records in the Library of the First Church, Danvers, Massachusetts.

WPA

"Salem Witchcraft, 1692. In three volumes. Verbatim Transcripts of Salem Witchcraft Papers, Compiled Under the Supervision of Archie N. Frost, Clerk of Courts (1938)." Copies of this typescript, compiled with financial support from the Works Progress Administration, are on deposit in the Essex County Courthouse and in the library of the Essex Institute, Salem, Mass. The pages are unnumbered.

Many of the documents on which this study is based, including the complete Salem Village Book of Record for the period 1672–97 and Samuel Parris's church records, are reprinted in Paul Boyer and Stephen Nissenbaum, eds., *Salem-Village Witchcraft: A Documentary Record of Local Conflict in Colonial New England* (Belmont, Calif., Wadsworth Publishing Co., 1972).

Prologue: What Happened in 1692

It began in obscurity, with cautious experiments in fortune telling. Books on the subject had "stolen" into the land; and all over New England, late in 1691, young people were being "led away with little sorceries." Fearful of the future, they began to cast spells and to practice "conjuration with sieves and keys, and peas, and nails, and horseshoes." [1]

In Essex County, Massachusetts, and particularly in the little community of Salem Village, it was mainly young girls who met in small informal gatherings to discuss the future. Their concern came to focus on that point where curiosity about future love merged with curiosity about future status: the nature of their own marriage, "what trade their sweethearts should be of." One of the girls devised a primitive crystal ball—the white of an egg suspended in a glass—and received a chilling answer: in the glass there floated "a specter in the likeness of a coffin." [2] What had begun as fearful curiosity was turning to sharp panic. The magic they had tried to

1. Cotton Mather, *The Life of His Excellency, Sir William Phips, Knt., Late Captain General and Governor in Chief of the Province of the Massachusetts Bay, New England* (Boston, 1697; reissued, New York, Covici-Friede, 1929), pp. 130–131.

2. John Hale, *A Modest Enquiry into the Nature of Witchcraft, and How Persons Guilty of That Crime May Be Convicted: And the Means Used for Their Discovery Discussed, Both Negatively and Affirmatively, According to Scripture and Experience* (Boston, 1702), pp. 132–133; testimony of Sarah Cole of Lynn, WPA, I ("what trade their sweethearts should be of"). These occult experiments are sensitively described in Chadwick Hansen's *Witchcraft at Salem* (New York, George Braziller, Inc., 1969).

harness was beginning, instead, to ride them: visibly, dramatically, ominously.

Nobody knew then, or knows now, precisely what it was the girls were experiencing. They never told; perhaps they did not know themselves. By February 1692 it was the grownups who began to try to put into words what was happening to their children: "odd postures," "foolish, ridiculous speeches," "distempers," "fits." [3]

Witchcraft

At first, the Villagers tried through informal and quiet means to bring this strange behavior under control. It was the local minister, the Reverend Samuel Parris, father of one of the first two girls to be afflicted and uncle of the other, who took the initiative. (He considered it "a very sore rebuke, and humbling providence," Parris would admit a few years afterward, ". . . that the Lord ordered the late horrid calamity . . . to break out first in my family.") Parris first called in a local physician, one William Griggs. But Griggs was at a loss to understand the behavior of nine-year-old Betty Parris or her eleven-year-old cousin, Abigail Williams, and warned Parris that he suspected the "Evil Hand" or, in more technical parlance, malefic witchcraft.[4]

If this were indeed the case, the problem was not medical at all, but legal. Those who suffered from witchcraft, after all, were the victims of a crime, not a disease. Still Parris did not turn to the civil authorities. Instead, he took counsel with several nearby ministers who, sharing Griggs's fears, advised him to "sit still and wait upon the Providence of God, to see what time might discover."[5]

But rumors had already coursed through Salem Village, and not everybody was content with such a passive response. At the suggestion of one young Village matron named Mary Sibley, a witch cake—rye meal mixed with the urine of the afflicted girls—was baked by Tituba and John Indian, a West Indian slave couple in

3. Robert Calef, *More Wonders of the Invisible World: Or, The Wonders of the Invisible World Display'd in Five Parts* (London, 1700), excerpted in George Lincoln Burr, ed., *Narratives of the Witchcraft Cases, 1648–1706* (New York, Charles Scribner's Sons, 1914; reissued, New York, Barnes and Noble, 1968), p. 342; Hale, *Modest Enquiry*, pp. 23, 133.

4. Calef, *More Wonders*, in Burr, *Narratives*, p. 342; Hale, *Modest Enquiry*, p. 23; Samuel Parris, "Meditations for Peace," Church Records, Nov. 26, 1694.

5. Hale, *Modest Enquiry*, p. 25.

Parris's household. The cake was then fed to a dog, evidently in the belief that if the girls *were* bewitched, the animal would experience torments similar to their own. A few weeks later, Parris denounced Mary Sibley from the pulpit for suggesting such a "diabolical" stratagem.[6]

By this time, more than a month had elapsed since the girls' strange behavior began, and still no legal action had been taken. By this time, too, the afflictions were beginning to spread ("plaguelike," as Parris later put it) beyond the minister's house; soon they would come to affect about seven or eight other girls as well, ranging in age from twelve to nineteen, and including three from the household of Thomas Putnam, Jr. For a time, even several young married women became afflicted. At last the troubled Village resorted to the law. On February 29, 1692, warrants went out for the arrest of three Village women whom the girls, under the pressure of intense adult questioning, had finally named as their tormenters: Sarah Good, Sarah Osborne, and Tituba herself.

The next day, Jonathan Corwin and John Hathorne, the nearest members of the upper house of the provincial legislature, made the five-mile trip out from Salem Town to conduct a public examination of the three women in the Village meetinghouse. Osborne and Good denied that they were witches, but Tituba confessed, volubly and in great detail, even volunteering a description of the devil as "a thing all over hairy, all the face hairy, and a long nose." After their examination, all three women were committed to Boston jail—where, on May 10, Sarah Osborne would die of natural causes.[7]

6. Deodat Lawson, *A Brief and True Narrative of Some Remarkable Passages Relating to Sundry Persons Afflicted by Witchcraft, at Salem Village Which Happened from the Nineteenth of March, to the Fifth of April, 1692* (Boston, 1692), reprinted in Burr, *Narratives*, pp. 162–163; Church Records, March 27, 1692.

7. W. Elliot Woodward, *Records of Salem Witchcraft Copied from the Original Documents*, 2 vols. (Roxbury, Mass., Privately printed, 1864; reissued, New York, Da Capo Press, 1969), I, 11, 17–23, 41–42 (warrants), 43–48 (examinations); II, 215 (jailing in Boston); Samuel G. Drake, *The Witchcraft Delusion in New England: Its Rise, Progress, and Termination* (Roxbury, Mass., 1866), III, 187–195 (Tituba's examination as recorded by Jonathan Corwin; quoted passage on p. 191); Charles W. Upham, *Salem Witchcraft*, 2 vols. (Boston, 1867), II, 32 (death of Sarah Osborne). A note on our form of citation for the witchcraft testimony: although Woodward's edition of the witchcraft documents is incomplete and often inaccurate, we nevertheless cite it where possible, simply because it is more accessible and more easily usable than the unpublished and unpaginated WPA volumes at the Essex Institute, Salem, Massachusetts. But while our citations are to Woodward, we have in fact checked most of the quotations in the carefully edited WPA typescript, and sometimes silently corrected Woodward's version.

At this point, anyone familiar with the pattern of earlier witch-craft outbreaks in New England—one or two accusations, arrests, and perhaps convictions—would surely have predicted that the matter was now at an end. But, for once, the pattern did not hold. Even with the three women in prison, the bizarre behavior of the girls continued. Once again, the Village strove to deal with the crisis in its own way. Parris held several "private fasts" in his own household, and on March 11 he invited the neighboring ministers for a day of prayer. But in the very presence of these men of God, the children began to behave "strangely and ridiculously"; one even suffered a "convulsion fit, her limbs being twisted several ways, and very stiff." [8]

Several days later, the Reverend Deodat Lawson, a former minister in the Village, came out from Boston to observe things for himself and to give what help he could to his erstwhile parishioners. Stopping at the inn of Nathaniel Ingersoll in the Village center, Lawson by candlelight examined a mysterious set of teeth marks on the arm of one of the troubled girls, seventeen-year-old Mary Walcott. Later that evening, as Lawson was visiting with Samuel Parris, Abigail Williams raced through the house, arms outstretched, crying "Whish! Whish! Whish!" Next she began to pull burning logs from the fireplace and toss them about the room. [9]

In the face of such a display, Parris had no difficulty in recruiting Lawson to help bring these manifestations to an end. On Sunday, March 20, the visiting clergyman delivered an earnest anti-witch-craft sermon in the Village meetinghouse. But even as he prepared to speak, Abigail Williams shouted out, "Now stand up and name your text." When Lawson did so, she added mockingly, "It is a long text." Another Village girl, twelve-year-old Ann Putnam, chimed in too, despite the efforts of those nearby to hush her, crying out that she could see a yellow bird perched on Lawson's hat as it hung from a hook by the pulpit. That Wednesday, when Deodat Lawson paid a call on the Putnams, it was to find young Ann's *mother* prostrate on the bed, "having had a sore fit a little before." [10] Adults as well as children were falling victim to the spell.

Mrs. Putnam rallied somewhat after Lawson read a passage of

---

8. Hale, *Modest Enquiry*, p. 25; Calef, *More Wonders*, in Burr, *Narratives*, p. 342.
9. Lawson, *Brief and True Narrative*, in Burr, *Narratives*, p. 153.
10. *Ibid.*, pp. 154, 157.

scripture, but despite such temporary respites it was increasingly clear that prayers and sermons were not the answer. The community was by now intensely agitated, and once again recourse to the law seemed unavoidable. On the Monday following Lawson's sermon, the fourth person to be arrested, Martha Cory of Salem Village, was examined by Hathorne and Corwin before a throng of several hundred in the Village meetinghouse. As she was led into the room, the afflicted girls, sitting together at the front, cried out in "extreme agony"; when she wrung her hands, they screamed that they were being pinched; when she bit her lips, they declared that they could feel teeth biting their own flesh. In the general hubbub, a Village woman named Bethshaa Pope flung first her muff and then her shoe at Martha, striking her on the head.[11]

Martha Cory joined the three other women in jail, but still the outbreak showed no signs of abating, and now the arrests began to accelerate. On March 23 Dorcas Good, the four-year-old daughter of accused witch Sarah Good, was sent to Boston prison, where for nine months she remained in heavy irons. (Eighteen years later her father would declare: "She hath ever since been very chargeable, having little or no reason to govern herself.") The day after Dorcas was jailed, at the packed examination of still another Village woman, Rebecca Nurse, the torments of the afflicted produced near pandemonium: Deodat Lawson, walking some distance from the meetinghouse, was amazed by the "hideous screech and noise" that poured from the open window.[12] When it was all over, Goody Nurse, too, was committed to jail in Salem Town.

By this time it had become impossible any longer to treat the outbreak as a local Salem Village matter. The next examinations, on April 11, were held not in the Village but in Salem Town, and not before Hathorne and Corwin only, but before the deputy governor, six magistrates, and a "very great assembly" which included several ministers. Ten days later, Thomas Putnam, Jr., whose daughter and wife were both among the afflicted, dispatched a

11. *Ibid.*, pp. 154–156; see also Woodward, *Records of Salem Witchcraft,* I, 50–51, for the arrest warrant.

12. *Ibid.*, I, 74–75 (Dorcas Good warrant); II, 215 (jailing); Calef, *More Wonders,* in Burr, *Narratives,* pp. 345 (Dorcas's age) and 349n (irons); 35 *New England Historical and Genealogical Register* (1881), 253 (William Good's 1710 statement); Lawson, *Brief and True Narrative,* in Burr, *Narratives,* p. 159 (Nurse examination). In this period, "Goodwife," usually shortened to "Goody," was the term most generally applied to married women. The more honorific "Mrs." was reserved for those of higher social standing.

letter to the magistrates in Salem Town hinting at "high and dreadful" news—a "wheel within a wheel, at which our ears do tingle." The news was dreadful indeed: Abigail Williams had charged that George Burroughs, a former minister in the Village who had moved away to a frontier parish in Maine, was himself a wizard—indeed, that he was the mastermind behind the entire outbreak. In a matter of days, an officer was on his way to Maine with a warrant for Burroughs's arrest. A few days after that, the Massachusetts legislature, the General Court, ordered that a public fast be observed through the length and breadth of the colony.[13]

It was now early spring. The prisons were overflowing; exhausting demands were being placed upon magistrates, jailers, sheriffs, and constables; and the entire apparatus by which the accused had been arrested, examined, and imprisoned was showing distinct signs of strain. The basic problem was that while more and more suspected witches and wizards were being arrested, not one trial had yet been held. Indeed, there *could* be none, for during these months Massachusetts was in the touchy position of being without a legally established government! Eight years earlier, in 1684, its original form of government had been abrogated by the English authorities, and in 1689 the administration with which the King had replaced it was overthrown in a bloodless *coup d'état*. Between 1689 and 1691 the colonists had lobbied vainly at court for a restoration of their original pre-1684 charter.

Finally, early in 1692 the colony learned that a new governor, Sir William Phips, would arrive shortly, bearing with him a new charter. But until Phips—and the new charter establishing the future form of government—were physically present in Massachusetts it would be illegal (and quite possibly fruitless) to proceed with formal prosecution of the accused witches.[14] Ironically, then, the most severe challenge to confront the judicial system of Massa-

13. Woodward, *Records of Salem Witchcraft*, I, 101 (the April 11 examination); II, 125–126 (testimony of Benjamin Hutchinson *vs.* George Burroughs, reporting Abigail Williams's charges); Calef, *More Wonders*, in Burr, *Narratives*, p. 346; Samuel Sewall diary entry, April 11, 1692 ("very great assembly"), Massachusetts Historical Society, *Collections*, fifth series, 5 (1878), 358; Upham, *Salem Witchcraft*, II, 139–140 (Thomas Putnam letter), 150 (arrest of Burroughs); Hale, *Modest Enquiry*, pp. 25–26 (the colony-wide fast).

14. Emory Washburn, *Sketches of the Judicial History of Massachusetts from 1630 to the Revolution in 1775* (Boston, Charles C. Little and James Brown, 1840), pp. 132–136. See also, for a more general survey of these developments, Wesley Frank Craven, *The Colonies in Transition, 1660–1713* (New York, 1968), pp. 223–225, 244–246.

chusetts during the entire colonial period came at a moment when that system was nearly immobilized. For the crucial first three months of the Salem witchcraft outbreak, the authorities had no official recourse except to throw suspects into jail without a trial.

Such was the crisis that confronted Sir William when he sailed into Boston harbor from England on May 14, 1692, new charter in hand. Phips's response was swift and bold, if of somewhat dubious legality. Within a few days of his arrival he constituted six members of his advisory council as a special Court of Oyer and Terminer to "hear and determine" the enormous backlog of witchcraft cases. As chief justice of this court, Phips named his lieutenant governor, William Stoughton.[15]

On Friday, June 2, after what must have been a rather hectic two weeks of preparation, the Court of Oyer and Terminer held its first session in Salem Town. The first trial produced the first sentence of death. On June 10, Bridget Bishop, a Salem Village woman who had been in prison since April 18, was hanged.[16] The place of execution—it would come to be called "Witches' Hill"— was a barren and rocky elevation on the western side of the town.

The court sat a second time on June 29. By now it had firmed up its procedures and was able to try the cases of five accused women in a single day. All five were sentenced to die. The jury at first acquitted one of them, Rebecca Nurse, but Chief Justice Stoughton sent it back for further deliberation, and this time it returned with a verdict of guilty. On July 19 the five condemned witches went to their deaths. (When the assistant minister of the Salem Town church urged one of them, Sarah Good, to confess, she shot back from the scaffold: "I am no more a witch than you

15. Washburn, *Judicial History of Massachusetts*, pp. 140–141. Phips's arrival and the creation of the Court of Oyer and Terminer are also dealt with in Calef, *More Wonders*, in Burr, *Narratives*, p. 348; William Phips to William Blathwayt, clerk of the Privy Council, Oct. 12, 1692, 9 *EIHC*, part II (1868), 86–88; Samuel Sewall, diary entry, May 14, 1692, Mass. Hist. Soc., *Coll.*, fifth series, 5 (1878), 360. Since, as Washburn points out, the new Massachusetts charter authorized only the provincial legislature to establish judicial courts, Phips was clearly exceeding his legal authority when he set up the Court of Oyer and Terminer.

16. Calef, *More Wonders*, in Burr, *Narratives*, pp. 355–356 (first session of the court); Woodward, *Records of Salem Witchcraft*, I, 140, 170–172 (Bridget Bishop death warrant). The actual records of the Court of Oyer and Terminer have for the most part disappeared; what are now generally characterized as the "records of Salem witchcraft" are the preliminary examinations of accused persons and the subsequent testimony and depositions presumably submitted in evidence at the trials. (We cannot, however, be sure that all the testimony taken was in fact offered in evidence.)

are a wizard, and if you take away my life, God will give you blood to drink.") [17]

Six more trials on August 5 produced six more convictions. Only five of these resulted in executions, however; Elizabeth Proctor was reprieved by reason of pregnancy, the authorities being unwilling to snuff out an innocent life along with a guilty one. At the execution of the five, two weeks later to the day, the Reverend George Burroughs solemnly protested his innocence and concluded with a recitation of the Lord's Prayer. Afterwards, the bodies (four female, two male) were thrown into a nearby crevice and partially covered with dirt. [18]

And the trials went on. In early September Stoughton's court passed sentence of death upon another half dozen persons. This time, however, two of the condemned managed to cheat the hangman: one was reprieved and the other, the wife of a Salisbury ship captain, was helped to escape from prison. Not so fortunate was Rebecca Nurse's sister Mary Easty, despite the moving appeal to the court she composed after her trial. "I petition your honors not for my own life," she wrote, "for I know I must die, and my appointed time is set; but . . . , if it be possible, that no more innocent blood be shed." [19]

On the seventeenth of the month, at what would prove to be the final sitting of the Court of Oyer and Terminer, nine more persons were condemned. Five of them, however, confessing to the charges, were reprieved. Two days later, Giles Cory of Salem Village (the husband of Martha), was pressed to death by heavy weights progressively piled upon his body. An accused wizard, Cory had stood mute before the authorities, his refusal to plead to the charges constituting an implicit denial of the court's right to try him. His torture, known as *peine forte et dure*, was an established English procedure designed to force recalcitrant prisoners to enter a plea so their trials might proceed. [20]

On September 22 the little company of eight who had been convicted at the two September sittings of the court went together to the gallows. As the cart in which they were riding creaked up the

17. Calef, *More Wonders*, in Burr, *Narratives*, pp. 357–358; Woodward, *Records of Salem Witchcraft*, II, 214–215 (death warrants); Upham, *Salem Witchcraft*, II, 268 (date of the Court's sitting).

18. Calef, *More Wonders*, in Burr, *Narratives*, pp. 360–361.

19. *Ibid.*, pp. 366–367 and 368–369 (Easty petition). Abigail Faulkner of Andover was reprieved, like Elizabeth Proctor, because of pregnancy.

20. *Ibid.*, pp. 366–367.

hill, one of its wheels lodged in a rut; at once a hovering cluster of "afflicted girls" cried out that the devil was trying to save his servants. And when one of the condemned, Samuel Wardwell of Andover, choked on the smoke from the hangman's pipe while making a final appeal to the crowd, the taunting girls shouted that it was the devil who was hindering him from speaking.[21] With these final small dramas, the hangings came to an end—not for that day alone, but for good.

Stopping the Trials: Ministers and the Question of Evidence

But just as prayers and sermons in Salem Village had failed to check the outbreak at its start, so the stern justice of the Court of Oyer and Terminer failed to check it once it had become a matter of colony-wide concern. Even in late September, after nineteen hangings, and with the jails still bursting with more than 100 suspected witches, the accusations and arrests went on. What finally *did* put a stop to the whole process was the direct and organized intervention of the principal ministers of eastern Massachusetts.

From the outset, to be sure, both within Salem Village and beyond, there had been a strong undercurrent of opposition to the arrests, examinations, and trials. Testimony and petitions had been introduced on behalf of several of the accused, and other evidence had called into question the character or veracity of some of the bewitched girls. Daniel Elliot, for example, testified that late in March one of the girls had boasted to him that "she did it for sport; they must have some sport." And after the hanging of Bridget Bishop in June, one member of the Court of Oyer and Terminer itself, Nathaniel Saltonstall, had resigned.[22]

But it was the ministers, at first hesitantly, and finally with a telling stroke, who levied the decisive pressure. Cotton Mather of Boston's First Church, while publicly supporting the trials, through-

21. *Ibid.*, p. 367.
22. Thomas Brattle to "Reverend Sir," Oct. 8, 1692, in Burr, *Narratives*, p. 184 (resignation of Saltonstall); Woodward, *Records of Salem Witchcraft*, I, 115–116 (Daniel Elliot testimony). For petitions on behalf of accused witches, see Upham, *Salem Witchcraft*, II, 272 (Rebecca Nurse) and Woodward, I, 115 (John and Elizabeth Proctor). For a number of testimonies casting doubt on the character or veracity of one or more of the accusers, see Paul Boyer and Stephen Nissenbaum, eds., *Salem-Village Witchcraft: A Documentary Record of Local Conflict in Colonial New England* (Belmont, Calif., Wadsworth Publishing Co., 1972), pp. 92–94.

out the summer addressed a succession of private communications to friends on the Court of Oyer and Terminer mingling encouragement with cautious reservations. On a somewhat more public level, a group of Boston ministers on June 15 submitted a brief letter of advice to Governor Phips and his council. This letter, also from the pen of Cotton Mather, urged "vigorous prosecution" of proven witches but also recommended "a very critical and exquisite caution" in the use of evidence. With this message, the ministers lapsed into an all but total silence that would persist through July, August, and September, while the trials and the hangings went on.[23]

In early October, finally, they acted. They did so under the leadership of Increase Mather of Boston, father of Cotton Mather and himself one of the most influential men in Massachusetts. (It was Increase who had been the colony's chief lobbyist in London between 1689 and 1692, and who had more or less hand-picked William Phips as the new governor; when Phips sailed for Boston, Increase Mather had been on the ship with him.) In a sermon which he preached to a formal gathering of ministers in Cambridge, Massachusetts, on October 3 and which was soon published as *Cases of Conscience Concerning Evil Spirits Personating Men,* Increase Mather delivered an open and forceful challenge to the Court of Oyer and Terminer. The overriding point of the sermon was conveyed in a single sentence: "It were better that ten suspected witches should escape, than that one innocent person should be condemned."[24]

The specific concern of *Cases of Conscience,* as of the ministers'

23. The ministers' letter first appeared in print as part of a "Postscript" attached to *Cases of Conscience Concerning Evil Spirits Personating Men* (Boston, 1693), a work written by Cotton Mather's father Increase. For the younger Mather's other, more private, comments on the witchcraft outbreak while it was still in progress, see Cotton Mather to John Richards, May 31, 1692, and Cotton Mather to John Foster, Aug. 17, 1692, in *Selected Letters of Cotton Mather,* compiled with commentary by Kenneth Silverman (Baton Rouge, Louisiana State University Press, 1971), pp. 35–40, 41–43. On August 1, 1692, a group of eight ministers, including Increase Mather, did gather at Cambridge and unanimously endorse the following cautiously phrased statement: "The Devil may sometimes have a permission to represent an innocent person as tormenting such as are under diabolical molestations. But . . . such things are rare and extraordinary, especially when such matters come before civil judicatures." Quoted in Increase Mather, *Cases of Conscience,* p. 32. This statement seems to have been kept private, however, and not until October did Mather or the other ministers take a further public stand on the trials.

24. I. Mather, *Cases of Conscience,* p. 66. As was usual for important and timely works, *Cases of Conscience* circulated in manuscript before publication.

June letter, was a legal one: what constitutes admissible evidence in witchcraft cases? "It is . . . exceeding necessary," declared the preface, "that in such a day as this, men be informed what is evidence and what is not." The fourteen ministers who signed this preface (thereby endorsing the work) did not deny the Biblical injunction that witches must be "exterminated and cut off," but at the same time (and with considerably more passion) they emphasized that every conviction must be based on water-tight proof of guilt.[25] And Mather reiterated the point in the sermon proper, asserting without qualification that in witchcraft cases "the evidence . . . ought to be as clear as in any other crimes of a capital nature."[26]

In thus focusing his discussion on the issue of evidence, Mather was picking up on a matter that had worried many educated men—the court included—since the first pre-trial examinations half a year before. For although witchcraft was indisputably a crime according to the word of God, the common law of England, and the statutes of Massachusetts, it was, for those concerned with the law, the most maddening and frustrating crime imaginable. This was because the evil deeds on which the indictments rested were not physically perpetrated by the witches at all, but by intangible spirits who could at times assume their shape. The crime lay in the initial compact by which a person permitted the devil to assume his or her human form, or in commissioning the devil to perform particular acts of mischief. And yet these private and secret transactions, conducted, really, in the mind of the witch, were exceptionally difficult to prove.

The voluminous examination records of 1692 constitute a remarkable testament to the magistrates' efforts to seek out proofs that would conform to the established rules of courtroom evidence—that is to say, evidence that was empirically verifiable and logically relevant. While much of the testimony accepted by the magistrates seems today naive or superstitious at best, it becomes more comprehensible if viewed as part of the attempt to fit this ancient crime into a rational intellectual framework.

Of the various kinds of evidence the magistrates sought, the simplest and most desirable was outright confession. Over and over again, the record shows the examiners almost frantically trying to draw a confession from the lips of a person whose guilt they

25. *Ibid.*, [p. ii].
26. *Ibid.*, p. 52.

clearly do not doubt but against whom they recognize they do not yet have a legal case.[27]

A confession was particularly weighty when buttressed by corroborating detail, and it was the effort to secure such corroboration which led the magistrates to probe for those vivid minutiae which comprise the popular image of what witchcraft was all about: broomsticks, blasphemous rituals, signatures in blood. When the Reverend John Hale of nearby Beverly visited one of the confessing witches in prison, he took care to quiz her closely on such matters: "I asked her if she rode to the meeting on a stick. She said yea. I enquired what she did for victuals. She answered that she carried bread and cheese in her pocket."[28] In a community where the reality of witchcraft was universally accepted, the persuasive power of such homely little details must have been very great.

Ranking just behind confession in the arsenal of damaging evidence was trustworthy testimony to some supernatural attribute of the accused. No fewer than six persons, for example, testified that George Burroughs, the wizard-minister, had performed such superhuman feats of strength as lifting a heavy gun at arm's length with a single finger thrust into the barrel. Another man revealed that Burroughs could "tell his thoughts."[29]

Along with these supernatural abilities went certain compensating supernatural weaknesses believed to characterize a witch, notably the inability to recite prayers, even of the simplest sort, with perfect accuracy. Thus Sarah Good, when so required, could only "mutter . . . over some part of a psalm" and appeared reluctant to "mention the word God." Recitation of the Lord's Prayer became a favorite test in 1692. One unfortunate, upon reaching the words "hallowed be thy name," said "hollowed" instead. And thus, when George Burroughs ended his final speech from the scaffold by delivering a perfect rendition of the Lord's Prayer, the

27. See for example, in Woodward, *Records of Salem Witchcraft*, the examinations of Sarah Good (I, 17–19); Sarah Osborne (I, 36–38); Dorcas Hoar (I, 237–240); Elizabeth How (II, 69–71); George Jacobs, Senior (I, 255–258); and Susannah Martin (I, 196–203).

28. Hale *Modest Enquiry*, p. 31. See also, in Woodward, *Records of Salem Witchcraft*, the confessions of Abigail Hobbs (I, 173–176); Samuel Wardwell (II, 148–150); Richard Carrier (II, 198–199); Rebecca Eames (II, 143–146); Ann Foster (II, 136–138); Mary Lacey (II, 140–141), and, of course, that of the first confessing witch, Tituba Indian (I, 44–48).

29. *Ibid.*, II, 113, 119–120, 123–124, 127–128. For another example of alleged mind-reading, see Elizabeth Balch's testimony against Edward and Sarah Bishop (*ibid.*, I, 167–168), mistakenly included by Woodward and others as part of the Bridget Bishop case.

assembled spectators grew restive. Only a forceful counter-speech by Cotton Mather, who was in attendance that day, enabled the authorities to proceed with Burroughs's hanging.[30]

A somewhat different form of supernatural attribute was the "witch's tit"—an abnormal physical appendage, ordinarily quite small, through which the witch or wizard was thought to give suck to the devil in the form of a bird, a turtle, or some other small creature. While the "witch's tit" was part of the vulgar lore which the authorities generally tried to suppress in 1692, it did have the advantage, like supernatural strength or the inability to pray, of being empirically verifiable, and thus it, too, figured prominently in the evidence. The accused were subjected to exhaustive and conscientious bodily examinations by physicians or midwives searching for this evidence of guilt. On the morning of June 2, for example, a committee of nine reputable women (probably midwives) administered physical examinations to five accused women and reported that on three of them they had discovered "a preternatural excrescence of flesh between the pudendum and anus, much like to teats, and not usual in women." But to confirm their finding they re-examined the three that afternoon, and this time reported that all of them appeared normal.[31]

These two categories of evidence, direct confession and empirical proof of supernatural attributes, were by far the strongest and most acceptable. Indeed, they are the only two which Increase Mather unqualifiedly endorsed as sufficient to justify conviction and execution.[32]

30. *Ibid.*, I, 19 (Sarah Good); Calef, *More Wonders*, in Burr, *Narratives*, pp. 347 ("Hallowed be thy name") and 361 (Burroughs' execution).

31. Woodward, *Records of Salem Witchcraft*, I, 146–148. For an interesting discussion of this form of medical evidence, relating it to the current state of gynecological knowledge, see Sanford J. Fox, *Science and Justice: The Massachusetts Witchcraft Trials* (Baltimore, The Johns Hopkins University Press, 1968), pp. 75–90.

32. I. Mather, *Cases of Conscience*, pp. 59, 65–66. The one 1692 conviction Mather explicitly endorsed was that of George Burroughs, the only executed person against whom non-spectral testimony of supernatural strength figured prominently. "I was not myself present at any of the trials, excepting one, *viz.*, that of George Burroughs; had I been one of the judges, I could not have acquitted him." *Ibid.*, unpaginated "Postscript." Interestingly, however, while Mather cited "conjuring," the use of "spells and charms," and the performance of feats "which are above human strength" as examples of empirically verifiable proofs (p. 66), he did not include the "witch's tit" in this category. On the other hand, he neglected to refer to unusual physical appendages when discussing the various "tests" he did not consider sufficient for conviction. It would appear that Mather made a deliberate decision, in composing *Cases of Conscience*, to pass in silence over this troublesome and controversial issue.

But although Mather was unwilling to accept it, there was another form of empirical evidence which, at least to magistrates caught up in the press of actual examinations, seemed only slightly less persuasive: anger followed by mischief. Typically, such testimony would recount how the accused witch, at some point in the past, had become angered at a second party—so angered as to express or imply a threat—and how this encounter had been shortly followed by some misfortune befalling the threatened party. Sometimes the damage was to his property—livestock which took sick, most often[33]—but just as frequently it was to his person or to the person of a relative.

One elderly Salem Villager, Bray Wilkins, reported a particularly painful instance of such personally directed mischief. His granddaughter's husband, John Willard, finding himself accused of witchcraft, had come to visit Wilkins to ask for prayer; but the latter, pleading the press of other responsibilities, had denied the request. When the two men next met, Willard had given Wilkins a piercing glance and almost at once, the old man later testified, "my water was suddenly stopped and I had no benefit of nature, but was like a man on a rack."[34] This bladder difficulty persisted until Willard was safely in irons, when Bray Wilkins finally had relief.

At its most serious, such demonic mischief actually took the life of the victim. It was, for example, doubly damning to John Willard when, a few days after his encounters with Bray Wilkins, another kinsman, Daniel Wilkins, died an unexpected and agonizing death at the age of seventeen. Thus the protean crime of witchcraft could involve murder itself, sometimes even mass murder: Mrs. Ann Putnam accused Rebecca Nurse of bewitching to death no fewer than fourteen people![35]

33. See, for example, the testimony of Samuel and Mary Abbey against Sarah Good in Woodward, *Records of Salem Witchcraft*, I, 25.

34. Wilkins' account of his ordeal is in *ibid.*, II, 8–10; quoted passage on p. 9.

35. *Ibid.*, II, 6–8, 11–18 (the death of Daniel Wilkins). Mrs. Putnam's testimony (*ibid.*, I, 94–95) is worth quoting: "[T]he apparition of Rebekah Nurse told me she had killed Benjamin Holton and John Fuller and Rebekah Shepard, and she also told me that she and [two other witches] . . . had killed young Jno. Putnam's child . . . . And immediately there did appear to me six children in winding sheets . . . and they told me that they were my sister Baker's children of Boston, and that Goody Nurs and [two other witches] . . . had murdered them, and charged me to go and tell these things to the magistrates or else they would tear me to pieces, for their blood did cry out for vengeance. Also there appeared to me my own sister Bayley and three of her children in winding sheets, and told me that Goody Nurs had murdered them."

But powerful as such evidence might be, it was flawed, and Increase Mather for one recognized the flaw. For although two steps in the process could be empirically verified—the anger and the mischief—the third (that is, the actual performance of the evil deed by the accused), was extremely hard to prove since it was carried out through a supernatural intermediary. Accordingly, in the examinations, evidence of anger followed by mischief was clearly most weighty when the connection was most direct: the piercing glance or its equivalent followed *immediately* by the evil consequences. It was widely noted that as Bridget Bishop was led into the Salem Town courthouse for her trial, she cast her eye on the place of worship across the square and *at that very moment* a heavy roof timber inside the meetinghouse came crashing to the floor. John and Hannah Putnam testified that at just the time John was accusing Rebecca Nurse of witchcraft, their eight-week-old infant, "as well and as thriving a child as most," fell into "strange and violent fits" and within forty-eight hours was dead. And Samuel and Mary Abbey, after describing what seemed to them a long-standing correlation between their relations with Sarah Good and the health of their livestock, concluded with a clinching piece of evidence: at the very hour of Sarah Good's arrest, a cow which had lain dying that very morning suddenly recovered "and could rise so well as if she had ailed nothing." [36]

In their effort to establish a probable connection between instances of misfortune and the malefic will of particular persons, the authorities introduced the practice of stationing the afflicted girls together in the examination room and observing them closely for signs of pain when an accused witch was brought in. (In an extension of this process, the accused witch would then be required to touch the sufferers, and their response—usually instant recovery—would again be noted and entered as part of the record.)[37]

While these public tests helped create the bedlam which emerges so vividly from surviving accounts of the examinations, and although these tests ultimately did much to discredit the entire proceedings, they were, in fact, rooted in the magistrates' determina-

36. Cotton Mather, *The Wonders of the Invisible World. Observations as well Historical as Theological, upon the Nature, the Number, and the Operations of the Devil* (Boston, 1693), excerpted in Burr, *Narratives*, p. 229 (Bridget Bishop and the crashing timber); Woodward, *Records of Salem Witchcraft*, I, 95–96 (testimony of John and Hannah Putnam), and 25 (testimony of Samuel and Mary Abbey).

37. See, for example, the account of Captain John Alden (an accused wizard) in Calef, *More Wonders*, in Burr, *Narratives*, p. 354.

tion to accept only evidence which they could verify or which, as in this instance, they could observe with their own eyes. It was consistent with their larger effort to cope with this most baffling of all crimes without betraying their sense of due process and empirical method.

But once again, Increase Mather emphatically rejected such tests. In the first place, they involved a dangerous toying with Satan's power; but also, and equally important, they too easily lent themselves to fakery and deception. *Cases of Conscience* called attention to an obvious fact that had become blurred in the quest for empirical proof: central to the validity of any evidence was the trustworthiness of its source and the circumstances under which it was secured. Thus Mather repeatedly emphasized the importance of relying only upon "credible" witnesses who were willing to testify under oath, and he pointedly related the story of a 1664 English witchcraft case in which a supposedly bewitched child had practiced blatant deception.[38]

There remained one final category of evidence, and it was the one which caused by far the greatest difficulty to the authorities in 1692. This was spectral evidence: testimony about supernatural visitations from some demonic creature—perhaps Satan himself?—who appeared in the specter (that is, shape) of an accused witch. At times these specters attempted actual bodily harm, as they did when "afflicting" the bewitched girls, and as one did against John Cook: "One morning about sun rising, as I was in bed before I rose, I saw Goodwife Bishop [that is, her specter] . . . stand in the chamber by the window. And she looked on me and grinned on me, and presently struck me on the side of the head, which did very much hurt me. And then I saw her go out under the end window at a little crevice about so big as I could thrust my hand into."[39]

---

38. I. Mather, *Cases of Conscience*, pp. 43–45. Other instances of false and malicious accusations are cited by Mather on pp. 27 and 64. In addition to stressing the danger of malicious deception and the hazard of relying on Satanically-inspired displays as evidence (pp. 49, 50), Mather also pointed out (p. 51) that the seizures experienced by the afflicted in the presence of the accused might "proceed from nature and the power of imagination." In developing these ideas, and in stressing the importance of relying only on "credible" witnesses, Mather came very close (though only by inference) to repudiating entirely the testimony of the afflicted girls of Salem Village. Individuals suffering from such fits and visions, he says (p. 41), are "Daemoniacks" and "no juror can with a safe conscience look on the testimony of such as sufficient to take away the life of a man."

39. Woodward, *Records of Salem Witchcraft*, I, 165.

In a variant form of spectral testimony, the witness would describe how the images of recently deceased persons had appeared and identified the individual who had caused their death. In early May 1692, for example, young Ann Putnam testified that a pair of female figures had appeared to her: "The two women turned their faces towards me, and looked as pale as a white wall, and told me that they were Mr. Burroughs's first two wives, and he had murdered them. And one told me that she was his first wife, and he [had] stabbed her under the left arm and put a piece of sealing wax on the wound. And she pulled aside the winding sheet and showed me the place." [40] In its dense specificity—the precise time of day, the grin, the left arm, the sealing wax, the shroud—such testimony possessed a superficial resemblance to firm empirical evidence. Yet this kind of evidence was, for two reasons, especially tenuous and uncertain. First, how could anyone be certain that Satan would not appear in the shape of an innocent or even a godly person? (After all, what would more satisfy his demonic purposes than to besmear the reputations of his enemies, God's pious servants?)

Second, even if it could be agreed that Satan lacked the power to deceive in this way, spectral evidence remained almost impossible to verify. For the specters were usually visible only to the person or persons for whom the visitation—vision, really—was intended. Others might be present, but they could see nothing. For example, Benjamin Hutchinson was with young Abigail Williams at eleven o'clock on the morning of April 21, 1692, when Abigail spotted the figure of a short, dark man. It turned out to be George Burroughs, who was in Maine at the time. When Hutchinson asked her "whereabout this little man stood," she replied: "Just where the cart wheel went along." Hutchinson went on to report:

> I had a three-tined iron fork in my hand and I threw it where she said he stood. And she presently fell in a little fit, and when it was over she said, "You have torn his coat, for I heard it tear." "Whereabouts," said I. "On one side," said she. Then we came into the house of Lieut. Ingersoll, and I went into the great room and Abigail came in and said, "There he stands." I said, "Where? Where?" and presently drew my rapier. But he immediately was gone, as she said. Then said she, "There is a gray cat." Then I said, "Whereabouts doth she stand?" "There!" she said,

40. *Ibid.*, II, 115–116.

"There!" Then I struck with my rapier. Then she fell in a fit, and when it was over she said, "You killed her." [41]

No issue was more troublesome in 1692 than that of spectral evidence. In actual practice, spectral testimony was included as part of the dossier assembled before the trials, but it was clearly considered somewhat suspect, and the magistrates always took pains to buttress it where they could with other, more empirical, forms of evidence.

To Increase Mather, however, even this compromise was unpalatable. In *Cases of Conscience,* Mather condemned without qualification the use of spectral evidence. Like the tests by which the sufferings of the afflicted were turned on or off with a glance or a touch, it was a dangerous dependence on the devil himself for evidence. To those who contended that spectral evidence could be trusted because a just God would surely not allow innocent persons to suffer because of it, *Cases of Conscience* pointed out that such assumptions implied a restraint upon God's absolute power and were thus "bold usurpations upon [His] spotless sovereignty." [42] The God of John Calvin would not be held accountable to the requirements of merely human justice.

And so, with the inexorable logical thoroughness of the Puritan sermon form, Increase Mather examined each of the kinds of evidence being used in the witchcraft cases—and found most of them wanting.

This is not to portray Mather as a lone and heroic figure battling for a return to reason in a society gone mad with witch hysteria. He was speaking soberly and calmly to men who shared his fundamental concerns, pointing out to them where they had gone off the track. It was this core of shared assumptions about the legal process

41. *Ibid.,* II, 125–126.
42. I. Mather, *Cases of Conscience,* [p. ii]. (This quoted passage is from the preface signed by the fourteen ministers, but Mather himself makes the same point on p. 17 of *Cases of Conscience.*) Robert Middlekauff develops this idea in his *The Mathers: Three Generations of Puritan Intellectuals, 1596–1728* (New York, 1971), pp. 154–155. Interestingly enough, the Mathers' opponent, Robert Calef, makes a similar point in challenging the trials: Robert Calef to Cotton Mather, November 24, 1693, quoted in Calef, *More Wonders,* in Burr, *Narratives,* p. 331. While the attack on spectral evidence is Mather's concern throughout much of *Cases of Conscience,* his position is perhaps most forcibly and succinctly stated on p. 34: "This then I declare and testify, that to take away the life of anyone, merely because a spectre or devil in a bewitched or possessed person does accuse them, will bring the guilt of innocent blood on the land."

and the nature of evidence which gave such great force to *Cases of Conscience*. Nobody disputed its conclusions, for it was simply the summing up and clarification of an intellectual process that was already well underway when it appeared. Throughout 1692, under implacable and unrelieved pressure to act, successive levels of authority in Massachusetts had been trying to formulate procedures and standards of evidence for dealing with an unprecedented social and legal crisis. Their effort has sometimes been portrayed as little more than thinly disguised hysteria and superstition bent on extinguishing as many lives as possible.

By twentieth-century standards, of course, the entire episode was simply a matter of "superstition." Undeniably, too, there were instances of gross injustice—injustice by the standards of that day as well as those of our own. But when all this has been conceded, what emerges most strongly from the record is the sense of a society, confronted with a tenacious outbreak of a particularly baffling crime at a time of severe political and legal disruption, nevertheless striving, in an equitable way, to administer justice and to restore order. The sober conclusion of the Reverend John Hale, in a work written shortly after the episode and in fact sharply critical of some of its legal aspects, cannot be ignored: "I observed in the prosecution of these affairs that there was in the justices, judges, and others concerned, a conscientious endeavor to do the thing that was right."[43]

Since the trial records have not survived, no one knows how much weight the Court of Oyer and Terminer gave to the spectral testimony gathered by the magistrates in their preliminary investigations. But as the summer wore on, a general uneasiness emerged, especially as it became apparent that executions were no more successful than fasting and prayer in putting a stop to things.

Cases of Conscience crystallized that growing uneasiness. On October 12 Phips informed the Privy Council that he had forbidden any further imprisonments or trials for witchcraft. On the twenty-sixth a bill was introduced in the Massachusetts legislature calling for a formal convocation of ministers to advise the civil authorities on the best way to deal with the accused witches who were still in

43. Hale, *Modest Enquiry*, p. 27. One modern legal historian, commenting generally on the decisions in all the witchcraft cases in colonial Massachusetts (acquittals as well as convictions) goes so far as to call them "the product of self-conscious and progressive lawmaking by a deeply ethical and religious people in an era of unparalleled scientific accomplishment." Fox, *Science and Justice: The Massachusetts Witchcraft Trials*, p. 8.

prison. The bill passed by a vote of thirty-three to twenty-nine. Coming when it did, this motion was presumably intended to lay the framework for a formal endorsement of Mather's position, with its emphasis on leniency, restraint, and a scrupulous regard for due process. Three days later, Phips dissolved the Court of Oyer and Terminer.[44] In November some of the bewitched girls were sent for by a man who believed that his ailing sister was under an evil spell; but "the validity of such accusations being much questioned, they found not the encouragement they had done elsewhere, and soon withdrew."[45]

Early in the new year a special court of judicature convened at Salem to dispose of the remaining cases. Although four of its five members had served on the Court of Oyer and Terminer, and although William Stoughton was again chief justice, its mandate was sharply circumscribed by Governor Phips: no one was to be convicted by spectral evidence. Forty-nine of the remaining prisoners were acquitted outright. The jury convicted three others, but these three were immediately reprieved by Phips. In a letter to the Earl of Nottingham in February 1693, Governor Phips struck a generally sanguine note: "People's minds, before divided and distracted by different opinions concerning this matter, are now well composed." Three months later Phips felt free to discharge all the remaining prisoners and issue a general pardon.[46]

William Phips may have convinced himself that the episode would quickly fade into obscurity, but the families of the victims could hardly have shared his feelings, and subsequent generations have amply proven him wrong. For historians, the continuing fascination and challenge of the Salem witchcraft outbreak has lain in the fact that a simple review of the events of 1692 raises so many more questions than it answers. The most fundamental of these questions, and the one that really encompasses all the others, is this: since there so clearly existed, at all levels and from the very outset, a powerful will in Massachusetts to end the cycle of accusations—why did they go on and on . . . and on? No one could have realized, back in February, or even as late as April or May, that the

44. Samuel Sewall, diary entries, Oct. 26 and Oct. 29, 1692, Mass. Hist. Soc., *Coll.*, fifth series, 5 (1878), 367, 368; William Phips to William Blathwayt, clerk of the Privy Council, Oct. 12, 1692, 9 *EIHC*, part II (1868), 87.

45. Calef, *More Wonders*, in Burr, *Narratives*, p. 373.

46. William Phips to Earl of Nottingham, Feb. 21, 1693, in Mass. Hist. Soc., *Proceedings*, second series, I (1884), 341–342.

traditional responses of prayer and prosecution would not speedily put an end to the outbreak. Something was subtly different about the situation in Salem Village in 1692, something which no one anticipated beforehand and which no one could explain at the time. What was it? This is the problem which will be engaging us in all the pages that follow.

1 1692: Some New Perspectives

Salem witchcraft. For most Americans the episode ranks in familiarity somewhere between Plymouth Rock and Custer's Last Stand. This very familiarity, though, has made it something of a problem for historians. As a dramatic package, the events of 1692 are just too neat, highlighted but also insulated from serious research by the very floodlights which illuminate them. "Rebecca Nurse," "Ann Putnam," "Samuel Parris"—they all endlessly glide onto the stage, play their appointed scenes, and disappear again into the void. It is no coincidence that the Salem witch trials are best known today through the work of a playwright, not a historian. It was, after all, a series of historians from George Bancroft to Marion Starkey who first treated the event as a dramatic set piece, unconnected with the major issues of American colonial history. When Arthur Miller published *The Crucible* in the early 1950's, he simply outdid the historians at their own game.

After nearly three centuries of retelling in history books, poems, stories, and plays, the whole affair has taken on a foreordained quality. It is hard to conceive that the events of 1692 could have gone in any other direction or led to any other outcome. It is like imagining the *Mayflower* sinking in midpassage, or General Custer at the Little Big Horn surrendering to Sitting Bull without a fight.

And yet speculation as to where events might have led in 1692 is one way of recapturing the import of where they did lead. And if one reconstructs those events bit by bit, as they happened, without too quickly categorizing them, it is striking how long they resist settling into the neat and familiar pattern one expects. A full month, maybe more, elapsed between the time the girls began to exhibit strange behavior and the point at which the first accusations of witchcraft were made; and in the haze of those first uncertain weeks, it is possible to discern the shadows of what might have been.

Bewitchment and Conversion

Imagine, for instance, how easily the finger of witchcraft could have been pointed back at the afflicted girls themselves. It was they, after all, who first began to toy with the supernatural. At least one neighboring minister, the Reverend John Hale of Beverly, eventually became convinced that a large measure of blame rested with these girls who, in their "vain curiosity to know their future condition," had "tampered with the devil's tools."[1] And Hale's judgment in the matter was shared by his far more influential colleague Cotton Mather, who pinpointed as the cause of the outbreak the "conjurations" of thoughtless youths, including, of course, the suffering girls themselves.[2]

Why then, during 1692, were the girls so consistently treated as innocent victims? Why were they not, at the very least, chastised for behavior which itself verged on witchcraft? Clearly, the decisive factor was the interpretation which adults—adults who had the power to make their interpretation stick—chose to place on events whose intrinsic meaning was, to begin with, dangerously ambiguous.

The adults, indeed, determined not only the direction the witchcraft accusations would take; it was they, it seems, who first concluded that witchcraft was even in the picture at all. "[W]hen these calamities first began," reported Samuel Parris in March 1692,

1. John Hale, *A Modest Enquiry into the Nature of Witchcraft, and How Persons Guilty of That Crime May Be Convicted: And the Means Used for Their Discovery Discussed, Both Negatively and Affirmatively, According to Scripture and Experience* (Boston, 1702), pp. 132–133.

2. Cotton Mather, *The Life of His Excellency, Sir William Phips, Knt., Late Captain General and Governor in Chief of the Province of the Massachusetts Bay, New England* (Boston, 1697; reissued, New York, Covici-Friede, 1929), p. 130. As early as 1689, Mather had suggested that afflicted persons might in some way be responsible for their own torments, and that such affliction might in itself occasionally be evidence that the sufferer had had dealings with Satan. Cotton Mather, "A Discourse on Witchcraft" in *Memorable Providences Relating to Witchcrafts and Possessions* (Boston, 1689), p. 19.

". . . the affliction was several weeks before such hellish operations as witchcraft was suspected."[3] Only in response to urgent questioning—"Who is it that afflicts you?"—did the girls at last begin to point their fingers at others in the Village.

It is not at all clear that the girls' affliction was initially unpleasant or, indeed, that they experienced it as an "affliction" at all. Unquestionably it could be harrowing enough once witchcraft became the accepted diagnosis, but the little evidence available from late February, before the agreed-upon explanation had been arrived at, makes the girls' behavior seem more exhilarated than tormented, more liberating than oppressive. One of the early published accounts of the outbreak, that of Robert Calef in 1700, described the girls' initial manifestations as "getting into holes, and creeping under chairs and stools . . . , [with] sundry odd postures and antic gestures, [and] uttering foolish, ridiculous speeches which neither they themselves nor any others could make sense of."[4]

Had Samuel Parris and his parishioners chosen to place a different interpretation on it, the "witchcraft episode" might have taken an entirely different form. This, in fact, is what almost happened, miles away from Salem Village, in another witchcraft case of 1692: that of Mercy Short. Mercy was a seventeen-year-old Boston servant girl who in June 1692 was sent by her mistress on an errand to the Boston town jail, where many accused Salem

3. Samuel Parris, Church Records, March 27, 1692.

4. Robert Calef, *More Wonders of the Invisible World: or, The Wonders of the Invisible World, Display'd in Five Parts* (London, 1700), in George Lincoln Burr, ed., *Narratives of the Witchcraft Cases, 1648–1706* (New York, Charles Scribner's Sons, 1914; reissued, New York, Barnes and Noble, 1968), p. 342. Our suggestion that the "affliction" of the Salem Village girls initially had its pleasurable and even euphoric aspect is reenforced by the evidence available on another witchcraft case in Massachusetts four years earlier. In the summer of 1688, the six children of a Boston mason named John Goodwin began to display unusual physical manifestations. The eldest of them, thirteen-year-old Martha Goodwin, eventually named an elderly neighbor woman, one Glover, as the source of their bewitchment, and Glover was duly arrested, tried, and executed. Young Cotton Mather took a keen interest in the Goodwin case from the first, and it was he who prepared a detailed account of the incident. In addition to noting the children's apparent sufferings, Mather's record includes such passages as this: "They would bark at one another like dogs, and again purr like so many cats. . . . They would sometimes be as though they were mad, and then they would climb over high fences, beyond the imagination of them that looked after them. Yea, they would fly like geese; and be carried with an incredible swiftness through the air, having but just their toes now and then upon the ground, and their arms waved like the wings of a bird." Mather, *Memorable Providences*, pp. 1–9, quoted passage on pp. 14–15.

witches happened to be held pending their trials. When one of them, Sarah Good, asked Mercy for tobacco, the girl, belying her name, threw a handful of wood shavings in the prisoner's face and cried: "That's tobacco good enough for you!" Soon after, Mercy Short began to exhibit the strange physical behavior that people had by now come to think of as proof of bewitchment.[5] Cotton Mather, as her minister, was interested in Mercy's case from the beginning, and through the winter of 1692–93 he spent much time with her, offering spiritual counsel and maintaining a detailed record of her behavior. Mather's notes make clear that what Mercy experienced was far from unmitigated torment. At times, in fact, "[h]er tortures were turned into frolics, and she became as extravagant as a wildcat," her speech "excessively witty" and far beyond her "ordinary capacity."[6] On other occasions, she delivered long religious homilies and moral exhortations.

Although it was generally agreed that Mercy was bewitched, what is interesting is that Mather directed the episode into quite another channel. He treated it not as an occasion for securing witchcraft accusations but as an opportunity for the religious edification of the community. As word of Mercy's condition spread, her room became a gathering place, first for pious members of Mather's congregation and then for local young people. These boys and girls, who had already organized weekly prayer services apart from the adults, "now adjourned their meetings . . . unto the Haunted Chamber." With Mather's encouragement, as many as fifty of them would crowd into the room, praying and singing psalms (sometimes until dawn) and occasionally themselves displaying unusual physical manifestations. At one point during the winter of 1692–93 they assembled every night for nearly a month.[7]

The entire Mercy Short episode, in fact, suggests nothing so much as the early stages of what would become, a generation later,

5. Cotton Mather, "A Brand Pluck'd Out of the Burning," in Burr, *Narratives*, pp. 259–260. This thirty-eight page account remained in the Mather family until 1814, when it was given to the American Antiquarian Society in Worcester, Massachusetts. It first was published a century later, in 1914, in Burr's *Narratives*.

6. *Ibid.*, pp. 271–272, 275. Mather observed similar behavior in Martha Goodwin, whom he took into his house for observation in 1688 (see note 4 above). During what he called her "frolics," which sometimes lasted all day, Martha would appear to be in a state verging on ecstasy, moving about rapidly and talking constantly, "never wickedly, but always wittily, beyond herself." Mather, *Memorable Providences*, p. 19.

7. Mather, "A Brand Pluck'd Out of the Burning," Burr, *Narratives*, pp. 275, 285.

a looming feature of the American social landscape: a religious revival. Mather himself made the point: "[T]he souls of many, especially of the rising generation," he wrote, "have been thereby awakened unto some acquaintance with religion." [8] Nor was this "awakening" simply a Matherian conceit; in his diary the minister recorded that "some scores of young people" (including Mercy herself) had joined his church after being "awakened by the picture of Hell exhibited in her sufferings." [9] Such a mass movement toward church membership, coming on a tide of shared religious experiences, had been almost unknown up to that time in New England and indicates how close the town of Boston may have been, that winter of 1692–93, to a full-scale revival.

When viewed not simply as freakish final splutters in the centuries-old cycle of witchcraft alarms, but as overtures to the revival movement, both the Boston and the Salem Village episodes emerge in a fresh light and take on a new interest. With a slight shift in the mix of social ingredients, both communities could have fostered

8. *Ibid.*, p. 322.

9. *The Diary of Cotton Mather*, 2 vols. (New York, Frederick Ungar Publishing Co. [1957]), I, 161. That the Mercy Short case under Mather's influence nearly turned into a religious revival is not surprising, for Mather consistently treated such episodes not primarily as occasions to expose and destroy individual witches but as opportunities to call attention to the more pervasive social and religious ills of New England. His concern with witchcraft was simply one dimension of his concern with society. In a 1688 sermon occasioned by the Goodwin case (see note 4 above), Mather declared that this outcropping of witchcraft in Massachusetts was merely a symptom of the deeper ills of a society where great numbers of people were "murmuring and repining at the Providence of God" because they were "discontented with their state . . . , their poverty, or their misery." Similarly, in his assessment of the Salem Village outbreak, *The Wonders of the Invisible World* (London, 1693), Mather tried to put this episode to a "good and right use" by treating it simply as evidence of deeper disorders in New England society which needed remedying. The Salem accused, he commented, were "impudent" persons already notorious for their "discontented" frame of mind; the "fierceness" of many social encounters and debates over public issues in Massachusetts, he added, was itself almost demonic in character. But there was a crucial difference about Salem Village: unlike the Goodwin or the Mercy Short episodes, the Salem outbreak was on so vast a scale—involving an entire community and, indeed, the governmental structure of the entire colony—that it was not so readily manipulable as a metaphor for the less tangible threats which Mather found alarming. It was itself, in a literal and direct way, an immediate source of social dissension and disruption. This helps us understand both the urgent whispers of caution which Mather addressed to the legal authorities throughout 1692 and the uncertain, hesitant tone of *The Wonders of the Invisible World*. Mather, "A Discourse on Witchcraft" in *Memorable Providences*, p. 23; *The Wonders of the Invisible World*, pp. 48, 59, 126, 140.

scenes of mass religious questing in 1692. In Salem Village, the afflicted girls occasionally displayed an inclination to ascribe their supernatural visitations to a divine rather than a demonic source. On April 1, according to Deodat Lawson's first-hand account, Mercy Lewis "saw in her fit a white man, and [she] was with him in a glorious place, which had no candles nor sun, yet was full of light and brightness, where was a great multitude in white glittering robes."[10] Similar heavenly visions, Lawson noted, appeared to the other girls as well. And as for the "foolish, ridiculous speeches which neither they themselves nor any others could understand," do they not suggest, in inchoate form, the Pentecostal gift of tongues which would figure so prominently in later revival outbreaks?

Even the more obviously painful symptoms which the girls manifested in their "fits"—the convulsive paroxysms, the hysterical muscular spasms—foreshadow the characteristic behavior of "sinners" in the agonizing throes of conversion.[11] How would the girls have responded if their ministers, their neighbors, or their families had interpreted their behavior as the initial stages of a hopeful religious awakening?

The parallel is underscored if we turn a full 180 degrees and examine, from the perspective of 1692, the first mass outbreak of religious anxiety which actually *was* interpreted as a revival: the so-called "Little Awakening" which began in the western Massachusetts town of Northampton in 1734. Here, as in Salem Village, a group of people in the town began, unexpectedly and simultaneously, to experience conditions of extreme anxiety. They underwent "great terrors" and "distresses" which threw them into "a kind of struggle and tumult" and finally brought them to "the borders of despair." Nineteen-year-old Abigail Hutchinson felt such "exceeding terror" that "her very flesh trembled"; for others

---

10. Deodat Lawson, *A Brief and True Narrative of Some Remarkable Passages Relating to Sundry Persons Afflicted by Witchcraft, at Salem Village Which Happened from the Nineteenth of March, to the Fifth of April, 1692* (Boston, 1692), reprinted in Burr, *Narratives*, p. 161.

11. The extreme physical reaction of people caught up in the grip of a religious revival is well documented both for the Great Awakening and, especially, for the so-called Second Great Awakening which spread eastward from Kentucky early in the nineteenth century. See, for example, the autobiography of the evangelist Peter Cartwright as extracted in William G. McLoughlin, ed., *The American Evangelicals, 1800–1900: An Anthology* (New York, 1968), pp. 47–51. See also Bernard A. Weisberger, *They Gathered at the River: The Story of the Great Revivalists and Their Impact upon Religion in America* (Boston, 1958), pp. 34–35.

the terror took such vivid forms as that of a "dreadful furnace" yawning before their eyes. Even a four-year-old girl, Phebe Bartlet, took to secreting herself in a closet for long periods each day, weeping and moaning.[12]

As in Salem Village, some people of Northampton began to whisper ominously that "certain distempers" were in the air. The town soon became the talk and concern of the entire province, and there were even those who spoke of witchcraft. And, again as in Salem Village, the episode eventually culminated in violent death: not executions, this time, but suicide. On Sunday, June 1, 1735, after two months of terror and sleepless nights, Joseph Hawley slit his throat and died. In the wake of this event many other persons were tempted to the same course, impelled by voices which urged: *"Cut your own throat, now is a good opportunity. Now! Now!"*[13]

In Northampton in 1735 as in Salem Village a generation earlier, the young played a central role. In both episodes, the catalyst was a group of young people who had taken to spending long hours together, away from their homes. In Salem Village, these gatherings began as fortune-telling sessions and soon took a scary turn; in Northampton, they started as "frolics" but were soon transformed, under the influence of the town's young minister, Jonathan Edwards (later to become the greatest theologian of his era), into occasions for prayer and worship.[14] In both places, too, the preoccupations of these youthful meetings soon spread to the community as a whole, and became the overriding topic of conversation. In Salem Village, the afflicted girls dominated the packed gatherings where the accused were examined. In Northampton, church services and household routines alike were disrupted by crying and weeping, again with the younger generation taking the lead.

In a reversal of status as breathtaking in 1735 as it had been in 1692, the young people of both Northampton and Salem Village at least momentarily broke out of their "normal" subservient and deferential social role to become the *de facto* leaders of the town

12. Jonathan Edwards, *A Faithful Narrative of the Surprising Work of God* (London, 1737), reprinted in Jonathan Edwards, *Works*, ed. S. Austin, 8 vols. (Worcester, Mass., 1808), III, 62, 36, 28, 57–58, 70–71.

13. *Ibid.*, 77–78.

14. At this time Edwards was still an unknown young minister; indeed, it was the publication of his account of the Northampton revival that first brought him fame. See Perry Miller, *Jonathan Edwards* (New York, 1949), pp. 136–137.

and (for many, at least) the unchallenged source of moral authority.[15]

Nor were the young the only group whose social position was temporarily altered by the traumatic episodes they had helped engender. The ministers, too, were profoundly affected. In Salem Village, it was to Samuel Parris—who had been experiencing difficulty in filling the Village meetinghouse for weekly worship and even in persuading the congregation to pay his salary—that most Villagers turned during 1692 for an understanding of what was happening. In Northampton, where Jonathan Edwards (the author of the account from which we have been quoting) had been going through comparable difficulties, attendance and involvement in the public worship also picked up noticeably, with "every hearer eager to drink in the words of the minister as they came from his mouth." Even on weekdays, Edwards received unaccustomed attention: "the place of resort was now altered, it was no longer the tavern, but the minister's house."[16]

By encouraging and even exploiting the unusual behavior of the young people in their communities, both ministers had managed to turn a potentially damaging situation to their own benefit. Both drew upon the energies, ostensibly disruptive and anti-authoritarian, of a hitherto subdued and amorphous segment of the population to shore up their own precarious leadership. In each case, the effort was dramatically successful—but only for a time; as it turned out, Parris and Edwards were both dismissed from their jobs only a few years after the events they had done so much to encourage.

But the differences are as significant as the similarities, for when all is said and done, the fact remains that Northampton experienced not a witchcraft outbreak, but a religious revival. With the backing of his congregation, Edwards chose to interpret the entire episode not as demonic, but as a "remarkable pouring out of the spirit of God." Under his guidance, most of the sufferers passed through their terrors to a "calm of spirit" and the "joyful surprise" of dis-

15. The status of the young people involved in the Northampton revival was imaginatively explored in two papers presented at a symposium on religion and society in the Connecticut valley held at Old Deerfield, Massachusetts, on November 18, 1972: Kevin M. Sweeney, "The Rising Generation: The Great Awakening in the River Towns," and Patricia Tracy, "Northampton during the Little Awakening." See also Stephen Nissenbaum, "Cosmos and Social Order: The Sermons of Jonathan Edwards," Senior Honors Essay, Harvard College, 1961, *passim*, esp. pp. 6–9.

16. Edwards, *Faithful Narrative* in *Works*, III, 17–26.

covering Christ afresh "in some of his sweet and glorious attributes."[17] Little Phebe Bartlet emerged from the closet to become
a spiritual mentor to her playmates and her family. When a neighbor reported the mysterious disappearance of a cow, Phebe emotionally bade her father show a Christlike spirit and give the man
a cow from his own herd. (In Salem Village in 1692, such a mischance would surely have produced an accusation of witchcraft.)
Abigail Hutchinson came through her spiritual torments to enjoy,
in the weeks before her death of a lingering illness, "a constant
ravishing view of God and Christ."[18] In short, several hundred
people of Northampton had been . . . not bewitched but converted.

Why is it that Northampton in 1735 ranks in American history
as a prelude to what would become known as the Great Awakening
rather than being bracketed with Salem Village as the scene of an
anachronistic outbreak of witchcraft hysteria? The crucial difference between the two episodes is the interpretation which the adult
leadership of each community placed upon physical and emotional
states which in themselves were strikingly similar. In Northampton
they were viewed in a divine and hopeful light; in Salem Village
they were seized upon as sinister and demonic. While the "afflicted
girls" of 1692 often showed signs of shifting their fantasies to
Christ, describing angelic messengers and glorious visions, their
cues were not "picked up" by the adults, and the girls invariably
lapsed back into reports of agonies and sufferings.

In each of these communities, in other words, the behavior of
groups of young people (whatever may have produced it) served as
a kind of Rorschach test into which adults read their own concerns
and expectations. To understand why Salem Village responded as
it did, we clearly need to know more about the Village. One way
to approach such an investigation is to return to the witchcraft
accusations themselves, looking this time not at the reaction of outsiders or at the surface flow of events, but probing for underlying
patterns which may deepen our understanding of the witchcraft
outbreak and of the community it made notorious.

Some Patterns of Accusation

Pace. By the time the storm subsided in October, several hundred persons had been accused of witchcraft, about 150 of them

17. *Ibid.*, 20, 37, 42, 38.
18. *Ibid.*, 72–76, 65.

formally charged and imprisoned, and nineteen executed. But when it first broke out in February, there had been no indication that it would reach such proportions, or that it would be any more serious than the numerous isolated witchcraft outbreaks that had periodically plagued New England since at least 1647—outbreaks that had resulted in a total of only fifteen or so executions.[19] The initial accusations at the end of February had named three witches, and most people outside Salem Village, if they heard of the matter at all, probably assumed that it would end there. But the symptoms of the afflicted girls did not subside, and toward the end of March the girls accused three more persons of tormenting them. Still, by early April (a month and a half after the accusations began) only six people had come under public suspicion of witchcraft.[20]

It was at this time, however, that the pace of accusations picked up sharply, and the whole situation began to assume unusual and menacing proportions. Twenty-two witches were accused in April, thirty-nine more in May. After a dip in June, probably reflecting the impact of the first actual execution on June 10, the arrests picked up again and increased steadily from July through September. Indeed, toward the end of the summer, accusations were being made so freely and widely that accurate records of the official proceedings were no longer kept.

Status. But it was not only in the matter of numbers that the episode changed dramatically as it ran its course; there was a qualitative change as well. The first three women to be accused could be seen as "deviants" or "outcasts" in their community—the kinds of people who anthropologists have suggested are particularly susceptible to such accusations. Tituba, as we have seen, was a West Indian slave; Sarah Good was a pauper who went around the Village begging aggressively for food and lodging; "Gammer" Osborne, while somewhat better off, was a bedridden old woman.[21]

19. Information on the number of pre-1692 executions has been supplied by John Demos.

20. Our data on the pace of accusations is derived from W. Elliot Woodward, *Records of Salem Witchcraft Copied from the Original Documents*, 2 vols. (Roxbury, Mass., Privately printed, 1864), supplemented by the three-volume WPA typescript, "Salem Witchcraft," in the Essex Institute, Salem, Mass. For a chart showing all the known arrests, with dates, see Paul Boyer and Stephen Nissenbaum, *Salem-Village Witchcraft: A Documentary Record of Local Conflict in Colonial New England* (Belmont, Calif., Wadsworth Publishing Co., 1972), pp. 376–378.

21. For more on Good and Osborne, see Chapter 8.

In March, however, a new pattern began to emerge. Two of the three witches accused in that month—the third was little Dorcas Good—were church members (a sign of real respectability in the seventeenth century) and the wives of prosperous freeholders. This pattern continued and even intensified for the duration of the outbreak: the twenty-two persons accused in April included the wealthiest shipowner in Salem (Phillip English) and a minister of the gospel who was a Harvard graduate with a considerable estate in England (George Burroughs). By mid-May warrants had been issued against two of the seven selectmen of Salem Town; and by the end of the summer some òf the most prominent people in Massachusetts and their close kin had been accused if not officially charged. These included:

Several men with "great estates in Boston";

a wealthy Boston merchant, Hezekiah Usher, and the widow of an even wealthier one, Jacob Sheafe;

a future representative to the General Court;

the wife of the Reverend John Hale of Beverly (a man who had himself supported the trials);

Captain John Alden, one of the best-known men in New England (and son of the now legendary John and Priscilla of Plymouth Colony);

the two sons of a distinguished old former governor, Simon Bradstreet, who were themselves active in provincial government;

Nathaniel Saltonstall, a member of the Governor's Council and for a time one of the judges of the witchcraft court;

and Lady Phips herself, wife of the governor.

Indeed, according to one account, a specter of Cotton Mather and another of his mother-in-law were spied late in the summer. As the attorney who prepared the cases against the accused wrote at the end of May, "The afflicted spare no person of what quality so ever." [22]

22. Thomas Newton to "Worthy Sir," May 31, 1692, 135 Mass. Arch., p. 25; Burr, *Narratives*, p. 377 note, citing John Whiting, *Truth and Innocency Defended* (Boston, 1702) on the men "with great estates in Boston"; Thomas Brattle to "Reverend Sir," Oct. 8, 1692, in Burr, *Narratives*, pp. 177 and 178 (Hezekiah Usher and the widow Sheafe); Charles W. Upham, *Salem Witchcraft*, 2 vols. (Boston, 1867), II, 248 (John and Dudley Bradstreet); Robert Calef, *More Wonders*, in Burr, *Narratives*, pp. 201 (Lady Phips), 353–355 (John Alden) 369 (Mrs. John Hale); Samuel Sewall, *Diary*, in Massachusetts Historical Society, *Collections*, fifth series, 5 (1878), 373 (Saltonstall).

True, none of these persons of quality was ever brought to trial, much less executed. Some escaped from jail or house arrest, others were simply never arraigned. Nevertheless, the overall direction of the accusations remains clear: up the social ladder, fitfully but perceptibly, to its very top. Whatever else they may have been, the Salem witch trials cannot be written off as a communal effort to purge the poor, the deviant, or the outcast.

Geography. Just as the accusations thrust steadily upward through the social strata of provincial society, so, too, they pressed outward across geographic boundaries. Beginning within Salem Village itself, the accusations moved steadily into an increasingly wide orbit. The first twelve witches were either residents of the Village or persons who lived just beyond its borders. But of all the indictments which followed this initial dozen, only fifteen were directed against people in the immediate vicinity of Salem Village. The other victims came from virtually every town in Essex County, including the five which surrounded the Village. (In the town of Andover alone, there were more arrests than in Salem Village itself.)[23]

While almost all these arrests were made on the basis of testimony given by the ten or so afflicted girls of Salem Village (although in some cases they merely confirmed the validity of others' accusations), it is clear that the girls themselves did not actually know most of the people they named. The experience of Rebecca Jacobs—arrested only to go unrecognized by her accusers—was far from unique. Captain Alden, for example, later reported that at his arraignment in Salem Village, the afflicted girls who had named him were unable to pick him out until a man standing behind one of them whispered into her ear. After finally identifying Alden, the girl was asked by one of the examiners if she had ever seen the man before; when she answered no, her interrogator asked her "how she knew it was Alden? She said, the man told her so."[24]

Accusers and accused, then, were in many if not most cases personally unacquainted. Whatever was troubling the girls and those who encouraged them, it was something deeper than the kind of chronic, petty squabbles between near neighbors which seem to

23. Again our data are drawn from Woodward, *Records of Salem Witchcraft* and the WPA volumes at the Essex Institute. The arrest warrant usually gives place of residence.

24. Alden's account of his experience is in Calef, *More Wonders*, in Burr, *Narratives*, p. 353. On the Jacobs case, see *ibid.*, p. 371.

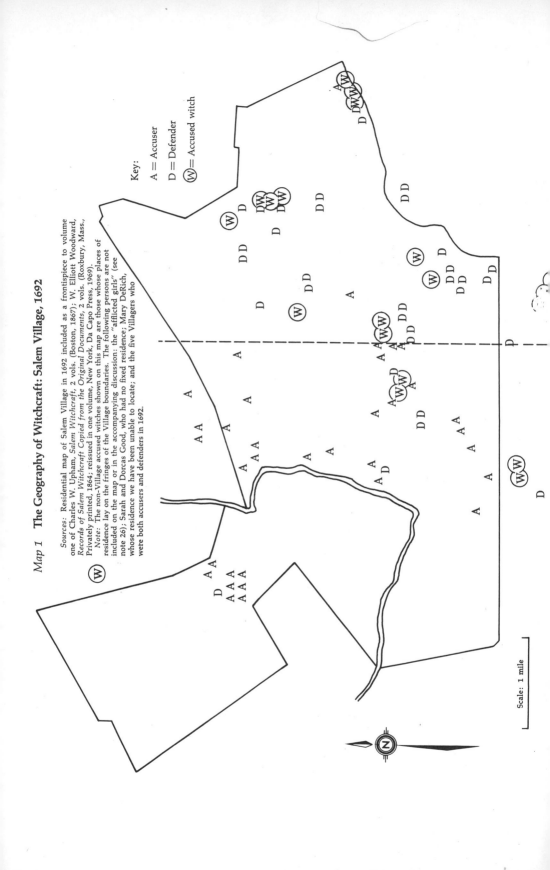

Map 1 **The Geography of Witchcraft: Salem Village, 1692**

Sources: Residential map of Salem Village in 1692 included as a frontispiece to volume one of Charles W. Upham, *Salem Witchcraft*, 2 vols. (Boston, 1867); W. Elliott Woodward, *Records of Salem Witchcraft Copied from the Original Documents*, 2 vols. (Roxbury, Mass., Privately printed, 1864; reissued in one volume, New York, Da Capo Press, 1969).

Note: The non-Village accused witches shown on this map are those whose places of residence lay on the fringes of the Village boundaries. The following persons are not included on the map or in the accompanying discussion: the "afflicted girls" (see note 26); Sarah and Dorcas Good, who had no fixed residence; Mary DeRich, whose residence we have been unable to locate; and the five Villagers who were both accusers and defenders in 1692.

Key:

A = Accuser

D = Defender

Ⓦ = Accused witch

Scale: 1 mile

have been at the root of earlier and far less severe witchcraft episodes in New England.

But if the outbreak's geographic pattern tends to belie certain traditional explanations, it raises other, more intriguing, interpretive possibilities. More than a hundred years ago, Charles W. Upham, a public figure in Salem whose lifelong avocation was the study of the witch trials, published a map which located with some precision the home of nearly every Salem Village resident at the beginning of 1692.[25] Using Upham's careful map as a basis, it is possible to pinpoint the place of residence of every Villager who testified for or against any of the accused witches and also of those accused who themselves lived within the Village bounds (see Map 1). A pattern emerges from this exercise—a pattern which further reinforces the conclusion that neighborhood quarrels, in the narrow sense of the phrase, played a minor role indeed in generating witchcraft accusations:

There were fourteen accused witches who lived within the bounds of Salem Village. Twelve of these fourteen lived in the eastern section of the Village.

There were thirty-two adult Villagers who testified against these accused witches.[26] Only two of these lived in that eastern section. The other thirty lived on the western side. In other words, the alleged witches and those who accused them resided on opposite sides of the Village.

There were twenty-nine Villagers who publicly showed their skepticism about the trials or came to the defense of one or more of the accused witches. Twenty-four of these lived in the eastern part of the Village—the same side on which the witches lived—and only five of them in the west. Those who defended the witches were generally their neighbors, often their immediate neighbors. Those who accused them were not.

25. "Map of Salem Village, 1692," by W. P. Upham, in Upham, *Salem Witchcraft*, I, following p. xvii, with accompanying key.

26. This figure does not include the eight "afflicted girls" who were living in the Village or its immediate environs: Sarah Churchill; Elizabeth Hubbard; Mercy Lewis; Elizabeth Parris; Ann Putnam, Jr.; Mary Warren; Mary Walcott; and Abigail Williams. (A ninth, Sarah Bibber, was from Wenham, and the residences of two remaining, Elizabeth Booth and Susanna Sheldon, have not been positively identified.) We have excluded these eight—even though their inclusion would not substantially alter the geographic pattern which emerges—because, as we have earlier explained, we think it a mistake to treat the girls themselves as decisive shapers of the witchcraft outbreak as it evolved. There is an important additional reason as well: six of the eight were not living in their parents' households in 1692.

What are we to make of this pattern? To begin an answer, we must take a close look at Salem Village before its moment of notoriety. For while outsiders suddenly became aware of the Village in 1692 and pondered the implications of its ordeal for their world, it was the men and women of the Village itself, and its children too, who were most directly and profoundly implicated in the event, and it is their history we must understand if we ever hope to understand 1692.

2 In Quest of Community, 1639–1687

For all the Biblical resonances of its name, the town of Salem, Massachusetts, began as a commercial venture. From the first its gaze was directed outward toward Europe, the West Indies, and the sea. This fine natural harbor, with its network of rivers providing access to the interior, was selected in 1626 by Roger Conant as a likely spot to found a fishing station and trading post. Conant and thirty or forty others had just come from further north on Cape Ann, where a similar venture, established two years earlier with the financial backing of a group of Dorsetshire merchants, had proven unsuccessful.[1]

With the tide of Puritan immigrants to Massachusetts after 1630, Salem prospered, soon outgrowing the narrow neck of land that was its original site; furthermore, the soil there proved insufficiently fertile to supply the food needs of a growing population. Responding to these pressures, the Town selectmen began to make grants of land several miles in the interior: thirty acres to "the widow Scarlett" in 1636, 300 acres to Samuel Sharp early in 1637, 150 acres to William Pester in 1638. After 1639, when the General Court gave the Town of Salem the legal right to settle its hinterland as far west as the Ipswich River (a distance of about seven miles

---

1. Charles M. Andrews, *The Colonial Period of American History*, 4 vols. (New Haven, Yale University Press, 1934–38), I, 344–362.

Map 2 **Salem: Town and Village**

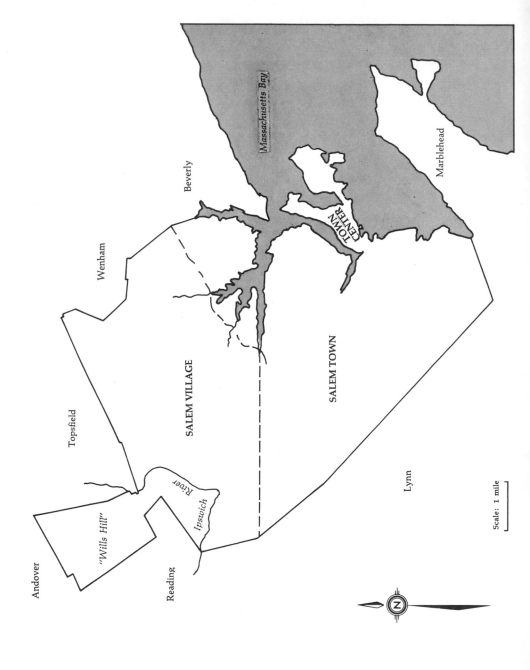

Massachusetts Bay

Beverly

Wenham

Topsfield

Andover

"Wills Hill"

Ipswich River

Reading

SALEM VILLAGE

SALEM TOWN

TOWN CENTER

Marblehead

Lynn

N

Scale: 1 mile

into the interior), the number of such grants increased still more rapidly.[2]

Few of these original grantees actually made the move into the interior, but they soon sold out to men who did; men bearing names —Prince, Putnam, Swinnerton, Porter, Hutchinson, Ingersoll— which would appear over and over again on the witchcraft documents of half a century later. For this was the beginning of what in time would be called Salem Village and then, still later, the town of Danvers. (See Map 2.)

The Place Called Salem Village

But at first the new settlement had no name and no legal existence apart from the Town of Salem. Colloquially it was called "Salem Farms," and its inhabitants "the Farmers." Yet at least some of these farmers (for reasons we shall be exploring more fully in Chapter 4) soon began to chafe beneath the power which Salem Town held over them and to work for a greater degree of autonomy. Salem Town had her own interests in the matter, however; interests that differed sharply from those of the farmers to the west. Though crowded onto a few square miles of coastal land so chopped up by rivers and inlets that it looked like the frayed edge of a ragged piece of cloth, Salem Town still possessed the natural assets that had first attracted Roger Conant, a deep harbor and an excellent network of waterways, and as early as the 1640's the Town had become a thriving commercial and fishing center.

But while it was becoming steadily more mercantile, Salem had no wish to lose control of the rural hinterland which not only increased her tax revenues but provided the food which the Town proper could not supply. The Town's concern over the separatist tendencies of her agricultural regions was intensified when several of these regions did, in fact, break away to become independent towns: Wenham in 1643, Manchester in 1645, Marblehead in 1648, and Beverly in 1668.[3] Clearly this trend needed to be checked, and

<hr>

2. On the General Court's 1639 order, see Charles W. Upham, *Salem Witchcraft*, 2 vols. (Boston, 1867), I, 238. The early land grants are referred to in Sidney Perley, "The Plains: Part of Salem in 1700," 54 *EIHC* (1918), 296, 300, 308.

3. Sidney Perley, *The History of Salem, Mass.*, 3 vols. (Salem, 1924–28), I, 316–317. This work, compiled by a meticulous and incredibly industrious Salem antiquarian, contains extensive genealogical information, verbatim extracts from various public records, and similar primary materials.

when the Salem Farmers showed signs, late in the 1660's, of going in the same direction, the Town determined to take a stand.

From this early and fundamental divergence of interest sprang more than a century of conflict between the Townsmen and the "Farmers"; scores of petitions, resolutions, depositions, and protests bear witness to the tenacity and ingenuity with which both sides pursued that conflict. Sometimes the immediate question seems petty, but the larger issue at stake was never far from view. In 1667, for example, several Salem Farmers appeared at Essex County court asking to be released from the duty of providing men for the Salem Town night watch. The court so ordered, but the Town continued to require this service all the same. Again the Farmers went to court but received no satisfaction. Finally, in October 1667, thirty-one of them petitioned the General Court in Boston for release from the watch, "considering how remote our dwellings are from the Town."

> Some of us live ten miles, some eight or nine; the nearest are at least five miles from Salem meeting-house (upon the road)— and then 'tis nearly a mile farther to the sentry-place . . . , so that some of us must travel armed eleven miles to watch—which is more than a soldier's march that is under pay. And yet [we are] not excused from paying our part to all charges, both ecclesiastical and civil, besides the maintenance of our families these hard times, when the hand of God is heavy upon the husbandman.

In response, the General Court exempted from the military watch "all farmers dwelling above four miles from the meeting-house." Nevertheless, early in 1669 two Salem Farmers were brought to county court by the Town for refusing to participate in the watch and for "highly affronting and abusing" the militia officers. One of them, Nathaniel Putnam, was ordered to make public apology or pay a fine of £20.[4]

Because the Salem Farmers had no ecclesiastical apparatus of their own—no church, no minister, no meetinghouse—they and their families were expected to travel to the Town center each week for religious services. It was on this issue that their separatist impulses often focused and it was here, too, that they finally received some measure of satisfaction. In 1666 a group of Farmers who

---

4. 112 Mass. Arch., 175–177 (1667 petition); 4 *EQC*, 92–93 (1669 court action).

were, in fact, full members of the Town church asked its elders and minister to give them permission to hire a minister of their own, again citing their "great distance from the meeting house." This request met no response, but the issue surfaced again three years later, when the Town voted a special tax for the construction of a new meetinghouse.

Twenty-eight of the Farmers signed a manifesto refusing to pay this special tax "unless you likewise of the Town will share with us when we shall build one for ourselves." But when two Farmers, John and Thomas Putnam, went to the Salem Town meeting to present this petition, they were first ignored by the moderator, George Corwin (a leading merchant), and then, when they insisted, sharply informed that they were out of order.[5] This rebuff was one of many similar experiences which helped convince a large number of Salem Farmers that the powers in control of the affairs of Salem Town were hostile to their interests.

Turning again to the General Court, the Farmers asked permission to build a meetinghouse and hire their own minister. In October 1670 the deputies of the lower house agreed to this request, but the assistants in the upper house refused to go along. In March 1672, however (under pressure from the General Court), the Salem Town meeting at last did authorize the Farmers to take this step, agreeing to release them from paying the church taxes of Salem Town if they did so. The Town leaders carefully noted, however, that for all other tax purposes, the Farmers would continue to be treated as residents of the Town.

The General Court ratified this arrangement, and instructed the Farmers annually to choose a five-man Committee to assess each householder's share in the support of a minister. Holding their first legal meeting on November 11, 1672, the men of Salem Village (as it now began to be called) quickly elected their Committee, laid plans for a meetinghouse, and hired a preacher.[6]

But Salem Village was still far from being an independent town. Indeed, for all its continuing efforts it did not achieve autonony for another eighty years—until 1752. For every purpose other than

5. "Records of the First Church of Salem," typescript, Essex Institute, Salem, Mass., p. 238 (1666 petition); 5 *EQC*, 272–274 (1669 petition and subsequent events).

6. Village Records, Nov. 11, 1672. On the 1670 petition and the General Court's response: 5 *EQC*, 273, and Perley, *History of Salem*, II, 439. Throughout our text we have capitalized the word "Committee" when it refers to the five-member body elected annually in Salem Village for the purpose of assessing taxes.

support of the ministry, it remained a part of Salem Town. Village residents continued to pay their civil taxes to the Town. Their constables were chosen by the Town and usually lived in it. The Villagers were still represented in the General Court by men chosen at Salem Town meeting. It was the Town selectmen who continued to hold the power of establishing the prices at which certain grains and other farm products from the Village could be sold in the Town, of appointing men to handle such ad hoc but important tasks as determining the layout of new roads, and of granting previously undistributed lands in the Village itself. (The only piece of land the Village did control, a tract donated to it in 1673 as the site for a meetinghouse and parsonage, was irrevocably bound over for that sole purpose.)[7]

And even in the ecclesiastical realm, the settlement of 1672 left the Villagers in a far from autonomous situation. To be sure, they could now have their own minister and meetinghouse, but this did not make them a "church" in the contemporary Puritan understanding of the word. For seventeenth-century Puritans, the church was neither a building nor a social institution, but a select fellowship of persons "gathered" out of the total population, those "visible saints" who had felt the infusion of divine grace and banded together in testimony to the power of their experience. Only a minority of people within a given community, even a Puritan community, were entitled to join the church. Those who were not so qualified—collectively termed the "congregation"—were obliged to support the ministry with their material goods and to attend meetings at which God's word was expounded, but the church itself, as an elite cadre within the community, met separately (usually after the congregation was dismissed) to partake of the privileged rite of communion.

As the farmers of Salem Village would have understood the terms, they were now a "parish" within the Town of Salem, but

---

7. Village Records, Nov. 14, 1673; Dec. 27, 1681. Frequent references to Town actions that in one way or another affected the Farmers can be found simply by reading through the Town records for the seventeenth century. They are printed in *EIHC*, vols. 9, 40–43, 48, 49, 62–69, 83, and 85. See, for example, *EIHC*, 41 (1905), 301, for a 1669 measure regulating the transport of wood beyond Town boundaries, and *ibid.*, 83 (1947), 68, for a 1692 Town vote empowering the selectmen to regulate the price at which wheat could be sold in the Town market. On the other hand, Villagers continued to hold most of the rights and prerogatives of full-fledged residents of the Town. They could, for example, participate and vote in Town meetings, and they were eligible for election to Town offices.

even so they had no *church* of their own. They were free to build a meetinghouse and to hire a man who would preach to them and "minister" to their needs, but he could neither usher them into the inner sanctum of church membership nor administer the sacrament of communion; and this was true even of those people who had already joined neighboring churches but who would soon begin to attend services at the Village meetinghouse as a matter of physical convenience. Such persons, when they wished to take communion, had to do so with their home churches.

For years after 1672, then, Salem Village was a distinct community without its own town government, and a distinct parish without its own church. This subordinate status was reflected in a variety of subtle ways—including even gestures of goodwill. The pulpit and deacons' bench in the Village meetinghouse, for example, were second-hand pieces passed on by Salem Town when the Town built its new meetinghouse in the early 1670's. Implicitly acknowledging their ambiguous position, some Salem Villagers continued for years to identify their place of residence, for legal purposes, as simply "Salem."

From the outset, the tensions inherent in this anomalous legal and ecclesiastical situation acted as a seriously disruptive force in Village affairs. And these tensions were magnified by the existence of a split, increasingly apparent over the years, within the Village itself: while some residents strove to define the political and religious power of the Village ever more broadly, others continued to identify themselves primarily with Salem Town. The Town leadership, in turn, playing upon these differences, proved extremely hesitant to cut the apron strings entirely. One chronic source of discontent and controversy, for example, was the fact that the Town persisted well after 1672 in including the Villagers when it levied taxes for the repair and improvement of the Town meetinghouse. In 1674, two years after the Villagers had built their own place of worship, a Town constable seized two and one-half acres of Nathaniel Putnam's land—land which lay directly in front of his house—because of his refusal to pay such a meetinghouse tax imposed by the Town.[8]

8. 5 *EQC*, 271 (seizure of Nathaniel Putnam's land); 42 *EIHC*, 267 (1672 Salem town meeting vote donating old pulpit and deacon's seat to Salem Village). Only in the spring of 1713, after innumerable petitions, was this issue finally resolved and the Salem Villagers definitely released from the obligation to help pay for the maintenance of the Town meetinghouse—Salem Town Records, typescript, Vol. II (1713), Essex Institute, Salem, Mass. We should like to thank Mrs. Nell Baum for calling this to our attention.

Early in 1690, reciting this and other grievances, the Village Committee (the five-member body elected annually to assess the parish taxes) explicitly requested that the Town permit Salem Village to become a fully independent township; at a Salem Town meeting that March, however, this petition was voted down. Taking its complaint to the General Court, the Village Committee noted its frustration: "We have several times made our application to the Town of Salem, but can get no relief." In reply, the selectmen of the Town dismissed the issue as trivial and deplored "the restless frame of spirit" which characterized the Salem Villagers.[9]

It was a characteristic response. On almost every occasion during these years, outside authorities—whether the selectmen in Salem or the General Court in Boston—denied the reality of any substantive political problems in the Village by attributing whatever complaints the Villagers might make solely to some collective defect in their social temper. This was a convenient way of avoiding the issues—a "restless frame of spirit" was an explanation frequently resorted to in Puritan culture—but it hardly contributed to a resolution of the very real problems of political and ecclesiastical identity which these same outside authorities had helped to create and which they were now helping to perpetuate.

The Village's problems were further complicated by the acrimonious boundary disputes it carried on during these years with the surrounding towns of Topsfield, Andover, and Wenham. (These disputes were serious matters, involving as they did the question of whether a given group of householders—or sometimes a single wealthy householder—would pay taxes to one jurisdiction or another.) Through the 1670's and 1680's, by face-to-face negotiation, lawsuits in the county court, appeals to the colonial legislature, and even occasional threats of violence, Salem Village representatives tried to defend what they felt to be the lawful bounds of the Village.[10] But always hovering in the background were the funda-

9. 11 Mass. Arch., 57–60.
10. On the Wenham dispute: 8 *EQC*, 159–161; on Topsfield: *ibid.*, 319–323, and Nathaniel B. Shurtleff, ed., *Records of the Governor and Company of the Massachusetts Bay in New England*, 5 vols. (Boston, 1853–54), V, 415. These disputes often involved the most personal kinds of confrontations. At the time of the dispute with Wenham, the wife of John Dodge of Salem Village declared that "if Wenham men came there for rates [that is, taxes] she would make the blood run about their ears." When a Wenham neighbor taunted her by telling her that she didn't frighten him, she "caught him by the hair of his head and with her other hand struck him on the face in a furious manner." Less violent, but no less serious, was the testimony of two Salem Villagers describing their accidental encounter in the woods with a party of Wenham

mental questions of the Village's *own* legitimacy and its right, as nothing more than a parish district, to assume in this way some of the prerogatives of an independent town. Somewhat defensively, the Villagers always prefaced their petitions with a lengthy set of historical documents aimed at establishing that the Village did have at least a tenuous legal existence of its own. In 1685, when the town of Topsfield claimed some lands occupied by Salem Villagers, the Village asked the Salem Town selectmen to confirm that Salem Village was, indeed, a legitimate part of Salem which had been settled with the blessing of the Town. The selectmen inexplicably delayed for a year and a half before giving this simple assurance, without which the Village was unable to confront directly the challenge posed by Topsfield. One gets the distinct sense that in its early years Salem Village was not taken altogether seriously. In a deposition of June 1679, for example, two Wenham officials spoke in a mildly patronizing way of the dispute between their town and "the *place* called Salem Village."[11]

Neighbors against Neighbors

Salem Village's uncertain status seems, too, to have contributed to a strikingly high level of internal bickering and disarray. In 1679 the Village minister spoke of the "uncomfortable divisions and contentions" which plagued the settlement; three years later a Salem Villager named Jeremiah Watts characterized the community as one in which "brother is against brother and neighbors [are] against neighbors, all quarreling and smiting one another."[12] The Village's experiences with a succession of ministers—James Bayley, George Burroughs, Deodat Lawson, and Samuel Parris—shed some light on the sources of this "quarreling and smiting."

The first of the four, the Reverend James Bayley, a native of Newbury, Massachusetts, began his services in the Village in October 1672—only three years after his graduation from Harvard College. Although the issue later became crucial, the records do

officials who were surveying a line to support their claims. When the compass of the Wenham man proved faulty, so the Salem Villagers reported, "they shook it and turned it the way it would best answer their ends." Depositions in 8 *EQC*, 21–22.

11. Village Records, Feb. 2, 1685, and Sept. 25, 1686. The disparaging Wenham deposition is in 8 *EQC*, 160–161. Italics added.

12. The Reverend James Bayley to the inhabitants of Salem Village, Feb. 11, 1679: 10 Mass. Arch., 140; Jeremiah Watts to the Reverend George Burroughs, April 11, 1682: 8 *EQC*, 294.

not show what procedures were followed in the initial decision to bring Bayley to the Village. The subsequent charge by his opponents that he had come merely "upon invitation of a few" suggests that those procedures may have been quite informal and irregular, though it is difficult to imagine how they could have been otherwise under the circumstances. Still, things seemed to go well enough at first. In June 1673, at a "public meeting" of the Village householders, Bayley was invited to remain in his post. At about the same time, five farmers of Salem Village gave him as a gift forty acres of prime Village land, on which he proceeded to build a house. But that same year also brought the first evidence of discontent with Bayley's ministry when fourteen Villagers fell into arrears in the taxes they owed for his support, and the Village Committee unsuccessfully brought suit against one of the delinquents.[13]

By 1679 a significant minority within the Village, led by Nathaniel Putnam and Bray Wilkins, had turned against Bayley, and that February the minister sent a letter to the Village meeting in which he acknowledged the dissension his presence seemed to be generating but stressed the depth of his commitment by pointing out, in a revealing phrase, that he had invested a "considerable estate" in the Village. In reply, fourteen men of the Village avowed in writing their discontent with Bayley and added sarcastically: "If upon invitation of a few—and that but for one year—if Mr. Bayley should have carved out a considerable estate, we think he might have been better advised." The fourteen concluded with a plea (to be echoed many times in the succeeding decades) for a restoration of "peace and order."[14] But peace by what means, and order on whose terms?

After several additional manifestoes on both sides (and the filing of a suit for slander against one of Bayley's critics), an appeal was taken to the Salem Town church to help resolve the controversy. Accordingly, the Salem church in April 1679 submitted a letter of advice to the Village written by its minister, John Higginson. Concluding that Bayley was favored by "the generality of the people" of the Village, as well as by "a considerable number of such as belong to Salem [Town] still, who do hear him sometimes for their

---

13. 6 *EQC*, 45–46. The various documents cited are in 10 Mass. Arch., 140a, 141, and 142. For biographical information on James Bayley, see John L. Sibley, *Biographical Sketches of Graduates of Harvard University*, 3 vols. (Cambridge, Mass., 1873–85), II, 291–299.

14. 10 Mass. Arch., 140 (Bayley letter), 142 (anti-Bayley petition).

ease," Higginson advised the dissidents to submit to Bayley's continued ministry "without any further trouble." But late in July, noting that this advice had been ignored for "nigh four months," Bayley informed the Village that he was "seriously thinking" of leaving.[15]

At this point the dispute passed from the stage of bitter words to that of direct action. The Salem Village Committee of 1678 had been pro-Bayley to a man, but the dissidents were evidently able to pack the Village meeting of September 11, 1679, for it was there voted to dismiss Bayley at the end of the year, "or before, if he have a call to another place." This turn of events generated a spate of petitions to the General Court. In response, the upper house of that body drafted an edict directing "that Mr. Bayley be continued and settled the minister of that place." But the deputies of the lower house reversed the thrust of this ruling with the amendment that it remain in force for only one year, after which the Village would be free either to retain Bayley or replace him with "some other meet person." Both houses agreed that so long as Bayley *did* remain he should be paid, and warned that if the farmers could not tax themselves properly for this purpose, the power to do so would be restored to Salem Town—a threat which made painfully obvious the Village's contingent and precarious political status.[16]

Difficult as it is to follow today, the protracted "Bayley dispute" is in fact crucial to an understanding of the witchcraft outbreak which occurred thirteen years later. This dispute both exposed and intensified certain destructive patterns of political behavior in the Village which were to surface again and again in the years to come, most dramatically in 1692. For this reason, a simple chronology of the events of 1679 is not enough; we must also try to identify and untangle the issues which provoked those events.

On the face of things, the sole issue was James Bayley himself. Specifically, Bayley was accused of neglecting his church duties and omitting family prayers in his own household. But these charges were never advanced with any real conviction, and they were vigorously denied by Bayley's friends. The sober John Higginson, speaking for the church of Salem Town, concluded that "setting

15. *Ibid.*, 143a (appeal to Salem Town church), 144 (additional manifestoes), 145 (Higginson letter), 146 (Bayley letter); 7 *EQC*, 248–249 (slander suit).

16. 10 Mass. Arch., 146a (Village action of September 11, 1679); 150 (General Court ruling).

aside human frailties, we find not any just exception against Mr. Baily." In the slander suit, only one witness could be produced to testify against Bayley, while four declared that he had been exemplary in performing his domestic religious duties. (Two people even testified that Bayley was in the habit of testing his sermons on his own family before delivering them in public.)

In fact, discontent over Bayley as an individual soon yielded to a broader debate over the nature and legitimacy of his appointment. While some Villagers wholeheartedly backed the procedures that had been followed, others charged that his call had been irregular from the first, and that the wrong had been compounded by Bayley's efforts to put down roots in the community.

In this way the Villagers arrived at what quickly became the central issue: who, in fact, had the authority to call or dismiss a minister in Salem Village? Was this authority restricted to those Villagers who belonged to one of the neighboring churches, or was it held by all the householders, whether church members or not, who regularly attended the Village meetinghouse? The opposing points of view were summed up in a set of petitions in February 1679. "[We] cannot find," said Bayley's opponents, "that Mr. Bayley was called at all by those that were capacitated to do so"— that is to say, by the church members who lived in the Village. But his supporters rejected this argument: "Mr. Bayley was called by a general consent and vote of the inhabitants [that is, all the inhabitants, not just the church members], who by order of the General Court had power and liberty so to do." [17]

For all the other issues that were raised, it was mostly on this one that the dispute turned. Salem Town minister John Higginson, in his April letter of advice, took the position that the General Court's 1672 action permitting the Salem Villagers to call a minister "was not granted to any of them under the notion of church members, but to the whole number of inhabitants there." Higginson advised that those who wished to see a church established in the Village should first "seriously apply themselves to join the church here [that is, in the Town]"; not until some point in the future, "when by mutual consent there shall be a competent number to be a church there of themselves," said Higginson, could a minister be called and a church established, "according to the order of the gospel and the law of the General Court."

But the Villagers, particularly those hostile to Bayley, were un-

17. *Ibid.*, 142.

willing to accept Higginson's advice as the final word. In October 1679 a committee from the Village asked the General Court for "an explanation of the former Court's order [of 1672] concerning our liberty about voting." Specifically, they inquired "who they are that may vote for calling a minister, and for the choice of a Committee." The legislature, unable to recognize (or to admit) that this query stemmed from anything other than ignorance or obstinacy, simply replied that the Villagers should "attend the law regulating voters in this and all other cases, as other towns are enjoined to do." [18]

But this was precisely the point: Salem Village was *not* a town. Twenty-four of the Villagers who had supported Bayley all along replied in a lengthy petition which expressed their eagerness to allow "the law to be our guide," if only they could ascertain what statute or custom actually applied to their case. They readily conceded that in normal circumstances "the law directs only church members to call a minister" but iterated once more the central fact of their peculiar situation: "We have neither township nor church, but belong to Salem, both town and church." They further made the practical point that the "11 or 12 church members" who happened to reside within the Village bounds were themselves evenly divided over Bayley, so that the decision by default fell to the non-church members. In a crucial passage, the signers of this petition urged the General Court to grant its approval to the de facto situation which had developed in the Village:

> Our humble request is that this honored Court will be pleased to give liberty to all our freeholders that aren't scandalous to vote about the calling, settling, or maintaining of a minister amongst us, with the approbation of the church at Salem, and their direction and advice to be attended by us till we come to be a town, or have a church amongst us. [19]

This time, the General Court did manage to confront the issue. In its response, the Court in effect endorsed the proposal made by Bayley's supporters, by declaring that until a church was founded in the Village, the whole body of "inhabitants" was empowered to call a minister, subject only to the consent of Salem Town and its church. In an obvious effort to create out of thin air something

18. *Ibid.*, 147.
19. *Ibid.*, 148.

paralleling the structure of a church, the General Court added that the Villagers should elect two persons "to supply the place of deacons for the time." These ersatz deacons would be responsible for transmitting the proceeds of the ministry tax from the Village Committee to the minister. In conclusion, the General Court tried to underscore the ad hoc nature of the highly unusual arrangements to which it had just given its official stamp of approval: "[T]his settlement [is] to continue until this court take further notice, or that there be a church of Christ orderly gathered and approved in that place. Then the choice of the minister and officers doth resolve upon them according to law."[20]

It is impossible to recover at this distance what bit of gossip, what hasty word, or what real or imagined slight may have caused some Salem Villagers initially to turn against Bayley, but in any case it is striking how quickly the issue mushroomed to such proportions that the colonial legislature itself became involved. The explanation seems to lie in the fact that all three Village institutions —the regular meeting of the householders (the Village's equivalent of a town meeting), the elected Village Committee (its equivalent of a Board of Selectmen), and the ecclesiastical apparatus, were all practically useless as instruments for the resolution of differences. We have already shown that the Village lacked a church that could provide institutional legitimacy for the minister and congregation. As for the Village meeting, the Bayley dispute clearly shows how readily particular groups within the community could, by energetic organization, turn that institution to their own purposes. Increasingly over the years, Village meetings were called and dominated by partisans of one cause or another who would then proceed to promulgate decisions in the name of the "inhabitants." The apparent resolution of an issue at a Village meeting often meant only that one faction or another happened to be in the driver's seat at the moment.

And even when one faction did manage to maintain control over a period of time, it often lacked the ability to enforce its will on the whole community. Both the Village meeting and the five-man Committee it elected annually were, after all, only pallid shadows of the "town meeting" and "Board of Selectmen" which governed full-fledged towns. As we have already noted, Village affairs remained largely the responsibility of institutions in Salem Town. Strictly speaking, the only power of the Village meeting was to

20. *Ibid.*, 150.

elect the five-member Committee, and the only power of that Committee, in turn, was the assessment and collection of the ministerial tax. Control of either or both of these institutions, therefore, hardly provided adequate political leverage to settle even "ordinary" disputes.

Outsiders often judged, even before 1692, that the intensity of conflict within the community was the consequence of some collective defect in the social temperament of its inhabitants (an analysis implicit in most later accounts of the witchcraft outbreak). But it is altogether possible that the level of internal bickering in Salem Village was, at least to begin with, no higher than that in many other New England communities of the late seventeenth century. What made Salem Village disputes so notorious, and ultimately so destructive, was the fact that structural defects in its organization rendered the Village almost helpless in coping with whatever disputes might arise. It is probably in this way alone that Salem Village may be considered a "deviant" community among its New England neighbors.

It is puzzling that contemporary observers persisted in attributing Salem Village's problems to a moral source rather than an institutional one, for these observers could hardly have failed to recognize that the Village's institutional arrangements were unusual—indeed, nearly unprecedented—in seventeenth-century Massachusetts. Salem Village was virtually the first Massachusetts community to enter for a protracted period this gray area in which its separate existence was given legal recognition, but in such a way as to deny it any real autonomy.[21] In another generation, such an arrange-

21. Before 1700 or so, outlying areas were either granted full autonomy at once as separate towns, or they were granted no legal recognition at all. We have found only a single seventeenth-century parallel to the evolution of Salem Village: this is the slow and painful separation of "Cambridge Village" (later the town of Newton) from Cambridge Town. First (in 1656) came the establishment of a separate meetinghouse in Cambridge Village, with a corresponding tax abatement from the town; then (1664) the creation of a full-fledged church, with an ordained minister; and, finally (1688), the emergence of a wholly independent town. These developments were accompanied by petitions and counter-petitions to the General Court similar in some respects to those which were being generated by Salem Town and Salem Village. (There was a crucial difference between the two situations, though: Cambridge Village and Cambridge Town were both primarily agricultural communities similar in all essential respects, but this was not at all true of Salem Village and Salem Town.) S. F. Smith, *History of Newton, Massachusetts* (Boston, 1880), pp. 57–71.

There exists no study of the emergence of precinct status in colonial Massachusetts. The only work which even raises this general question, John Sly,

ment—it came to be known as "precinct" or "parish" status—would be accepted as a temporary compromise for outlying districts wishing to gain independence from parent communities that were reluctant to relinquish full control. In the late seventeenth century, however, this arrangement was too new to be accepted as legitimate,[22] and so both Salem Village and the outside authorities to whom she looked for assistance were left to feel their way through unfamiliar and even alarming terrain.

Given the ineffectiveness of the Village's institutional structures, private grievances and disputes escalated with a rapidity which must have startled even those embroiled in them, until the entire community, willy-nilly, was drawn in. In their frustration, the disputants turned outward for assistance: to the county courts, to the Salem Town church, to the governor and the General Court, sometimes even to prominent private citizens—to *anyone*, in short, who might help them in their chimerical quest for "peace and order." But these outside authorities, unable to be of much real assistance, often only made matters worse by trying to shame the Villagers into accepting personal moral responsibility for their troubles.

Finally, the institutional flaws in the Village structure meant that when disputes did arise, each side could plausibly introduce the most fundamental issues of civil and ecclesiastical polity. (Further, as such disputes percolated rapidly upward through the power structure of the colony, the disputants used such issues to make the

Town Government in Massachusetts, 1620–1930 (Cambridge, Mass., Harvard University Press, 1930) is inadequate. Our contention that Salem Village and "Cambridge Village" were unique in their time is based on an examination of the following sources: Commonwealth of Massachusetts, Division of Public Records, *Historical Data Relating to Counties, Cities, and Towns in Massachusetts* (Boston, 1920); Shurtleff, ed., *Records of the Governor and Company of the Massachusetts Bay*; and Harold Field Worthley, *An Inventory of the Records of the Particular (Congregational) Churches of Massachusetts Gathered 1620–1805* (Cambridge, Mass., Harvard University Press, 1970).

22. A recent study of the town of Dedham, Massachusetts, shows in dramatic detail the process by which one parent-town spawned a whole cluster of "precincts" late in the 1720's. Kenneth A. Lockridge, *A New England Town: The First Hundred Years* (New York, W. W. Norton Co., 1970), pp. 97–103. Sometimes, as in Dedham, the process was protracted and rancorous; sometimes, as with the emergence of the future town of Amherst as a precinct of Hadley in 1734, it was brief and apparently placid. *The History of the Town of Amherst, Massachusetts*, compiled and published by Carpenter & Morehouse (Amherst, 1896), p. 33. The point, however, is that in either case there existed by the early eighteenth century both a precedent and a term (precinct) for handling the problem of population growth and dispersion within a community.

controversy seem somehow worthy of all the attention being given to it by so many important men.) Thus even personal and perhaps petty disputes often came to involve debate over some very fundamental issues indeed. In the Bayley dispute the most important of these was the question of who had the power to call and dismiss a minister. Most Villagers appear to have agreed that in a "normal" situation this power should be exercised only by the church members. But, structurally speaking, Salem Village was not "normal." By voting to retain James Bayley as minister in 1673, the Villagers had taken a far-reaching step: that of giving all the householders power in what traditionally was thought of as strictly a church matter. In the next few years they began to grasp the implications of the change they had wrought, and when disagreement broke out in 1679 they debated it at the ideological level, with the majority contending that the power which the non-church members had assumed in 1673 should continue to be theirs by right. Initially, as a practical way of handling a situation unprecedented in their experience, the householders of Salem Village had assumed a function which they all felt to be anomalous and irregular. But once the new procedure became customary—even over the brief span of a few years—they came to view it as the proper and correct one, and to treat any challenge to it as a threat.[23] Throughout the 1680's all the "inhabitants" of the Village continued to play a direct role in ministerial affairs—a role in which they had been confirmed by the highest authorities of the colony. When Salem Village did, at last, gather a full-fledged church of its own in 1689, those same "inhabitants" were hardly willing to relinquish their power.

In pursuing the intricacies of the Bayley dispute we have almost lost sight of James Bayley—just as, one suspects, he was very nearly lost sight of during the controversy. But it was he who finally resolved the issue. With his opponents in control of the local political apparatus, and with the entire Village deeply divided over theoretical questions about the legitimacy of his call, Bayley simply gave up the fight and in 1680 left Salem Village. After a few years more as a minister in Killingworth, Connecticut, he eventually set himself up as a doctor in Roxbury, Massachusetts, perhaps concluding from his Salem Village ordeal that physical

23. This entire episode, in fact, is a classic illustration of the model which Bernard Bailyn has proposed for the American colonial experience as a whole. See his "Political Experience and Enlightenment Ideas in Eighteenth-Century America," 67 *American Historical Review* (1961–62), 339–351.

problems were more easily dealt with than social and political ones.[24]

But Bayley's departure did little to ease the dissension in Salem Village. In April 1680 a solidly anti-Bayley committee, headed by Nathaniel Putnam, was chosen by the "inhabitants" (that is, both church members and nonmembers) to "look out for a minister." In November it was voted "that *all our householders* for the future time shall have liberty to choose, and to be chosen on, the [Village] Committee, and to act in all other matters that concern us, until there be a church gathered among us." Later that same month, by vote of a "meeting of the inhabitants," the Reverend George Burroughs was hired.[25]

Burroughs, twenty-eight years old in 1680, came from a wealthy family of Suffolk County, England; indeed, he eventually inherited a "considerable estate" there, including property in Ipswich, Smithfield, and London. Brought early to America under circumstances which are now unclear, he seems to have been reared by his mother in Roxbury, Massachusetts. Graduating from Harvard in 1670, a year after James Bayley, young Burroughs soon went to Maine, where he preached in Falmouth (Portland), on Casco Bay, until that settlement was attacked by Indians in August 1676, during King Philip's War, at a cost of many lives. With other survivors, Burroughs returned to Massachusetts, settling in Salisbury, where he was still living when he received the call to Salem Village. As one of his conditions for coming, Burroughs stipulated "that in case any difference should arise in time to come, that we engage on both sides to submit to counsel for a peaceable issue."[26] The formula was familiar enough in seventeenth-century New England, but, for Burroughs, who had probably learned from Bayley something of what confronted him, it must have had a more than routine significance.

The differences were not long in arising. It was to Burroughs that Jeremiah Watts wrote his letter of April 1682 lamenting the

24. Sibley, *Harvard Graduates*, II, 296.

25. Village Records, April 6, Nov. 9, Nov. 25, 1680. Italics added.

26. 39 County Court Records, 81. On Burroughs' early life, see Sibley, *Harvard Graduates*, II, 323–334; "Memorial of the Representatives of George Burroughs—1749," American Antiquarian Society, *Proceedings*, 5 (April 1888), 270–273 (petition to the General Court from the heirs of Burroughs, with biographical information); William Willis, "The History of Portland from its First Settlement," Maine Historical Society, *Collections*, first series, 1 (Portland, 1865), 216, 222, 261–264; *Vital Records of Salisbury, Mass., to the End of the Year 1849* (Topsfield, 1915), p. 36.

disputes that were pitting "brother . . . against brother, and neighbors against neighbors." By early 1683 the minister's salary was not being paid, and in March Burroughs simply stopped meeting his congregation. Rumors circulated that he was about to leave Massachusetts altogether. (In fact, the settlement at Casco Bay was being reorganized, and Burroughs had accepted an offer to resume his ministerial duties there.) The Salem Village Committee quickly complained to the county court of Burroughs' "sudden breaking away from us," and asked the court to order his appearance for a balancing of accounts. The Village also prepared for legal action against Burroughs, choosing an ad hoc committee to represent it in such a suit.[27]

Burroughs did return, apparently voluntarily, and on May 2, 1683, less than two months after his abrupt departure, he met with the freeholders of the Village for a final accounting. But while this meeting was in progress, Burroughs was arrested by a marshal on complaint of Captain John Putnam, who had instituted a private action for debt against the minister. Several Villagers who were present at that meeting later gave a vivid account of it:

> [J]ust as . . . Burroughs began to give in his accounts, the marshal came in and, after a while, went to John Putnam, Senior, and whispered to him. And said Putnam said to him, "You know what you have to do; do your office." Then the marshal came to Mr. Burroughs and said, "Sir, I have a writing to read you." Then he read the attachment, and demanded goods. Mr. Burroughs answered that he had no goods to show, and that he was now reckoning with the inhabitants, for we know not yet who is in debt, but there was his body.
>
> As we were ready to go out of the meetinghouse, Mr. Burroughs said, "Well, what will you do with me?" Then the marshal went to John Putnam, Senior, and said to him, "What shall I do?" The said Putnam replied, "You know your business." And then the said Putnam went to his brother, Thomas Putnam, and pulled him by the coat, and they went out of the house together, and presently came in again. Then said John Putnam, "Marshal, take your prisoner, and have him up to the ordinary [the public house maintained in the Village by Nathaniel Ingersoll] and secure him till the morning."[28]

27. 39 County Court Records, 81–82; Willis, "History of Portland," pp. 262–263.

28. 39 County Court Records, 104–105. The particular document we have quoted is also printed in Upham, *Salem Witchcraft*, I, 258–259.

The timing of Putnam's suit makes clear that it was intended as a maneuver in the broader dispute between Burroughs and the Village. In 1681 and 1682, Captain John had on several occasions advanced credit to Burroughs so that he could make purchases from Boston merchants. It was, in fact, Putnam credit which had enabled Burroughs to provide the customary funeral wine at the time of his wife's death in September 1681. The understanding was that this credit represented an advance on salary for which Putnam would be reimbursed from the Village ministry tax. Thus, when the Village failed to pay Burroughs' agreed-upon salary, not only the minister but John Putnam too stood to lose.[29]

Putnam's suit, like the Village's, was eventually settled out of court, but it was on this acrimonious note, with George Burroughs driven ignominiously from the community, that his ministry came to an end. He returned to Maine, where he lived for nine years until brought back to Salem Village on May 4, 1692, a prisoner once again. Three and one-half months later, on August 19, he was executed as a convicted wizard.

The Burroughs dispute is less well documented than other Salem Village controversies of these years, since Burroughs' hasty departure forestalled the kind of full-scale petition campaign that had been mounted in the Bayley affair. It is interesting, however, that the one group identifiable as probably pro-Burroughs—the six Salem Villagers who posted bail for him after his arrest—had been almost unanimously pro-Bayley, or closely identified with pro-Bayley families.[30] Ministers came and went, but the basic lines of factional divisions in Salem Village were hardening year by year.

With the departure of Burroughs, the Village resumed its search for a minister who would be satisfactory to all groups. In the summer and autumn of 1683 three separate committees to choose Burroughs' successor were elected in rapid sequence. Early in 1684 the Reverend Deodat Lawson was engaged and a boat hired to transport his possessions from Boston to Salem. Son of a dissenting minister of Norfolk, England, Lawson had emigrated in the 1670's to Massachusetts where, through his father's influence, he was hired as minister of the church at Edgartown, on Martha's Vineyard. But his career suffered setbacks—the result, so he later

---

29. Testimony in 39 County Court Records, 104–105.
30. *Ibid.*, 104. The six were Nathaniel Ingersoll, John Buxton, Thomas Haynes, Samuel Sibley, William Sibley, and William Ireland, Jr.

claimed, of reverses his father had experienced in England—and in the early 1680's he pursued various secular occupations in Boston, none with any success. In 1684 he decided to make another try at the ministry and accepted the offer from Salem Village.[31]

The coming of Lawson, attended by such full deliberation and consultation, inaugurated a period of at least outward calm in the Village. In 1686, however, controversy broke out afresh. The precipitating issue seems to have been the decision of one group of Salem Villagers to press for the establishment of a full-fledged covenanted church at Salem Village, and also for the ordination of Lawson as its minister. (Neither Lawson nor his two predecessors had undergone this ceremonial rite by which a man assumed the full privileges and duties of the Christian ministry.) The Village Committee then in office, including Captain John Putnam and his nephew Thomas Putnam, Jr., supported, if it did not actually initiate, this move. The opposition to Lawson's ordination was led by four men whom we shall encounter again: Joseph Hutchinson, Job Swinnerton, Joseph Porter, and Porter's brother-in-law Daniel Andrew. In January 1687 these four men requested the Salem Village inhabitants to name a committee to confer with them about their "grievances relating to the public affairs of this place." Hutchinson expressed his dissatisfaction in a still more direct fashion: he began to fence in and farm part of the meetinghouse land which he had given to the Village in the more tranquil year 1673, a gift entered with his own hand in the Village Book of Record.[32]

The Village Committee promptly brought suit against Hutchinson, complaining that he "hath so hedged in our meeting house already that we are all forced to go in at one gate." Hutchinson responded with an indignant denial that he had ever reached any binding agreement with the Village about the ministry land:

[T]hey have no cause to complain of me for fencing in my own land; for I am sure I fenced in none of theirs. I wish they would

31. Village Records, Feb. 22, 1684; *Dictionary of National Biography*, XI, 739 (*s.v.*, "Lawson, Thomas"); Charles E. Banks, *The History of Martha's Vineyard, Duke's County, Mass.*, 3 vols. (Edgartown, Mass., 1966), II, 149–150; Upham, *Salem Witchcraft*, I, 268–269. Lawson's preface to his sermon *Christ's Fidelity the Only Shield against Satan's Malignity* (Boston, 1693) provides further biographical information.

32. Village Records, Nov. 14, 1673 (Hutchinson's gift), Jan. 14, 1687 (the request of the four aggrieved Villagers). The entire affair is described in a November 1686 court deposition by the Salem Village Committee in 46 County Court Records, 72.

not pull down my fences. . . . [A]s for blocking up the meeting-house, it was they did it, and not I, in the time of the Indian wars, and they made Salem pay for it. I wish they would bring me my rocks they took to do it with, for I want them to make fence with.[33]

Fences were going up all over Salem Village in the 1680's, literally as well as figuratively.

Significantly, the leadership of Salem Town threw its influence against the ordination move. In February 1687, at the initiative of the anti-ordination group, the dispute was laid before three arbitrators from the Town: Bartholomew Gedney, John Hathorne, and William Brown, Jr. These three representatives of the interests of Salem Town (all of them wealthy merchants) advised in no uncertain terms against Lawson's ordination, since the matter had "not been so inoffensively managed as it might have been."

Going beyond the immediate issues, however, the arbitrators made some revealing observations. The dispute, they noted, had been characterized by "uncharitable expressions and uncomely reflections tossed to and fro," suggesting "the effects of settled prejudice and resolved animosity." Such patterns of behavior, they went on, "have a tendency to make such a gap as we fear, if not timely prevented, will let out peace and order and let in confusion and every evil work." In conclusion they said: "If you will unreasonably trouble yourselves, we pray you not any further to trouble us."[34] Well before the witchcraft outbreak, Salem Village was becoming locally notorious. In their analysis of Salem Village factionalism and their prediction of future troubles, Gedney, Hathorne, and Brown were remarkably shrewd and prescient. Unfortunately, however, they themselves were hardly disinterested parties, and in any event they offered no specific recommendations as to how the Village might go about extracting itself from the tangled web of controversy which was pulling it steadily downward. Outsiders in these years always seemed more ready to deplore the symptoms of the Village's malaise than they were to examine its causes.

With the emergence of a strong anti-ordination group within the Village, and the weight of Salem Town influence brought to bear against the move, the plan for ordaining Lawson was abandoned. Desirous as they were of forming a church, the proponents of Lawson's ordination were still unprepared to proceed in the face of

33. *Ibid.*
34. The arbitrators' letter in Village Records, Feb. 28, 1687.

strong opposition both outside the Village and within it. As late as 1687, they continued to hope that formation of their church would be a way of somehow transcending the chronic divisions which plagued the community. The Village meeting had become wholly subject to the pressures of conflicting groups, but the men who were working for a church still visualized it as a union of brethren rather than an arena in which self-interested men struggled for primacy. That crucial shift, however, was not long in coming.

3 Afflicted Village, 1688-1697

Like James Bayley and George Burroughs before him, Deodat Lawson made a timely and voluntary exodus from the welter of conflicting interests of which he found himself the unwitting center. In 1688, at the conclusion of his period of contractual obligation, Lawson left Salem Village. After a few more years in Massachusetts, for a time as pastor of the church in Scituate, he abruptly returned to England where he passed the rest of his life in obscurity. He is mentioned cryptically in a 1727 English publication as "the unhappy Mr. Deodat Lawson."[1]

A Church Is Gathered

In the aftermath of Lawson's departure, those Salem Villagers who wanted an ordained minister and a full-fledged church in

1. Samuel Deane, *History of Scituate, Mass., From Its First Settlement to 1831* (Boston, 1831), pp. 195–197; Charles W. Upham, *Salem Witchcraft*, 2 vols. (Boston, 1867), I, 282–283, quoting a reference to Thomas Lawson in Edmund Calamy, *A Continuation of the Account of the Ministers, Lecturers, Masters, and Fellows of Colleges, and Schoolmasters Who Were Ejected and Silenced after the Restoration in 1660*, 2 vols. (London, 1727). In 1714, in desperate straits in London, with his family hungry and three of his children suffering from smallpox, Lawson wrote to two New Englanders resident in London begging for £5 so he could have printed a sermon on the coronation of King George I which he had recently preached before a small congregation of which he was evidently the pastor. The letter is printed in American Antiquarian Society, *Proceedings*, 5 (1888), 268–269.

Salem Village made some important decisions. Whether the hesitancy which had characterized their moves through 1687 resulted from a principled unwillingness to generate even more intense dissension within the Village or from the fear that such dissension might jeopardize those privileges the Village already possessed, one fact must have been depressingly evident: three ministers had now come and gone, and Salem Village seemed no closer to ecclesiastical autonomy than it had been in 1672. The proponents of ordination now abandoned the restraints under which they had hitherto operated, and determined early in 1689 to push ahead whatever the risks.

Their resolve may well have been hardened, too, by major political developments in London and Boston: for it was during these very months, in late 1688 and early 1689, that both the King of England and the imperial governor of Massachusetts, Sir Edmund Andros, were removed from office in a connected pair of bloodless *coups d'état*.[2] There followed a period of confusion during which those men in Boston and Salem who might ordinarily have objected to such a move remained uncertain of their own status and authority. In this situation it may have seemed possible for the Villagers to act, this once, without real fear of obstruction from without.

In any case, they found a willing collaborator in Samuel Parris of Boston, a man whose career we shall examine more fully later. After private negotiations an understanding was reached, and on June 18, 1689, a "general meeting of the inhabitants" of Salem Village—precisely which Villagers were present, or how many, is unknown—agreed to hire Mr. Parris as minister at an annual salary of £66.[3]

The proponents of ordination became still bolder a few months later. On October 10, 1689, another "general meeting of the inhabitants" voted to give outright to Samuel Parris "and his heirs" the Village parsonage together with its barn and two acres of land! This action flew directly in the face of a resolution adopted at a Village meeting in 1681. (In that year, seeking to ensure that this

2. One of many accounts of this familiar bit of history is Wesley Frank Craven, *The Colonies in Transition, 1660–1713* (New York, Harper and Row, 1968), pp. 223–225, 244–246.

3. Village Records, June 18, 1689. Although this gathering was duly entered in the Book of Record as a "general meeting of the inhabitants" (the usual formula employed to describe the regular Village meeting), it was later denounced as illegal, since no warrant for it had been entered in the Record Book as required. *Ibid.*, Oct. 16, 1691.

property would "stand good to the inhabitants of this place and to their successors forever, for the ministry," the Village had forbidden its future transfer "to any particular persons or person, not for any cause, by vote or other ways.")[4] The "general meeting" of October 1689 circumvented this seemingly ironclad prohibition by the simple and brazen expedient of nullifying it: "It was agreed and voted that the vote in our Book of Records of 1681, that lays as some say an entailment upon our ministry house and land, is hereby made void and of no effect."[5]

The men chosen to carry out this most unusual real-estate transaction were Nathaniel Ingersoll, Nathaniel Putnam, John Putnam, and two men closely connected to the Putnams by marriage: Jonathan Walcott and Thomas Flint. All were to emerge as strong members of the "pro-Parris" faction in the controversies of the next several years.

Preparations were now complete, and on November 19, 1689, in a solemn ceremony belying the unseemly maneuvers of the preceding months, Samuel Parris was ordained to the Christian ministry by the Reverend Nicholas Noyes, associate pastor of the church in Salem Town. On the same occasion, twenty-five Salem Villagers joined with Parris and his wife Elizabeth in putting their names to a covenant formally proclaiming themselves a Church of Christ. This group included three of the Village Committeemen who in 1687 had led the move to ordain Lawson, but it did not include any of the four leaders of the anti-ordination party of that year. By the following summer, twenty-six more Villagers had joined with them in covenant membership—for an overall total of fifty-three, or something under one-quarter of the community's adult population. In the context of all that had gone before, and was to follow, the vision summoned up in the Biblical cadences of the covenant's concluding paragraph is worth recording:

> And that we may keep this covenant, and all the branches of it inviolable forever, being sensible that we can do nothing of ourselves, we humbly implore [that] the help and grace of our Mediator may be sufficient for us, beseeching that whilst we are

4. *Ibid.*, Dec. 27, 1681.

5. *Ibid.*, Oct. 10, 1689. The agreement did specify that if Parris or his heirs should decide to sell the property, the Village would have first refusal of it, provided the Village was willing to match any other offer. The Record Book also notes that one Villager—his name is not recorded—dissented from this vote.

working out our own salvation, with fear and trembling, He would graciously work in us both to will and to do. And that he, being the Great Shepherd of our souls, would lead us into the paths of righteousness, for His own Name's sake. And at length receive us all into the inheritance of the Saints in Light.[6]

The year 1689 was doubly memorable to the Village, for the same impulse which in that year brought an independent church into being also underlay the first sustained effort since 1672 to achieve greater political independence as well.[7] Indeed, the creation of a full-fledged Village church is best understood as part of a broader strategy whose long-range goal was total separation from Salem Town.

In July 1689 (a little over two weeks after Parris's hiring) two Salem Village farmers who actively supported the new minister were chosen as selectmen of Salem Town—evidently the result of a concerted political effort there by a group of Salem Villagers. Following up this success, the Village "inhabitants" voted at a meeting in August to petition the Town selectmen for a total separation of Town and Village and the establishment of the Village as an independent township. But the political balance in the Town quickly shifted amidst the confusions of that year, so that the only result of this effort was a Town offer to reduce somewhat the tax demands it placed on the Villagers.[8]

Initially, as the move for political independence first gained headway early in 1689, it won at least apparent backing from a wide spectrum of Salem Villagers, including some who did not support the establishment of a separate church. In February 1689, for example, ten prominent Salem Villagers informed the Town by petition that they would support independence for the Village provided the Town would cede to the Village certain large and extremely valuable tracts of land lying on the Town side of the existing

6. "The Covenant Agreed Upon and Consented Unto [by] the Church of Christ at Salem Village at [its] First Embodying on the 19th of November, 1689," Church Records, first entry.

7. As we shall note in Chapter 4 below, hints of the interconnections between the Village's religious and political history had surfaced intermittently over the preceding decade. But it was in 1689 that the link became explicit.

8. Village Records, Aug. 23, 1689. The protracted negotiations over these concessions may be followed in the Village Records, especially the entries for December 9, 1690, and January 8 and March 1, 1692; see also documents in 11 Mass. Arch., 57–60.

boundary.[9] This group included seven men who would soon emerge as opponents of the move for political autonomy and as bitter enemies of Samuel Parris and his church. At first glimpse, this February petition seems difficult to explain, but in fact, these seven men did have certain interests distinct from the Town. With little genuine interest in separation, they were nevertheless disturbed by the Town's continued insistence on taxing the Villagers for maintenance of the Town meetinghouse, roads, and poor. Significantly, they concluded their petition by noting that if the Town found unacceptable the considerable enlargement in the Village bounds which they had suggested, then "we desire still to remain to Salem as we are, provided our just grievances may be removed."

But as 1689 wore on, Village opposition to the independence move—and to the church which was its ecclesiastical expression—rapidly coalesced, and the fragile and temporary coalition of interests within the Village splintered.[10]

What are we to make of all this? The political maneuvering surrounding the events of 1689 remains so intricate and obscure as to be almost impossible to piece together with any real confidence. What does seem clear, however, is that the various Villagers who initially backed the political autonomy move did so for differing and ultimately contradictory reasons. To some—the pro-Parris group—the move represented a desirable goal in itself; to others it was attractive chiefly as a bargaining tool for obtaining tax concessions from the Town. But the strategy of the latter group very nearly backfired, for the genuine advocates of independence proved unexpectedly determined and resourceful. In the Town, they displayed surprisingly strong, if fleeting, power; in the Village, their transfer of the parsonage to Parris showed to what lengths they were willing to go.

By the end of the year it must have been apparent to the emerging anti-Parris leadership that, far from manipulating the "independence" campaign for their own purposes, it was they who had been manipulated: the one firm result of the year's maneuverings was the emergence of a church which, if it went unchallenged,

9. Petition reprinted in J. W. Hanson, *History of the Town of Danvers from Its Early Settlement to the Year 1848* (Danvers, 1848), p. 37.

10. In August a broadly representative seven-member committee was chosen at the Village meeting to present an independence petition to the Town. That December, however, four of the seven men dropped out. All four would emerge in the years ahead as unqualifiedly anti-Parris in sympathy, while the three who remained proved equally strong in their support for the Village minister. Village Records, Aug. 23 and Dec. 17, 1689.

could become the single most powerful force for political autonomy in the Village. In this way, tacit acquiescence in the events of 1689 soon gave way to outspoken opposition.

The Church and Its Enemies

Samuel Parris, for one, recognized the ambiguous circumstances which had made him head of an independent church. In the very first sermon he preached after his ordination, from the Biblical text "Cursed be he that doeth the work of the Lord deceitfully," Parris came close to launching an explicit attack on the motives of those Villagers, soon to become his bitter adversaries, who had attempted to exploit the developments of 1689 for their own purposes: "[W]hen persons attend any duty, any service or ordinance . . . but yet aim at some private and carnal interest, some by-end of their own; if that be the principal weight that moves them, not the honor, service and glory of God . . . then these . . . are to be ranked among such as do the work of the Lord deceitfully." [11]

Only two weeks after the Village church was organized, then, Parris had publicly identified a group of Villagers as its enemies— and, by implication, as his. Although almost two years were to pass before these men were prepared to move against him, their attack, when it did come, was swift and brutal. At a crucial meeting of the Villagers on October 16, 1691, a decisive shift in the power balance occurred. At that meeting the existing Committee, dominated by supporters of Parris, was voted out and an entirely new slate chosen in its place: Joseph Porter, Joseph Hutchinson, Joseph Putnam, Daniel Andrew, and Francis Nurse. These five men would serve for more than a year, through the entire period of the witchcraft trials. Three of them had led the opposition to Lawson's ordination in 1687, and all five were members of what now openly emerged as the anti-Parris faction in the Village. (One, Daniel Andrew, was simultaneously serving as a selectman in Salem Town.)

In his usual meticulous hand, Samuel Parris noted the five names in the margin of the Church Book. At an evening gathering of seventeen church members held at his house two weeks later, the aggrieved minister declared: "I have not much to trouble you with now; but you know what Committee, the last town-meeting here, were chosen; and what they have done, or intend to do, it may be

11. Samuel Parris, sermon of Nov. 24, 1689, Sermon Book, p. 20.

[you know] better than I." Parris had good reason to fear the up-heaval that had taken place on October 16. Its proportions had been made unmistakeably clear not only by the political complexion of the newly elected Committee but by a further ominous vote passed at the same Village meeting: no tax would be assessed that year for the payment of Parris's salary.[12]

The surviving records yield frustratingly little documentation about the steps which led up to October 16, 1691. They do show clearly enough, however, that from the first a significant number of Villagers expressed their resistance to the course of events by the passive but effective expedient of simply refusing to pay their taxes. As early as September 1690 the Village Committee—still pro-Parris at that point—reported that 20 percent of the 1689–90 church tax remained unpaid fourteen months after it had been assessed. A new accounting in April 1691 revealed that the sta-tistics for the 1690–91 tax period were even worse, with 29 percent of the total still outstanding. (As the weather sharpened that winter, this indirect form of political action became even bolder: Parris's firewood supply, which the Villagers were obligated by contract to maintain, dwindled to the vanishing point.) Another clue to the Village situation in 1690–91 is the pace of church growth. From mid-1690 to the end of 1691, not a single Salem Village man, and only eight women, made the decision to seek membership.[13]

But while such evidence shows the climate of dissatisfaction and uneasiness prevailing in the Village, it tells little about how that dissatisfaction was mobilized politically to bring about the *coup* of October 1691. How are we to account for such dramatic shifts in power, which were to occur more than once in Salem Village during these years? Did a small group of uncommitted Villagers hold the balance of power in an evenly divided community? Did one faction or another, by energetic organizing or some other means, manage to pack the meetings with men of their own persuasion? How many Villagers, in any case, even attended these crucial meetings?

These are tantalizing and important questions, and it would be

12. Village Records, Oct. 16, 1691; Church Records, Nov. 2, 1691. For Daniel Andrew's simultaneous service as a Town selectman, see list of select-men in Sidney Perley, *The History of Salem, Mass.*, 3 vols. (Salem, 1924–28), III, 252.

13. Village Records, Sept. 23, 1690, and April 3, 1691 (the percentages were computed by comparing the taxpayers listed as delinquent on these occasions with the total number of men assessed); Church Records, Oct. 8, 1691 (fire-wood complaint), and *passim* (membership records).

as gratifying as it is difficult to answer them with any certainty. But the Village Book of Record is refractory on such matters: for a variety of reasons, those men who controlled the Village Committee in any given year were not inclined to record the mechanics by which they retained that control. For example, at only one meeting during these years was a record made of the number of persons in attendance: on December 17, 1689, there were "26 men householders" present—somewhat more than one-quarter of all those in that category, and perhaps 15 percent of the adult males in the Village.[14] As for the actual vote counts—not to mention the names of those on each side—these were never recorded except for the stylized and perhaps deliberately obscure phrase, "by a general concurrence."

There does exist, however, a single point at which the haze concealing some of these operations is partially lifted—a point, too, at which violent feelings in the Village were raised to their highest pitch. In December 1692 the pro-Parris leadership, in a petition to the county court, offered its own analysis of the means by which the minister's opponents had managed to capture control of the Village Committee in October 1691 and to hold it through the period of "sore tribulation" which followed. According to this analysis, the hard-core anti-Parris group initially contained just "a few" men, but these few, by shrewdly exploiting the problems of the Village, had "drawn away others who heretofore could not by any means join with them." In addition to this group, there were "several well-affected persons" who had been driven to "absent themselves" altogether from Village meetings "because they cannot bear the jars amongst us—by which means others, to our great disquietment and injury, obtain casting vote."[15]

Stripped of its self-serving verbiage, the hard political facts behind this analysis seem clear enough. Some Villagers, who had

14. Village Records, Dec. 17, 1689. The adult male population was computed from tax lists; from "Map of Salem Village, 1692," Upham, *Salem Witchcraft*, I, following p. xvii (with accompanying key); and from a variety of published family genealogies in the Essex Institute. See Abbey Miller and Richard Henderson, "Census of Salem Village in January 1692," in Paul Boyer and Stephen Nissenbaum, eds., *Salem-Village Witchcraft: A Documentary Record of Local Conflict in Colonial New England* (Belmont, Calif., Wadsworth Publishing Co., 1972), pp. 383–393.

15. Petition of the Salem Village church to the Court of Common Pleas, Dec. 27, 1692—Church Records. This petition focuses on the witchcraft outbreak as the principal cause of the pro-Parris group's disaffection with Village politics, but the power shift which it seeks to explain had occurred back in 1691.

previously been uncommitted or mildly pro-Parris, went over to the anti-Parris side in 1691–92. Others, while remaining vaguely sympathetic to the minister—or perhaps not wishing to reveal publicly that their sympathies for him had chilled—simply ceased coming to the Village meetings. In this way the anti-Parris faction, who may indeed have remained a minority in the Village, managed to gain and hold political control through the years of greatest turmoil.

They did so, however, only over the determined opposition of Parris's supporters. In November 1691 the elders of the Village church formally requested the Village to levy a tax for the payment of Parris's salary. A week later, no action having been taken, the church voted to sue the Salem Village Committee in county court.[16] By late 1691, then, the Village had reached the point of total institutional polarization: the church speaking for one group, the Village Committee for another.

In response to the church's suit, it would seem, the Village Committee late in November announced that a Village meeting would be held on December 1 to investigate the legality of the 1689 meetings at which Parris had first been hired and the ministry house and lands turned over to him.[17] Not only was this maneuver part of a sustained attack on the one Village institution dominated by Parris's supporters, but it had a more immediate significance as well: if the very arrangements by which the church had come into being could be discredited by action of the Village, the credibility of the legal moves the church was making against the Village Committee would be seriously undermined.

No record of this meeting survives. Was it held? Was it so turbulent that neither group could gain the upper hand to move either against Parris or in his behalf? The Book of Record is silent.

And silent it remains for most of the year 1692. The anti-Parris Village Committee called no meetings from early March to mid-December of that year; similarly, only a few sketchy entries for 1692 appear in Samuel Parris's normally voluble Church Records. Indeed, if we had only the usual sources for our guide, we would conclude that 1692 was the least eventful year Salem Village had experienced in more than a decade! In fact, of course, the Village's history for that year is recorded in other and far more somber documents. The flames of Village factionalism, smoldering away for years, now burst spectacularly into the open.

16. Church Records, Nov. 2, 10, and 18, 1691.
17. Village Records, warrant following entry for Oct. 16, 1691.

The witchcraft episode did not generate the divisions within the Village, nor did it shift them in any fundamental way, but it laid bare the intensity with which they were experienced and heightened the vindictiveness with which they were expressed. For some Salem Villagers, the witchcraft trials had brought suffering and even death to friends and kinfolk; for others, the trials had ended too soon, just when the magnitude of the evil afflicting the Village was being fully revealed.[18] Thus the events of 1692 were frustrating, if not tragic, for all who survived them; they had all the divisive effect, but little of the cathartic value, which such a burst of violence potentially contained.

With the return of a semblance of normality in the winter of 1692–93, the chronic struggles within the community revived. Indeed, the pro-Parris group was soon professing to see the witchcraft episode as little more than another incident in the frustrating history of their effort to provide for their minister and maintain their church. In a petition to the county court in December 1692, a committee of the Village church complained that as a result of the distractions caused by the recent witchcraft outbreak (which had taken twenty lives, shattered many families, and left scores of accused persons still in jail), "we have [had] no [Village] meetings to relieve our minister." The meetinghouse, too, had fallen into disrepair for want of funds, "so that by reason of broken windows, stopped up, some of them, by boards or otherwise, and others wide open, it is sometimes so cold that it makes it uncomfortable and sometimes so dark that it is almost un-useful."[19]

For all the pettiness of these complaints, they were in fact true enough. The anti-Parris group, through its continuing control of the Village Committee, had not only made no move to provide for Parris's support, but by the end of the year had renewed its demand for an investigation of what it now called the "fraudulent" conveyance of the parsonage and ministry land to Parris in 1689.[20] It was, in fact, this action which elicited the church's peevish complaint to the court.

In January 1693 the court did indeed declare the Committee derelict in its duty, and ordered the inhabitants forthwith to elect a new

18. In September 1693 Cotton Mather visited Salem Town, where a "Mrs. Carver" predicted "a new storm of witchcraft" because of "the wilful smothering and covering" of the 1692 outbreak—*The Diary of Cotton Mather*, 2 vols. (New York, Frederick Ungar Publishing Co., [1957]), I, 172.

19. Church Records, Dec. 26, 1692.

20. Village Records, Dec. 7, 1692.

one. In obedience to this court order a new Committee was duly elected on January 25, but it proved as determinedly anti-Parris as its predecessor. Returning once again to the courts, the church brought suit against this new Committee, whose members in March were found guilty and fined forty shillings each. The fines were paid, but still the Committee took no steps to collect a salary for their minister. The only authorities who might have enforced the court order—the local constables—took their orders from Salem Town; significantly, they made no move against the Village Committee.[21] With one civil authority confronting another, a solution would have to be sought elsewhere, and it was.

Throughout 1693 and 1694, the central aim of Parris's opponents was to maneuver the minister into calling a council of outside ministers and laymen to enquire into the Salem Village situation—a council they clearly expected would lead to Parris's departure from the Village. Since this was an ecclesiastical strategy, it was managed principally by the only anti-Parris men who were members of the Village church: John Tarbell, Samuel Nurse, Peter Cloyce, and Thomas Wilkins. But Parris's detailed record of the intricate maneuverings during this period makes clear that at every stage these four—whom Parris consistently referred to as the "dissenting brethren"—were advised and assisted by other men of the Village who did not belong to the Village church, notably Israel Porter, Joseph Putnam, and Joseph Hutchinson.[22]

Through a complex and protracted sequence of petitions, counter-petitions, tense public confrontations, and private meetings extending late into the night, the crucial issue was decided: would Parris and the leaders of the Village church agree to the calling of an ecclesiastical council, with all the risks for Parris which that implied? Moving first on the local level, the "dissenting brethren" met repeatedly with Parris in the spring of 1693 and requested that he call such a "Council of Elders." Not only did the minister refuse this request, but he publicly dismissed their list of grievances as a "libel" and, in the Church Book, condemned their behavior as "rough" and "exceeding unchristian." [23]

---

21. These legal moves are documented in County Court Records, "General Sessions Record Volume, July 1692–March 1695," 28–30; and Church Records, Dec. 26, 1692, and Jan. 15, 1693. The refusal of the constables to enforce the court order is mentioned in a petition of a later, pro-Parris, Village Committee to the General Court, Feb. 1695, 113 Mass. Arch., 103, 103a.

22. See, for example, Church Records, March 27, 1693, Oct. 23, 1693, and Nov. 18, 1694.

23. Church Records, April 20 and May 18, 1693.

Frustrated at the Village level, the dissenters turned outward. In a show of strength in July 1693, they secured the signatures of fifty Villagers on a petition asking Governor William Phips and the General Court to intervene in the dispute by appointing several disinterested outsiders to act as arbitrators. About this time, too, in meetings with the ministers of Boston, Salem, and other towns, the anti-Parris group urged these men to press Parris to call a council.[24]

These efforts bore fruit. In October 1693 the minister and assistant minister of the Salem Town church, John Higginson and Nicholas Noyes, together with John Hale of the Beverly church, wrote to Parris advising him to call a council of Massachusetts ministers to hear and arbitrate the dispute. Pointedly, these three noted that they were writing at the explicit request of "the Elders of Boston" who were alarmed about the Village situation. In an aggrieved response, Parris deplored the irregularity of the methods his opponents were employing against him, as well as the "amazing confused noises" about conditions in Salem Village which they were broadcasting throughout the province. But he recognized full well the import of the communication he had received: that he had become an embarrassment to the ecclesiastical leadership of Massachusetts and that they had decided to move against him. Accordingly, he concluded his reply by agreeing that a council should be summoned.[25]

Parris must have read the handwriting on the wall at least as early as October 1693, but he was never one to give in gracefully. As it turned out, by delays, stratagems, and the shrewd manipulation of procedural issues and fine points of protocol, he was able to delay convening the church council for another year and a half.

In November 1693 Parris drew up a statement of his grievances against the dissenters: the equivalent of a brief for the defense in the ecclesiastical trial which now seemed to be shaping up. In this document, he denounced not only the dissenters' "precipitate, schismatical, and total withdrawing from the Church; yea, and [from] the Congregation," but also "their withdrawing their purses as well as their persons." Indeed, continued Parris, not only had his opponents absented themselves from religious worship, but they had attacked him with a "factious and seditious libel," and carried their "impetuous pursuit" so far as to disturb him in his own home

24. The July 1693 petition is in 11 Mass. Arch., 76; the dissenters' meetings with outside ministers are referred to in the Church Records, Feb. 16, 1693.
25. Church Records, Oct. 23, 1693.

late at night. In sum, they were guilty of "extremely disturbing the peace of this church and many other good people amongst us, sadly exposing all to ruin." [26]

But still the crucial call for a council was not forthcoming from the Salem Village church. In June 1694, the Salem Town and Beverly ministers, openly joined this time by four ministers from Boston—James Allen, Samuel Willard, Samuel Cheever, and Joseph Gerrish—again pressed Parris to call such a gathering. (They were acting, they acknowledged, because they had been approached directly by "some persons of Salem Village.") In another letter three months later, the seven clergymen reiterated their call still more forcefully; and, driving home the point, they added that since Parris had ignored their earlier advice, "we . . . find it to be our duty to express our minds more plainly and particularly, that we may be the more clearly understood without mistake." [27]

But Parris and his supporters were now preparing one final tactic by which they might regain control of the situation. On November 26, 1694, without the intimidating presence of a delegation of outside ministers, Parris confronted his opponents in the Salem Village meetinghouse. This confrontation—surpassed for sheer drama only by the scenes enacted in that same meetinghouse in 1692—was witnessed by the entire "congregation" as well as the church members, together with several persons whom Parris identified simply as "strangers." The "dissenters" sat together, engaging in "frequent whisperings with comers and goers to them and from them." [28]

The occasion was carefully planned so that the focus throughout would be on Parris himself. He delivered the opening prayer; and it was he, over the objection of the dissenters, who read to the assembly the bill of grievances they had brought with them. Thus it was from the minister's own lips, oddly enough, that the Salem Villagers heard a stinging indictment of his role in 1692: his "easy and strong faith" in the accusations of the afflicted, his lack of "charity towards his neighbors," and his deep complicity in the legal actions against the accused, many of whom were members of his own congregation. Under these circumstances, declared the dissenters, they had withdrawn from the Salem Village church, with

26. Composed Nov. 13, 1693, recorded in Church Records after entry for Feb. 7, 1695.
27. *Ibid.*, June 14 and Sept. 20, 1694.
28. Parris gives a vivid picture of this meeting in the Church Records, Nov. 26, 1694, where the documents which were there read are also transcribed.

its "distracting and disturbing tumults," and started attending another church—which they did not name—"where we might hear the word in quiet."[29]

After he had finished reading this indictment, Parris delivered his response, a lengthy and carefully written document he entitled "Meditations for Peace." Far different in tone from his hostile utterances of 1693, "Meditations for Peace " reveals Parris at his most conciliatory, as he sought to rally the largest possible support in the Village. The mood of the document was established in its opening sentences, in which Parris declared that the initial outbreak of affliction in his own house represented to him "a very sore rebuke, and humbling providence." He admitted giving too much weight to spectral testimony in the witchcraft trials, and acknowledged that "in that sore hour of distress and darkness," he may have spoken "unadvisedly." Asking forgiveness for "every offense," Parris concluded with an appeal for unity which even in so divided a community as Salem Village must have evoked echoing phrases from hundreds of vaguely remembered sermons, prayers, and parental admonitions:

> And so again, I beg, entreat, and beseech you, that Satan, the devil, the roaring lion, the old dragon, the enemy of all righteousness, may no longer be served by us, by our envy and strifes . . . but that all from this day forward may be covered with the mantle of love, and we may on all hands forgive each other heartily, sincerely, and thoroughly, as we do hope and pray that God, for Christ's sake, would forgive each of ourselves. . . . Amen, Amen.

If the real issue had, in fact, been Parris himself, it is not impossible that, even at this late date, the eloquence of "Meditations for Peace" could have established Parris as a spiritual and moral leader honored by the entire community. Indeed, when one of the "dissenting brethren," John Tarbell, first heard Parris read his "Meditations" (at a private conference several days before the November 26 meeting) he was "much affected" and declared that "if half so much had been said formerly, it had never come to this."

But the divisions in Salem Village went deeper than the personal behavior of one man, and one man's eloquence was not enough to

29. The church which the dissenters were attending may have been Ipswich, where John Wise was pastor. Parris later made great efforts to keep Wise from being a member of the Ecclesiastical Council which convened in Salem Village in 1695. See Church Records, Feb. 12, 1695.

heal them. When Parris had finished reading "Meditations for Peace," the dissenters simply asked for a copy "to consider of it." He refused unless they, in turn, would allow him to retain the document listing *their* grievances. In this fashion, and "with no little difficulty," the two sides exchanged their manifestoes, "and so the meeting broke up." In an anti-Parris tract evidently written shortly after this meeting and circulated privately through the Village, "Meditations for Peace" was curtly dismissed as "a slender and general confession, without any proposals of reparations."[30]

Each group had now, in effect, submitted its brief, and plans for the long-delayed ecclesiastical council went rapidly forward. On April 3 and 4, 1695, an impressive convocation of seven ministers and ten church elders/ from Boston and other Massachusetts towns gathered in the Salem Village meetinghouse. Acting as moderator was Increase Mather, the best-known and most widely respected clergyman in the province. (It was his sermon, *Cases of Conscience Concerning Evil Spirits Personating Men*, which two-and-one-half years before had played a key role in bringing a stop to the witchcraft trials.) Increase's son Cotton Mather also sat on this council.

After hearing the presentations of the opposing sides, the seventeen dignitaries issued their report. Beginning at the homiletical level, they lectured the community—as had so many outsiders in the past—on the moral failings which had generated its divisions in the first place. The council members declared that they had discerned among the inhabitants "a spirit full of contentions and animosities, too sadly verifying the blemish which hath heretofore lain upon them." Should the Villagers continue so "to devour one another," they warned, Christ would "abandon them to all the desolations of a people that sin away the mercies of the gospel."

Turning to the immediate issue under contention, the council balanced its judgments very carefully, but in the end it supported those who wished to drive Parris from the Village. As minister, Parris should be "respected, honored, and supported"—neverthe-

---

30. "Meditations for Peace" may be found in the Church Records for Nov. 26, 1694. The anti-Parris tract from which we have quoted, evidently a handwritten document, was printed by Robert Calef in his *More Wonders of the Invisible World: Or, The Wonders of the Invisible World Display'd in Five Parts* (London, 1700) and is included in Samuel P. Fowler, ed., *Salem Witchcraft* (Salem, 1861), pp. 159–160. (Fowler's edition of Calef includes some sections omitted from the version in Burr's *Narratives*.) The original is not known to have survived; that it reached Calef's hands suggests that he was in close touch with the anti-Parris leaders in Salem Village as he composed *More Wonders* in the late 1690's.

less, he had taken "sundry unwarrantable and uncomfortable steps" in "the late and the dark time of the confusions." Thus for this reason the council urged "much compassion" toward the dissenters and, in the key sentence of the entire report, declared: "If the distempers in Salem Village should be (which God forbid!) so incurable that Mr. Parris, after all, find that he cannot, with any comfort and service, continue in his present station, his removal from thence will not expose him unto any hard character with us, nor, we hope, with the rest of the people of God among whom we live."[31] Clearly the council members were hinting that if Parris would make his exit voluntarily, they would do their best to help him put a good face on the entire episode—and perhaps even assist him in finding another position.

But the anti-Parris leaders in the Village were dissatisfied with this qualified support, and late in April they mustered their full strength to send to Increase Mather a petition signed by eighty-four Salem Villagers expressing disappointment with the council's conclusions. Describing themselves as "utterly frustrated," the signers urged that the erstwhile members of the council "plainly advise" Parris "to cease his labors and seek to dispose of himself elsewhere." This petition was taken most seriously by Mather and his colleagues, and on May 6 they informed the Salem Village church that in their judgment the anti-Parris group had become so "implacable" as to "render Mr. Parris's removal necessary."

But the quality of implacability was not monopolized by the anti-Parris faction. On May 20, 1695, a *pro*-Parris petition signed by

31. Parris transcribed this report in full in the Church Records under the date of April 3 and 4, 1695. Four years after this Salem Village council, one of its members, Cotton Mather, spoke publicly to the question of the circumstances under which a minister might legitimately resign his pastorate. These circumstances, he wrote, included "incurable prejudices, dissensions, animosities, and implacable offences between a Pastor and his People," as well as situations in which resignation was the only way to "avoid a storm of persecution" that was "purely personal." [Cotton Mather], *Thirty Important Cases Resolved with Evidence of Scripture and Reason. By Several Pastors of Adjacent Churches Meeting in Cambridge, New-England* (Boston, 1699), pp. 28, 29. A recent study suggests that pastoral turn-over, along with the contractualization of relations between minister and congregation, were becoming prevalent in New England toward the end of the seventeenth century, and that both developments were the result of widespread local "contentions." See David D. Hall, *The Faithful Shepherd: A History of the New England Ministry in the Seventeenth Century* (Chapel Hill, University of North Carolina Press, 1972), pp. 185–196. See also Daniel H. Calhoun, *Professional Lives in America: Structure and Aspiration, 1750–1850* (Cambridge, Harvard University Press, 1965), pp. 94–97. Here again we see that the problems of Salem Village were unique only in the intensity they ultimately reached.

105 Salem Villagers went off to Mather and the Boston elders. "The removing of Mr. Parris from his present station," it declared, "will not unite us":

> For we have had three ministers removed already, and by every removal our differences have been rather aggravated. Therefore, we justly fear that the removing of the fourth may rather prove the ruining of the interests of Christ amongst us, and leave us as sheep without a shepherd. Therefore we desire that Mr. Parris may continue in his present station.[32]

A few weeks later, the town of Suffield, Massachusetts, doubtless after prompting from Boston, inquired whether Parris might be available to fill their pulpit, but the Salem Village church elders, "after several hours debate," insisted that Parris remain at his post. "Seeing they would not let me go," Parris commented in recording this decision, "I pressed them to keep me, and make much of me." [33]

The Departure of Parris

The reason underlying Parris's new and surprising show of confidence is not difficult to find: his backers had regained control of the Village political apparatus. For fourteen months, from January 1693 to March 1694, the anti-Parris Village Committee had called no meetings of the inhabitants, thereby making certain that no ministry taxes could be voted or collected. But at last, in March 1694, the Committee called a general meeting at which a new—and solidly pro-Parris—Committee was elected.[34] While the tide outside the Village was turning against Parris, his supporters within the Village were consolidating their position.

How Parris's supporters thus regained power in 1694 is impossible to explain with any confidence; one strong possibility, however, is that as passions began to cool around the edges of the conflict, the process by which his opponents had taken control of the Village Committee three years earlier simply reversed itself: some of those men who had turned, perhaps reluctantly, against Parris in 1691–92 now reverted to his side, and those who had been stay-

---

32. Both these petitions were recorded by Parris in the Church Records, preceding the entry for June 2, 1695.
33. Church Records, June 3, 1695.
34. Village Records, March 20, 1694.

ing away from Village meetings now began to attend once again. In this way the fundamental pro-Parris majority reemerged naturally as an effective political force. This much is clear: by May 1695, when virtually the entire adult population of Salem Village publicly committed itself on the issue (by signing one of the two opposing petitions to the members of the recent church council), Parris's supporters dominated the Village numerically: they gathered 105 signatures on this occasion, while the opposition was able to win only eighty-four. (And if one counts only those signers who were eligible to vote in Village meeting—the householders— the pro-Parris majority is even more striking: fifty-four to thirty-six.)

But in any case, in a community as riven, and as immobilized, as Salem Village now was, control of the formal political apparatus was of only limited value, and Parris's supporters soon discovered the hollowness of their victory. In September 1694 the new pro-Parris Committee called a meeting of the inhabitants "to see if we can possibly agree together in peace and unity"—but again no trace of this meeting appears in the Village Book of Record: if it was held at all, the minutes were not deemed suitable for preservation. A tax for Parris's salary was at last voted on January 18, 1695 (the first in four years), but a few weeks later the Salem Village Committee complained to the General Court that it was unable to collect this tax because the local constables (officials chosen by Salem Town) were still refusing to prosecute the householders who did not pay.[35]

So despite the apparent upswing in his political fortunes within the Village (confirmed in December 1695 when another pro-Parris Committee was elected), Parris evidently concluded early in 1696 that his position had become untenable. Though his friends had regained control of the Village's institutional apparatus, his opponents had contrived to make that control virtually meaningless. The ecclesiastical leaders of Massachusetts had given up on him, at least while he clung to the Salem Village pulpit. On a personal level, the endless conflict, coupled with the emotional strain of the witchcraft period, had taken its toll. In the deep winter of early 1695, in a rare moment of (intentional) self-revelation, Parris had confessed that he was "spent and tired out with the multitude of meetings." Further, by early 1696 his wife, aged forty-eight, had probably already entered upon the illness from which she would

35. *Ibid.*, Sept. 15, 1694; Jan. 18, 1695; 113 Mass. Arch., 103, 103a.

die in mid-July.[36] In April 1696, then, Parris notified the elders of the Village church that he would not be continuing as its pastor after his current appointment expired on July first. Accepting this decision without recorded protest, the church began a search for his successor.[37]

Parris's resignation reduced the emotional level of the controversy, but it did not resolve the outstanding issues between himself and his opponents. He had received no salary (only individual contributions on a voluntary basis) for the years 1691–94, and only a partial salary for the 1694–96 period. On the other hand, he still held deed to the parsonage and two acres of land on which it stood. In March 1697, noting that Parris was still in the parsonage nine months after the termination of his services as minister, the Village Committee instituted a lawsuit against him. (In another of the seemingly endless pendulum swings, Parris's opponents had just regained control of the Committee.) The Village lost the case, however, and was ordered to pay costs. Parris, for his part, won a *countersuit* against the Village for back salary, and the court ordered the Village to pay him £125. The Village Committee at once appealed.[38]

Finally, in the summer of 1697, both sides agreed to accept the arbitration of three prominent Bostonians, Wait Winthrop, Elisha Cooke, and Samuel Sewall. That September, in accordance with their findings, the Village paid Parris £79 in back salary and Parris surrendered the deed to the parsonage.[39] Accounts were closed at last.

Parris moved on to a pulpit in the tiny western settlement of Stow, Massachusetts—where he and the townsmen promptly became embroiled in a salary dispute! Living on until 1720, he passed his final years in Sudbury, Massachusetts, where he earned his

36. Village Records, Dec. 13, 1695; Church Records, Feb. 7, 1695. On the death of Elizabeth Parris, see Perley, *History of Salem*, III, 360, and gravestone in Wadsworth burying ground, Danvers. In the midst of his troubles, Parris took time to compose an epitaph for Elizabeth's tombstone, praising her as "best wife, choice mother, neighbor, friend." In view of all she had undergone during her seven years in Salem Village, the "neighbor" and "friend" are not without poignancy.

37. Church Records, Apr. 9, 1696.

38. Village Records, Mar. 2, 1697; 28 County Court Records ("Court of Common Pleas, 1692–1719"), 12–14; Upham, *Salem Witchcraft*, I, 295–296.

39. Village Records, Sept. 14, 1697; Deed: Samuel Parris to Salem Village Committee, dated Sept. 24, 1697, recorded Jan. 16, 1699, printed in Danvers Historical Society, *Historical Collections*, 16 (1928), 8.

living as a schoolmaster, absentee landlord (he still owned property in Boston) and petty merchant, selling such articles as gloves to the townspeople.[40] Like James Bayley and Deodat Lawson before him, Parris had found the demands of the Puritan ministry in late-seventeenth-century Massachusetts too great, and had turned to secular pursuits.

In the meantime, back in Salem Village, a genuine effort was made by a chastened community to give voice to all factions in the search for Parris's replacement. Committees began to present a more balanced appearance than in the troubled years from 1689 to 1697. The long cycle of acrimony was at last winding down to a manageable level. Out of sheer exhaustion, perhaps, both sides had given up the quest for total dominance and accepted the prospect of more or less chronic factional divisions. When Parris's successor, the Reverend Joseph Green, managed further to soften animosities in the Village, it was less an evidence of the two factions' "reconciliation" than of their recognition that the sources of social and political diversity could never be wholly eliminated. The most that the Villagers could now hope for was to accommodate diversity within an essentially stable institutional structure, not to root it out altogether. Typical of the new mood was the Village meeting of April 1701 to discuss building a new meetinghouse. The gathering was characterized, Green noted in his diary, by "much contravening discourse, but a good issue [that is, outcome]." [41] The nineteen bodies that swung on Witches' Hill in the summer of 1692 were part of the price Salem Village paid for that "good issue."

40. Perley, *History of Salem*, III, 360; Samuel Parris's will and estate inventory, Middlesex County Registry of Probate, Courthouse, Cambridge, Mass., Docket 16951; Alfred Sereno Hudson, *History of Sudbury, Mass., 1638–1889* (Boston, 1889), p. 275. On the Stow interlude see the extracts from the Stow town records, Nov. 29, 1697–Nov. 21, 1698, in 12 *New England Historical and Genealogical Register* (1858), 63–64, and D. Hamilton Hurd, *et al.*, *History of Middlesex County, Mass.*, 3 vols. (Philadelphia, 1890), I, 642.
41. Diary of the Reverend Joseph Green, Apr. 28, 1701, 8 *EIHC* (1868), 220.

4 Salem Town and Salem Village: The Dynamics of Factional Conflict

Although the quartet of ministers who came and went—Bayley, Burroughs, Lawson, and Parris—often served as the immediate focus of factional conflict in Salem Village, it is clear that they themselves were not the ultimate source of that factionalism. Fortunately for us, the Villagers in their repeated appeals to outside authorities produced several sets of petitions and counter-petitions, many of them complete with signatures, which allow us to analyze the nature of the struggle by reconstructing the membership of the two competing groups. By far the most useful of these petitions, for such a purpose, are the two addressed to Increase Mather and other elders of the Massachusetts churches in the spring of 1695, a month after the ecclesiastical council at Salem Village.[1] The eighty-four Salem Villagers, male and female, who signed the anti-Parris petition and the 105 who put their names to the pro-Parris petition represent a high percentage of the adult residents of the Village. (Our own "census" of Salem Village in 1692 suggests a population of about 215 persons over the age of twenty-one.)[2] As this strik-

1. Parris entered verbatim transcripts of these petitions, with signatures, in the Church Records, preceding the entry for June 2, 1695.
2. Abbey Miller and Richard Henderson, "Census of Salem Village in January 1692," in Paul Boyer and Stephen Nissenbaum, eds., *Salem-Village Witchcraft: A Documentary Record of Local Conflict in Colonial New England* (Belmont, Calif., Wadsworth Publishing Co., 1972), pp. 383–393. Since some of the petition signers were under the age of twenty-one, the ratio of petition-signers (189) to the total over-21 Village population (*ca.* 215) was not quite so overwhelming as it might at first seem, but it was nevertheless strikingly high.

ingly full breakdown of the two factions is analyzed, certain patterns and correlations emerge which provide at least a beginning point for understanding the dynamics of Village factionalism in these years.

The Two Factions: A Profile

Church Membership. To begin with, there is a clear connection between membership in the Salem Village church and support for Samuel Parris. Of the sixty-two people who belonged to the Village church in May 1695 (not counting Parris himself and his wife), forty-two signed the pro-Parris petition and only eight the anti-Parris document. (Six of these eight were three of the "dissenting brethren" and their wives.) More striking still is the fact that of the twenty-five original members—those admitted when the church was formed on November 19, 1689—only one, Joshua Rea, Senior, opposed Parris in 1695.[3] Those who made the decision to cast their lot with the Salem Village church remained to the end overwhelmingly loyal to its minister.

But of the Villagers who retained their membership in other churches while worshiping with the Salem Village congregation, a far smaller percentage supported Parris. Of the eighteen such persons whose names appear on the petitions, only ten endorsed Parris, while eight opposed him.[4] Not church membership per se, but affiliation with the Salem Village church, is the decisive indicator of support for Parris.

Wealth. In December 1695 Salem Village imposed a tax for the support of the ministry. Assessments on individual property owners were apportioned on the basis of their landholdings and other wealth, in accordance with a scale set by the General Court.[5] Of the eighty-nine adult Village males who signed one of the two petitions of 1695, all but three appear on the tax rolls of that year. Thus it is possible to analyze with a high degree of precision the comparative economic standing of the two factions.

---

3. The names of members were entered by Samuel Parris in the Church Records at the time they joined.

4. These eighteen represent those who are identified by Parris as church members in his breakdown of the signers of the petitions, but who do not appear in the Church Records as members of the Salem Village church.

5. Village Records, Jan. 18, 1695. Developed land was taxed at one penny per acre, unimproved land at one-half penny per acre—*ibid.*, Nov. 11, 1672 and March 6, 1685.

Chart 1.   **Factionalism and Wealth in Salem Village, 1695**

Amount of 1695–96 tax	Number of householders in each tax bracket		Percentage of householders in each tax bracket	
	Pro-Parris (average tax: 10.9 shillings)	Anti-Parris (average tax: 15.3 shillings)	Pro-Parris	Anti-Parris
Under 10 shillings	31	15	61	43
10–20 shillings	16	12	31	34
Over 20 shillings	4	8	8	23
Total	51	35	100	100

Sources: Tax list, Village Records, Dec. 13, 1695; pro-Parris and anti-Parris petitions as transcribed by Samuel Parris in the Village Church Records preceding the entry for June 2, 1695.

As Chart 1 shows, of the twelve most prosperous men among the petition signers (those taxed more than twenty shillings), only four supported Parris, while eight opposed him. (If we exclude the members of the Putnam family, whose unique situation requires separate treatment, the contrast is even more striking: only one non-Putnam in this most wealthy category supported Parris, while seven opposed him.) At the other end of the scale, thirty-one of the poorer men of the Village (those taxed at under ten shillings) backed Parris, with only fifteen in opposition. In other words, the richest men in the Village opposed Parris by a margin of better than two-to-one, while the poorest supported him in almost precisely the same proportion.[6]

Breaking the data down in another way, the average tax of the pro-Parris householders was just under eleven shillings, in contrast to an average of more than fifteen shillings for the opponents of

6. Only sixteen known adult Village males failed to sign either petition. With one exception—Daniel Rea, who may have been out of the Village at the time—all sixteen were taxed in 1696 at under ten shillings, and six of them at three shillings, the rate normally assessed on propertyless individuals—Tax List, Village Records, Dec. 13, 1695.

Parris.[7] The fifty-one pro-Parris householders paid a total of £28 in the 1695 taxation, scarcely higher than the £26/15 paid by the considerably smaller number of householders (thirty-five) in the anti-Parris ranks. As these figures so vividly suggest, the opponents of Parris, while numerically a minority, owned virtually as much Village property as did his supporters.

Geography. In the first chapter we reported the striking pattern which emerges when the places of residence of accused, accusers, and defenders in the witchcraft outbreak are plotted. As Map 3 shows, a similar geographic pattern distinguishes the pro-Parris from the anti-Parris faction.[8] The petitioners who lived nearest Salem Town (or, in a few cases, just over the Village line in the Town) opposed Parris by a ratio of six-to-one. Those whose houses were in the northwestern half of the Village, most remote from the Town, *supported* Parris by a ratio of better than four to one. (In the central section of the Village the two factions divided much more evenly, with the pro-Parris group somewhat in the preponderance.)

Map 4 reveals that the actual acreage owned by the pro-Parris and anti-Parris factions was distributed in more or less the same geographic pattern as the places of residence: the land nearest the Town was owned mainly by Parris's opponents, that most distant from the Town owned primarily by Parris's supporters. There is a difference in the central area on the two maps, however, for while the pro-Parris signers were numerically dominant in this area, the land itself was divided almost equally between the two factions— suggesting larger individual holdings on the anti-Parris side. In

7. If each of these figures is reduced by three shillings (the amount of the "head tax" imposed on all adult males regardless of their landholdings), so that the figure represents Village landholdings alone, then the contrast between the average tax of the two groups becomes even starker: an average of seven shillings for the pro-Parris group, twelve for the anti-Parris group. The divergence in the relative economic standing of the two groups is confirmed on the Salem Town tax rolls as well. In the returns of the *Town* constables submitted in connection with a provincial tax levied by the General Court in October 1695, forty-six pro-Parris Villagers are assessed an average of 18.2 shillings, while the average for thirty-four anti-Parris Villagers is 23.3 shillings. See *Tax and Valuation Lists of Massachusetts Towns before 1776*, microfilm edition compiled by Ruth Crandall (Harvard University Library), reel 8: "Salem, 1689–1773." The tax from which the above statistics are derived is titled "1695. Rate Made by Virtue of an Act of Adjournment Made the 16th Day of October in the Sixth Year of Their Majesties' Reign, Entitled 'An Act for Payment of the Province Debt.'"

8. Residential information from "Map of Salem Village, 1692," in Charles W. Upham, *Salem Witchcraft*, 2 vols. (Boston, 1867), I, following p. xvii.

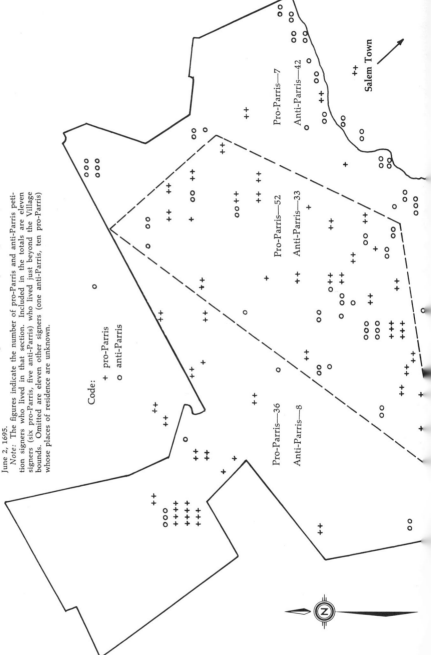

Map 3 **The Geography of Factionalism: Residential Pattern of the Signers of the Pro-Parris and Anti-Parris Petitions of 1695**

Sources: The residential map of Salem Village included as a frontispiece in volume I of Charles W. Upham, *Salem Witchcraft*, 2 vols. (Boston, 1867); the pro-Parris and anti-Parris petitions, with signatures, as transcribed by Samuel Parris in the Salem Village Church Records preceding the entry for June 2, 1695.

Note: The figures indicate the number of pro-Parris and anti-Parris petition signers who lived in that section. Included in the totals are eleven signers (six pro-Parris, five anti-Parris) who lived just beyond the Village bounds. Omitted are eleven other signers (one anti-Parris, ten pro-Parris) whose places of residence are unknown.

Code:

+ pro-Parris
o anti-Parris

Pro-Parris—7
Anti-Parris—42

Salem Town

Pro-Parris—52
Anti-Parris—33

Pro-Parris—36
Anti-Parris—8

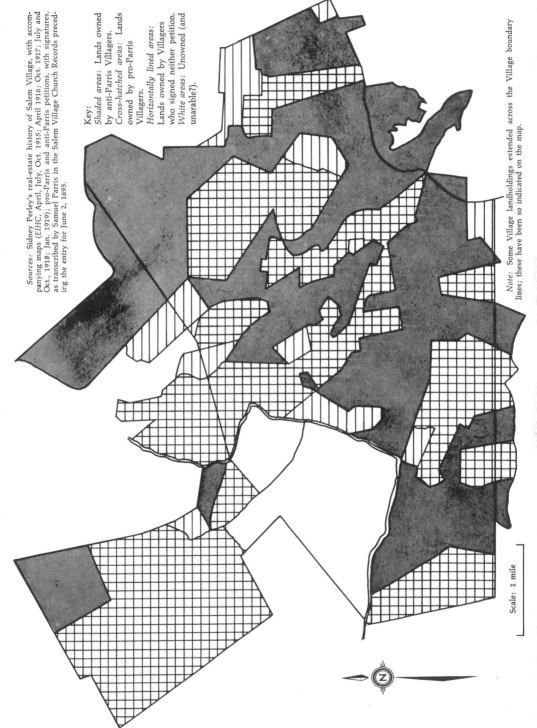

Map 4 **Land Ownership and Factionalism: Salem Village in 1695**

Sources: Sidney Perley's real-estate history of Salem Village, with accompanying maps (*EIHC*, April, July, Oct. 1915; April 1916; Oct. 1917; July and Oct. 1918; Jan. 1919); pro-Parris and anti-Parris petitions, with signatures, as transcribed by Samuel Parris in the Salem Village Church Records preceding the entry for June 2, 1695.

Key:
Shaded areas: Lands owned by anti-Parris Villagers.
Cross-hatched areas: Lands owned by pro-Parris Villagers.
Horizontally lined areas: Lands owned by Villagers who signed neither petition.
White areas: Unowned (and unarable?).

Note: Some Village landholdings extended across the Village boundary lines; these have been so indicated on the map.

Scale: 1 mile

N

general, the lands of the anti-Parris faction tended to enclose the Village on all but its westerly borders, and to hedge in the lands of those pro-Parris men whose farms lay in the heart of the Village.

Commercial Town, Agricultural Village: The Seeds of Discord

But simply to describe the distinguishing characteristics of the two factions is no more than a first step. The next, and more difficult one, is to try to make some sense of these factions, particularly in the context of the protracted political struggles of the period. Our point of departure must be a central fact of Salem Village life: the immediate presence, directly to the south and east, of Salem Town. From almost any point of view, whether geographic or institutional, Salem Town dominated the horizon of the farmers of Salem Village.[9]

What mattered was not simply the fact of the Town's power; it was also the quality of that power. By the 1690's Salem Town was a far cry from the community it had been, half a century earlier, when the first farmers had left it for the hinterland settlement which would become Salem Village. Prosperous from the start, the Town in the years after 1660 entered its great era of economic, and specifically mercantile, expansion. Well before the end of the century, that expansion had led (as one recent study puts it) to "a distinctly urban pattern of life" in Salem Town. The Town's growing commercial importance was officially recognized in 1683 when the General Court designated Boston and Salem as the colony's two "ports of entry" through which all imports and exports had to pass. Increasingly, Salem was gaining access to a broader trading orbit of which London was the center. Such evidence as the close correspondence during these years between grain prices in Salem and in London indicates that the "Atlantic Market" was becoming a reality—and the merchants of Salem Town were immersed in it, exporting cod and mackerel, furs, horses, grain, beef, pork, masts, and naval stores to the other American colonies, the West Indies, the Canaries, Newfoundland, and England, and importing tobacco, sugar, cloth, rum, and a host of other products. In the 1690's twenty-six Salem men owned twenty-one merchant vessels averaging nearly fifty tons each and comprising 12 percent of the total tonnage in Massachusetts. While this left Salem far

9. See above, pp. 41–43.

behind dominant Boston, it did make her—as the 1683 legislation had recognized—the only other really significant mercantile center in the colony.[10]

One consequence of these developments was a sharp rise in the Town's relative wealth. In the first thirty years of its settlement—the period before 1660—the average size of individual Salem Town estates recorded in probate court had actually been lower than the average for the rest of Essex County; in contrast, during the period 1661–81, the estates of Salem Town dwellers averaged almost one-third higher than those from the rest of the county.

But Salem's rising prosperity and cosmopolitan connections did not benefit equally all segments of the Town population. Quite the contrary: in the 1661–81 period (again on the evidence of probated wills), the richest 10 percent of Salem's population controlled 62 percent of its wealth—almost three times as much as it had controlled a generation earlier.[11] What had happened, in fact, was that the prosperity of the Town had polarized the distribution of its wealth and propelled into a position of clear dominance a single group of men: the merchants.

The rise of the merchant class was reflected in Salem Town politics. In the years before 1665, twice as many farmers as merchants had been elected Town selectmen; in the 1665–1700 period, the merchants among the selectmen outnumbered the farmers by six to one.[12] Only those few farmers with close merchant ties and affinities (like the Porter family, which we shall examine in the next chapter) continued to exercise any sustained political influence in the Town.

For the farmers of Salem Village, who represented about one-fifth of the Town's total population in this period,[13] these develop-

10. James Duncan Phillips, *Salem in the Seventeenth Century* (Boston, Houghton Mifflin, 1933), pp. 280–281; Donald Warner Koch, "Income Distribution and Political Structure in Seventeenth Century Salem, Mass.," 105 *EIHC* (1969), 51 ("distinctly urban pattern of life" quote); William I. Davisson, "Essex County Price Trends: Money and Markets in Seventeenth Century Massachusetts," 103 *EIHC* (1967), 183–185; Bernard and Lotte Bailyn, *Massachusetts Shipping: 1697–1714, A Statistical Study* (Cambridge, Mass., Harvard University Press, 1959), Table II, p. 79.

11. Koch, "Income Distribution and Political Structure," pp. 53, 59, 61.

12. Marcia N. Gold, "Sectaries in Puritan Society: A Study of Seventeenth Century Salem Quakers," M.S. thesis, University of Wisconsin, 1969. Appendix I (List of selectmen with occupational and other data), pp. 104–108.

13. Comparative population data from Miller and Henderson, "Census of Salem Village in January 1692," and, for Salem as a whole: William I. Davis-

ments were looming realities which simultaneously enlarged the figurative dimensions of the Town in their eyes and diminished the stature of their own community. The percentage of Essex County wealth represented by farm assets and equipment in the seventeenth century shrank steadily and dramatically through the 1680's (the last decade for which data have been compiled). In the 1650's, on the basis of probated estates, farm wealth averaged 40 percent of the total; thirty years later it was hovering at about 9 percent. Although it may be going too far to claim, as has one recent student of Essex County economic history, that agriculture was a "declining industry" in these years, it seems clear that it was no more than holding its own while the Town's commercial development shot ahead.[14]

Nor were these changes experienced merely as data buried in statistical tables; they were the vivid and tangible substance of everyday reality. In Salem no less than in Boston, the rise of an internationally oriented merchant class, connected by ties of marriage and mutual interest, spawned a style of life and a sensibility decidedly alien to the pre-capitalist patterns of village existence. The differences were becoming apparent even in the Town's physical appearance; while Salem in these years did not yet possess the breathtakingly beautiful mansions which the architect Samuel McIntire would design for its commercial aristocrats a century later, the trend was already clear. Even a Londoner who visited Salem Town in 1686, for example, was struck by the "many fine houses"

son, "Essex County Wealth Trends: Wealth and Economic Growth in Seventeenth Century Massachusetts," 103 *EIHC* (1967), p. 294. The 5:1 population ratio of Town and Village is confirmed in the Town's 1695 tax rolls. Of the 429 adult males assessed to pay the Provincial tax that year, a total of 92 (21.4 percent) were Villagers. *Tax and Valuation Lists of Massachusetts Towns before 1776* (microfilm), "Salem, 1689–1773."

14. Davisson, "Essex County Wealth Trends," pp. 325–326. Davisson's statistics also show a decade-by-decade decline in the average actual cash value of agricultural assets and equipment in estates probated from mid-century down to the 1680's: from just over £81 in the 1650's to about £31 in the 1670's to £17 for the early years of the 1680's, where his study ends. Though Davisson sees this as further evidence that agriculture was "declining," it could also reflect the greater availability, and consequent lower valuations, of such equipment. Considerable agricultural activity was certainly still being pursued within the bounds of Salem Town proper in these years, particularly in the "Northfields" section lying between the Wooleston and the North Rivers and in the area, south of Salem Village, which later became the Town of Peabody. In speaking of the way Salem Villagers perceived "Salem Town," however, we are thinking of the bustling mercantile center which increasingly dominated the Town and imparted to it its distinctive flavor.

he saw there.[15] If this was how the Town impressed an English cosmopolite, how must it have struck the farmers of Salem Village?

What may have made these farmers even more sensitive to the transformation of Salem Town was the fact that Salem Village itself was hardly a haven of social serenity. In its own way, the Village was almost as vulnerable as the Town to the pressures of change. Even in physical terms, the community had from the first lacked that stable and visually cohesive quality which many modern real-estate developers—and some historians—seek to summon up with the word *village*. Since it had never been "founded" as a separate entity, it lacked the central town common, surrounded by a square of substantial homes and dominated by the meetinghouse, which even today provides a focal point for many old towns of New England. Maps of Salem Village in the early years reveal no such systematic layout; houses are simply dotted here and there, almost at random it seems, throughout the Village bounds.[16]

By the 1680's and 1690's additional, more serious evidences of instability were beginning to emerge, not only in the record of political squabbling, but from other data as well. The matter of population turnover, for instance. Of the ninety-four Salem Villagers on the tax roll in 1681, forty-one do not appear on the 1690 list. In their places, one finds the names of forty-six other men, some of them sons come of age, some of them new arrivals.[17] Death took a few of those whose names are missing in 1690, but most simply disappear from the records without a trace.

Furthermore, for those who did remain in Salem Village, the diminished availability of land was becoming an increasingly serious problem.[18] Many men of Salem Village were already landless by the 1690's, and, as Chart 2 shows, those who did hold title to land usually owned less than the yeomen of the preceding generation. In the 1640's, the average landholding in "Salem Farms" was 180 acres. And in fact, over the next two decades, as new settlers

15. Extract from *The Life and Errors of John Dunton, Late Citizen of London, Written by Himself in Solitude,* Massachusetts Historical Society, *Collections,* second series, 2 (1814), 117.

16. Map of Salem Village in 1672, Sidney Perley, *The History of Salem, Mass.,* 3 vols. (Salem, 1924–28), II, facing p. 441.

17. Village Records, Dec. 27, 1681; Jan. 6, 1691.

18. As early as 1673 the Town selectmen appointed a committee to search out any remaining common lands which might be sold to increase the tax base. With the exception of a one-hundred-acre tract of somewhat dubious ownership, the committee found only ten small plots of undistributed land—Perley, *History of Salem,* III, 63.

Chart 2.   **Average Size of Salem Village Landholdings, 1640–1700   (in acres)**

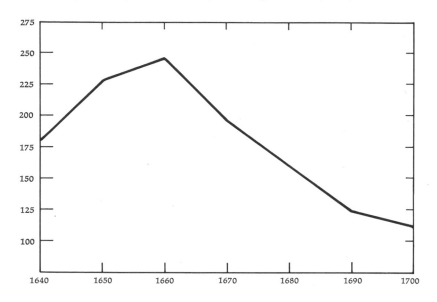

Source: Unpublished quantification of Sidney Perley's real-estate history
of Salem Village (*EIHC*, April, July, and Oct., 1915; April 1916; Oct. 1917;
July and Oct., 1918; and Jan. 1919) by Cynthia Paquette and Tamar Shelkan.

received substantial grants and as new tracts were distributed
among the farmers already on the scene, this figure increased to
nearly 250 acres. But from 1660 to the end of the century, as the
second and third generations established themselves within the
circumscribed confines of the Village, these large holdings were
increasingly broken down into smaller and smaller units of ownership. By 1690 the average Salem Village landholding stood at 124
acres—just about half what it had been in 1660. During the 1690–
1700 decade, as the witchcraft trials and the Parris controversy
wracked the Village, the average size of Village landholdings continued to shrink.[19]

The diminishing availability of land, a matter of general concern
in colonial New England, was felt here with particular intensity,

19. These statistics are based on an unpublished quantification of Sidney
Perley's real-estate history of Salem Village (see note on sources to Map 4)
by two of our students, Cynthia Paquette and Tamar Shelkan. For a recent
discussion of overcrowding in colonial New England, see Kenneth Lockridge,
"Land, Population and the Evolution of New England Society, 1630–1790,"
Past and Present (No. 39, April 1968), pp. 62–80.

for Salem Village, unlike some other communities facing this problem, could neither expand nor easily generate new settlements in contiguous open lands. The situation of the Village farmers was quite different, for example, from that of those men of Sudbury, Massachusetts, who, feeling the land squeeze in the 1650's, had secured from the General Court permission to establish a new town just a few miles to the west of Sudbury, and sharing a common boundary with it. From the earliest years, Salem Village was hemmed in by a circle of towns: Lynn, Reading, Andover, Rowley, Topsfield, Wenham, and Beverly, not to mention Salem Town itself. Significantly, as land grew scarcer in the late 1670's and the 1680's, the Villagers engaged in sharp boundary disputes with at least three of these: Andover, Wenham, and Topsfield.[20] With open lands unavailable, a new boundary settlement became the Village's only hope for expansion.

Although individual men and families were continually moving from the Village, it was only in the 1720's, when central Massachusetts was being opened to settlement, that group migration appeared a feasible solution to these land problems. In 1724 a number of Salem Villagers, describing themselves as "much straitened for land," petitioned the General Court for a grant in the west. The tract they received lay some eighty miles from Salem, in the range of hills forming the eastern rim of the Connecticut River Valley, and here they founded a town they called New Salem.[21] But all this came later, too late to alter the feeling of many Salem Villagers in the 1690's that their situation was growing bleaker, with no immediate prospects of relief, while the Town's commercial orientation rendered it less and less responsive to the problems of the farmer.

Even before the establishment of Salem Village in 1672, many of the residents of the area had recognized that it was more than geography that separated them from the Town of Salem. As early as 1667, in their petition to the General Court asking relief from

20. On the boundary disputes, see Chapter 2; on Sudbury: Sumner Chilton Powell, *Puritan Village: The Formation of a New England Town* (Middletown, Conn., Wesleyan University Press, 1963), Chapter IX.

21. Upham, *Salem Witchcraft*, I, 148–149. As early as 1676 a group of Salem men, including a number of Salem Villagers, received, in compensation for their services in King Philip's War, a grant of land in what would become the town of Amherst, N.H. But no actual settlement was made until the 1730's, presumably because of the continued presence of Indians in the area—Perley, *History of Salem*, III, 99; Daniel F. Secomb, *History of the Town of Amherst* (Concord, N.H., 1883), pp. 9–10, 32.

the burden of attending military watch in Salem, the thirty-one signatories did not stop with the obvious point that they lived five to ten miles from Salem center; they went on to compare the "compact town" to their own "scattered" settlement, always vulnerable to Indian attack because its houses were so widely separated "one from another, some a mile, some further," so that even "six or eight watches will not serve us." They proceeded to inquire sarcastically "whether Salem Town hath not more cause to send us help to watch among ourselves than we have to go to them?"[22] But no help came forth from this direction. Lacking it, yet legally powerless to strike out on their own, many Salem Village residents even as early as the 1660's came to feel both exploited and neglected by the Town. Envy mingled with resentment in those Villagers who had constant cause to remember the dynamic and vaguely hostile urban presence on their southeasterly border.

The Development of Village Factionalism

But the looming presence of Salem Town was not perceived as hostile by everyone in the Village. If the changes in the Town had affected all the Villagers in the same way, or to the same degree, the Village's affairs in the final quarter of the seventeenth century would surely have taken quite a different turn. But as it actually happened, not every Villager had reason to feel alienated from the Town. Indeed, the economic and social transformations of the Town in these years affected different Villagers in quite different ways. The very developments which threatened many of them gave others reason to take heart. It was this fact, above all, that produced the factional lines which from the beginning divided the Village.

From the 1670's on, proximity to the Town, and even a direct involvement in its economic life, repeatedly emerged as a determining factor in the divisions which plagued the Village. In the Bayley dispute, for example, there is a striking pattern in the geographic distribution of the minister's supporters and opponents—a pattern which neatly inverts that of 1695. James Bayley's supporters were clustered in that part of Salem Village which lay closest to Salem Town, while his opponents' farms lay in those regions of the Village most remote from the Town. Similarly, the evidence in the Deodat Lawson ordination dispute, though more sketchy, again

22. Perley, *History of Salem*, II, 436–438.

suggests that the line of cleavage was determined to a degree by one's relationship to Salem Town. Of the four men who took the lead in opposing Lawson's ordination and the creation of a Village church in 1687, three owned lots in Salem Town as well as in Salem Village. None of the five members of the Salem Village Committee which actively promoted the ordination owned land in the Town. Further, those Villagers who were fighting Lawson's ordination went so far as to challenge the legality of the pro-Lawson Village Committee by claiming, quite without foundation, that only Town men, not Villagers, were entitled to serve on the Village Committee![23]

All this points to the conclusion that these divisions pitted people who continued to identify with Salem Town against others for whom the Village, and what they saw as its distinctive interests, were paramount. Such an interpretation is strengthened by evidence that at crucial moments Salem Town influence, both ecclesiastical and secular, was brought to bear in support of the Town-oriented Village group and against those who were working for the independence of the Village. When the elders of the Salem Town church took Bayley's side at the critical moment in 1679, it may have been not only to support a colleague in distress but also to protect the broader interests of Salem Town in the matter. Recall, too, the 1693 letter of the minister and assistant minister of the Salem Town church clearly supporting the anti-Parris faction, and the fact that the Town-appointed constables refused in 1695 to cooperate in collecting Samuel Parris's salary arrears—even though the pro-Parris Committee in the Village explicitly requested them to do so.[24]

From this perspective, the geographic and economic profile of the two factions begins to take on meaning. For even though the Village's relationship to the Town was the crucial factor in the early history of the Village, that relationship was never simply a matter of Town versus Village. Within each, significant divisions were to be found. In the Town, as we shall see, the dominant merchant group was challenged dramatically on a number of occasions. Similarly, as the demarcation lines of the two Village factions so clearly

23. This fact was noted by the five Salem Town arbitrators (John Hathorne, Bartholomew Gedney, William Browne, Jr., John Higginson, and Nicholas Noyes) in their letter of advice to Salem Village—Village Records, Feb. 28, 1687.

24. Chapter 3, notes 21 and 25.

suggest, the Salem Villagers were by no means of one accord in their feelings toward the Town. To certain Salem Villagers, the urbanization and commercial growth of the Town seemed a promising and exciting development. The chance of a boundary line may have placed them in Salem Village, but their interests lay with the Town.

For they recognized that Salem Town required food, and that the Village was the nearest food-producing region. Furthermore, the Town's developing export trade was based in part on products which Salem Village could supply. While we do not know, because we lack the necessary commercial records, precisely how much Salem Village grain and beef went to fill the bellies of slaves and planters in Barbados, or how much Village timber helped build houses in Newfoundland or ships-of-the-line in England, we can be fairly certain that to some degree involvement in this larger market, or the possibility of such involvement, was a factor in the Village economy.

But Salem Village agriculture in these years was being pursued under certain adverse conditions: not only was productivity limited by primitive equipment, but the size of farms was shrinking as lands were divided among maturing sons of the third generation. Under these circumstances, relatively slight differences became crucial in determining which Village farmers would be able to cross the subsistence threshold and begin to profit by the Village's proximity to a populous trading center. In at least two important respects—quality of land and access to market—those farmers on the eastern (or Town) side of the Village had a significant advantage. Modern topographical maps show what any Salem Village farmer knew from first-hand experience: the best lands in the Village were the broad, flat meadows of the eastern part, nearest the coast, while the western part was increasingly broken up by sharp little hills and marshy depressions. The eastern side of the Village, too, was significantly closer to the network of roads and waterways which gave access to Salem Town and her markets. (The additional two or three miles may seem negligible today, but for the farmer who had to convey his goods by ox cart over rutted, muddy, and often flooded paths before reaching the better-maintained Ipswich Road, they certainly loomed large.) In both these respects, then, the farmers on this side of the Village had a crucial edge in supplying the needs of Salem Town and, to a limited degree, the broader Atlantic market of which it was a part. And Village geography, as we shall now see, had other effects as well.

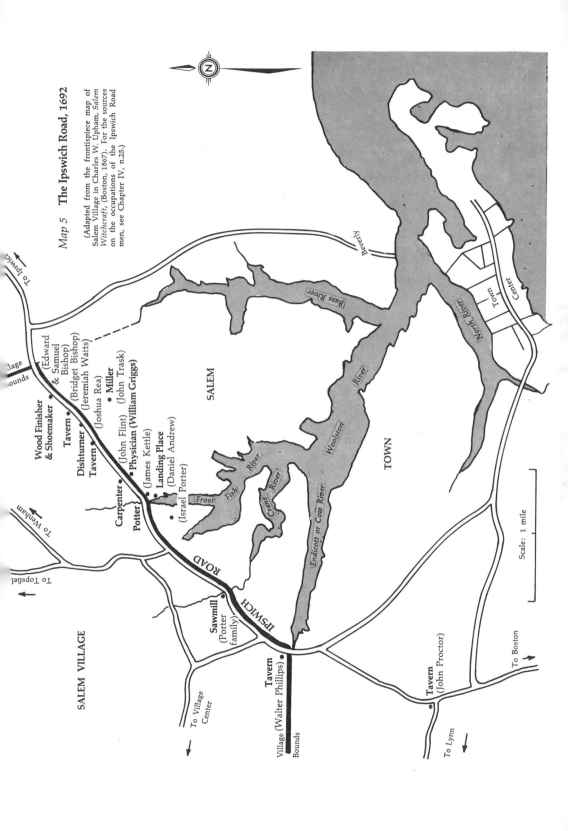

Map 5 **The Ipswich Road, 1692**

(Adapted from the frontispiece map of Salem Village in Charles W. Upham, *Salem Witchcraft*, (Boston, 1867). For the sources on the occupations of the Ipswich Road men, see Chapter IV, n.25.)

To Ipswich

SALEM

Bass River

Beverly

North River

Town Center

Woolston River

Endicott or Cow River

Crane River

Fish River

Frost River

TOWN

Scale: 1 mile

Village Bounds

Wood Finisher & Shoemaker (Edward & Samuel Bishop)

Tavern (Bridget Bishop)

Dishturner (Jeremiah Watts)

Tavern (Joshua Rea)

Miller (John Trask)

Physician (William Griggs)

(John Flint)

Carpenter (James Kettle)

Potter (Israel Porter)

Landing Place (Daniel Andrew)

To Wenham

To Topsfiel

SALEM VILLAGE

Sawmill (Porter family)

To Village Center

Tavern Village (Walter Phillips) Bounds

IPSWICH ROAD

Tavern (John Proctor)

To Boston

To Lynn

The Ipswich Road: An Anti-Parris Paradigm. The eastern section of Salem Village, because of its location, boasted an unusually high concentration of what little non-agricultural economic activity was to be found in the community during the 1690's. One way to make this point is to examine with some care those Villagers who lived on or near the Ipswich Road, which formed the boundary line between Salem Town and Salem Village, and which was the major northward route from Boston. Just south of the Village this thoroughfare was joined by an important spur road connecting it (and the Village itself) with the center of Salem Town. Even more important, the Ipswich Road—crossing, near their farthest point of navigability, no fewer than three rivers which flowed on into Salem harbor—was the site of several wharves and landing places from which goods and products could move by water between Village and Town. (See Map 5.)

More than any other inhabitants of the community, the Villagers who lived along the Ipswich Road were exposed to the Town and its concerns. Like a modern interstate highway, the road passed *by* the Village, not into it. With all kinds of travelers daily passing near their doors on the way to or from Salem Town, or Boston itself, town and province news were inevitably the common currency of conversation. The Village center, by contrast, well to the west, must have represented a considerably weaker pole of attraction.

It is not surprising that a number of the men living on or very near the Ipswich Road were engaged in occupations which brought them into regular contact with a wide range of individuals: occupations such as potter, physician, carpenter, innkeeper, sawmill operator, shoemaker, miller, sawyer (that is, wood finisher), and "dish-turner." Particularly important, in terms of the Townward orientation of this part of Salem Village, were the four taverns which stood along a short stretch of the Ipswich Road as it passed through Salem Village. Three of these actually lay within the Village: the licensed taverns of Joshua Rea, Jr. and Walter Phillips, and the un-licensed—but well known and well patronized—tavern of Edward and Bridget Bishop. The other, operated by John Proctor, stood about a mile south of the Village boundary.[25]

25. On the Ipswich Road taverns: Perley, *History of Salem*, III, 84 (Rea, Phillips), 266 (Bishop); 8 *EQC*, 231 (Proctor). On the other Ipswich Road occupations: Sidney Perley, "Rial Side: Part of Salem in 1700," 55 *EIHC* (1919), pp. 66 (James Kettle, potter), 67 (John Flint, carpenter), 69 (Jeremiah Watts,

The Ipswich Road, the part of the Village most intimately linked to Salem Town, boasted a particularly dense concentration of anti-Parris sentiment. Of the twenty-one Village householders who lived along this road or within one-quarter mile of it, only two signed the pro-Parris petition in 1695, while thirteen aligned themselves with Parris's opponents.[26] (From another angle, fully one-third of the householders in the anti-Parris faction lived along or near the Ipswich Road.)

The small entrepreneurs of the Ipswich Road were not the wealthiest or most prominent members of the anti-Parris group—those men we will be considering in the next chapter—but they shared to a particularly intense degree the feeling that their livelihood was linked to Salem Town more closely than to Salem Village. While the interests of the anti-Parris faction were far from identical to those of the merchants in the Town, they viewed the Town not as a threat, but as a center with which they might hope to establish a profitable commercial relationship. Conversely, they felt little sympathy—and ultimately much enmity—toward those who were working to widen the political gap between Town and Village. If the members of the pro-Parris faction had succeeded in breaking away from Salem entirely and establishing an independent town under their control, they could have acted in various ways to the disadvantage of the more commercially oriented Villagers, including the imposition of fees on the transport of products beyond the town boundaries. As early as 1666, when the separatist move was just getting underway, the Townsmen reported that even some

dishturner), and 63 (William Griggs, physician); Robert Calef, *More Wonders of the Invisible World* in George Lincoln Burr, ed., *Narratives of the Witchcraft Cases* (New York, Charles Scribner's Sons, 1914; reissued New York, Barnes and Noble, 1968), p. 370 (Samuel Bishop, shoemaker); 5 *EQC*, 385 (John Trask, miller); W. Elliot Woodward, *Records of Salem Witchcraft Copied from the Original Documents*, 2 vols. (Roxbury, Mass., Privately printed 1864; reissued in one volume, New York, Da Capo Press, 1969), I, 136 (Edward Bishop, sawyer, i.e., wood finisher). The only other Salem Village tavern was one lying in the heart of the Village, next to the meetinghouse and operated by the firmly pro-Parris Nathaniel Ingersoll. It may be noteworthy that Ingersoll's license was not renewed in 1691, and instead one was granted to Walter Phillips, on the Ipswich Road—Perley, *History of Salem*, III, 84. Ingersoll's residence continued to function as a hostelry, however, and in 1692 the initial examinations of some accused witches were held here.

26. There may have been three pro-Parris signers. Of the three men named "Edward Bishop" in the Village in these years, two lived along the Ipswich Road, and one did not. We have been unable to ascertain whether or not the one Edward Bishop who was pro-Parris (probably a step-grandson of Bridget Bishop's who married a Putnam) was one of the Ipswich Road Bishops.

inhabitants of the Farms were prepared to oppose any change which would force them to "forsake Salem." [27]

The Village Church: A Pro-Parris Paradigm. But, for the Salem Villager who would later join the pro-Parris faction, there was every reason to "forsake Salem." Remote from the Town, and cut off even from convenient access to it, he increasingly came to see his interests neglected by those in power there. Consistently, then, he opposed those in the Village who represented, or seemed to represent, the intrusive thrust of Salem Town and what it stood for, and just as consistently he worked to build up the Village as a strong and independent entity distinct from the Town. For him, the church which the Village lacked before 1689 promised more than religious solace; it loomed also as a potential counterweight, spiritual and political, to the unfamiliar developments which were gaining such force so near at hand.

Once the church did become a reality, it provided an institutional locus for all those Villagers who felt threatened by such developments. Predictably, these were not the richest men in the Village. Although our general impression of colonial New England communities is that those prosperous inhabitants at the top of the tax rolls tend to figure prominently on the church rolls as well, this was not the case in Salem Village. Of the thirteen Village householders taxed at more than one pound in December 1695, only three joined the Village church during Samuel Parris's tenure. (These three— John, Nathaniel, and Jonathan Putnam—were all members of the family which will receive separate consideration in the next chapter.) The Village church, in fact, was less an institution through which the wealthiest members of the community gave expression to their special status than a bulwark against precisely these people —and against the insidious infection with which they seemed to be tainted.

But neither is this to say that the church was dominated by the

---

27. J. W. Hanson, *History of the Town of Danvers* (Danvers, 1848), p. 36. As an example of the kind of steps a town might take to impede the commercial activities of its residents, note the following action of the Town of Andover on January 1, 1675: "[N]o man shall have liberty after the first of January, 1675, to sell, or transport any cedar out of the town, either in shingles or otherwise, but shall forfeit twenty shillings for every thousand of shingles, or quantity of cedar proportionable, unless the town shall upon some extraordinary occasion grant liberty to the contrary"—6 *EQC*, 323. For a similar, though less stringent, action by Salem Town in 1669, see Salem Town Records, 41 *EIHC* (1905), 301–302.

poorest Villagers. Of the sixty-two Villagers taxed in 1695–96 at under ten shillings, only seven, or about 11 percent, were members of the Village church. (See Chart 3.) It was, rather, the broad

Chart 3. **Wealth and Salem Village Church Membership**

	Tax Bracket, 1695–96	
	10–20 shillings	Over 20 shillings
	15	3
	14	10
	29	13

1695; membership information

he taxpayers in the 10–20
up the bulk of the church
an 50 percent of those in
h under Parris's ministry.
y large stake in the status
reaten it, yet not enough
commercial opportunities
p, politically conscious,
ng with several wealthy
core of Samuel Parris's

nent in this support: the
o signed the pro-Parris
.... wives made possible the forging
or a pro-Parris majority in the Village. As Chart 4 shows, these were primarily poor Villagers: twenty-one of the twenty-nine were taxed at under ten shillings in 1695, and two were not taxed at all. Some of them landless, some with only the most meager acreage, these were not, in the nature of things, men who have left us many clues as to the reasons for their political allegiance. But, whatever their motives for remaining outside the church, we may speculate that they nevertheless perceived this institution as a friendly and sheltering buffer against the world beyond the fragile boundary lines of Salem Village.

Chart 4. **Wealth and Salem Village Church Membership in the Pro-Parris Faction**

Taxpayers	Tax bracket, 1695–96			Average assessment
	Under 10 shillings	10–20 shillings	Over 20 shillings	
Pro-Parris church members (*n* = 21)	7	11	3	14.4 shillings
Pro-Parris non-church members (*n* = 27)	21	4	2	7.8 shillings

Sources: Tax list, Village Records, Dec. 13, 1695; pro-Parris petition as transcribed by Samuel Parris in the Village Church Records preceding the entry for June 2, 1695; membership information in the Church Records, *passim.*

The pro-Parris faction thus emerges as a coalition whose shared fears united it in support of Parris: a core group of Villagers of middling wealth who were also church members, supplemented by another group, approximately twice as large, of poorer Villagers who were not church members but who identified with the Village church and its minister. The church members provided the institutional structure and the political impetus, the others supplied the votes and the signatures.

Since the pro-Parris faction also played a leading role in the witchcraft prosecutions, it has typically been portrayed as a powerful and domineering clique. From the evidence, however, this group emerges as by far the more vulnerable of the two: less wealthy than its opposition, owning less land, quite literally hedged in by more flourishing anti-Parris neighbors and less able to benefit from the commercial developments centered in Salem Town.

If the Ipswich Road helped shape and define the anti-Parris faction, it also provided an objective focus for the amorphous fears of the pro-Parris group, for whom it would have seemed not so much the line which separated the Village from the Town, but the very channel through which the Town penetrated the Village. The road stood as a perpetual affront to those who felt the integrity of the Village to be menaced from just this quarter. Its residents, with their more commercial outlook and occupations, had in many cases already succumbed to the lure which menaced the Village as a whole.

The unusual concentration of taverns along the Ipswich Road dramatized the threat with particular vividness. The Puritans, of course, did not frown on alcohol as such, especially when it was consumed in the domestic circle; indeed, beer and wine were standard accompaniments to seventeenth-century New England fare. But they did fear, profoundly, the threat to social stability embodied in taverns and inns. As gathering places for wayfarers and strangers, they offered the individual at least partial and temporary escape from the overlapping restraints of family, church, and town. The obvious hesitation with which the courts licensed taverns, the close oversight the authorities exercised, and the haste with which licenses were revoked at any hint of disorderliness—all bear witness to the reality of this concern.[28]

A revealing glimpse into the social circumstances surrounding the establishment of one of these taverns emerges from John Proctor's request to the Salem selectmen in 1666 for a license to operate a tavern in his house on the Ipswich Road near the Salem Village line. His residence, he said, was "in the common roadway, which occasioneth several travelers to call in for some refreshment as they pass along." Since the free entertaining of these wayfarers was proving to be expensive, Proctor added: "I do therefore earnestly request you that you would be pleased to grant me liberty to set up a house of entertainment to sell beer, cider [and] liquors."[29] The court granted Proctor's petition, with the stipulation that he sell exclusively to strangers. Thus, from the Salem Village perspective, the Proctor house became a rendezvous point for outsiders—and *only* for outsiders.

For the pro-Parris Salem Villagers, with their particular anxieties, this generalized concern over taverns must have been especially intense. Given such a background, it is not surprising to find that three of the four Ipswich Road tavern keepers figured prominently in the climactic Village events of the 1690's—and two of these three as victims of those events. Joshua Rea, Jr., publicly expressed his opposition to the witchcraft trials in 1692 by signing a petition seeking to save Rebecca Nurse from the gallows. In 1695 Rea's

28. The Essex County court records, published and unpublished, are full of such cases.
29. 3 *EQC*, 377.

name appears on the anti-Parris petition.[30] Two of the other tavern keepers, Bridget Bishop and John Proctor, were unable to take a stand for or against Parris in 1695: they had been hanged three years before for committing witchcraft.

One of the witnesses against Proctor in 1692 was Joseph Bayley (a son-in-law of Captain John Putnam) who had a distressing experience to relate. Late in May of that year, riding along the Ipswich Road on horseback with his wife, he felt two very hard blows on his chest "which caused great pain in my stomach and amazement in my head." Pointedly, Bayley chose in his deposition to indicate the precise spots in his journey where he had suffered these unpleasant shocks to his system. The first occurred "when we came in sight of the house where John Proctor did live," and the second "when we came to the way where Salem Road cometh into Ipswich Road."[31]

Except, perhaps, for Samuel Parris, nobody in Salem Village came much closer than this in the 1690's to articulating publicly the depth of Village anxiety toward the Town. Curiously enough, the first explicit public expression of the economic basis of this anxiety appeared only decades later, in 1752, in a public document composed by the General Court of the province. After noting, in what was by then commonplace fashion, that the "great distance" between Town and Village made it difficult for Villagers to take part in the "public affairs" of the Town, the document proceeded to the heart of the matter: most of the inhabitants of the Town were "either merchants, traders, or mechanics," while those of the Village were "chiefly husbandmen." Consequently, "many disputes and difficulties" had arisen "in the managing their public affairs together." To prevent these "inconveniences" in the future, the court decreed that Salem Village "be erected into a separate and distinct district by the name of Danvers."[32]

With this action of 1752, Salem Village at last became an independent town. By the mid-eighteenth century, when the candid analysis which accompanied its formal separation became part of the public record of the province, tensions like these, rooted in economic differences, could be openly acknowledged and accepted even in so formal a document as an Act of Incorporation. During the 1690's and earlier, the essential nature of the conflict was never

30. Upham, *Salem Witchcraft*, II, 272.
31. Woodward, *Records of Salem Witchcraft*, I, 113.
32. Hanson, *History of Danvers*, p. 52.

articulated so explicitly, at least in print, and this has contributed to the obscurity in which so much of the history of Salem Village— and of Salem witchcraft—has been shrouded.

Village Factionalism: A Wider Perspective

But still we have not penetrated to the heart of the matter. For our narrative of Salem Village's ordeal, even supplemented by an examination of her two rival factions, raises as many questions as it answers. How, after all, could such a dispute have escalated to so bitter and deadly a level? Why were the two sides so long unable to find any political means of resolving the impasse? And, moving back one step further, why should the presence of differing economic interests have polarized the Village in the first place into such vindictive and implacable camps? Even granting the existence of two opposing sides, why did not each one simply pursue its particular interests and tacitly accept the right of the other to do the same?

In one sense, of course, Salem Village factionalism poses no "problem." There were, after all, concrete issues at stake, and significant, measurable differences between the two groups. And yet, as one follows these disputes over the years, their *intensity* so often seems out of proportion to the ostensible issues. In 1687, in one of many similar observations made over the years, a committee of outside arbitrators commented on "the settled prejudice and resolved animosity" which their probe of Village conditions had uncovered.[33] Samuel Parris's early church records made clear that conditions, if anything, grew worse in the period immediately preceding 1692. And, of course, the witchcraft trials themselves offer the most persuasive evidence of the passionate emotions which underlay these longstanding divisions.

To understand this intensity, we must recognize the fact—self-evident to the men and women of Salem Village—that what was going on was not simply a personal quarrel, an economic dispute, or even a struggle for power, but a mortal conflict involving the very nature of the community itself. The fundamental issue was not who was to control the Village, but what its essential character was to be. To the Puritans of seventeenth-century New England, no social or political issue was without its moral dimension as well. For a community was more than simply a collection of individuals

33. See Chapter 2, note 35.

who happened to live and work together; it was itself an organism with a reality and an existence distinct from that of its component parts.

John Winthrop, the first governor of colonial Massachusetts, fully articulated this theme as early as 1630 in his lecture aboard the ship *Arabella*, as the first large contingent of Puritan settlers was sailing toward New England. "[W]e must be knit together in this work as one man," he declared; "We must delight in each other, . . . rejoice together, mourn together, labor and suffer together, always having before our eyes our commission and community in the work, our community as members of the same body." [34] Since each community was almost literally a "body," the individuals who composed it could neither logically nor practically regard themselves as autonomous creatures with their own "particular" interests. For a person to pursue such a self-determined course was as destructive and, ultimately, as absurd as for one part of the human body to pursue *its* own good: for a hand to refuse to release to the mouth the food it held in its grasp, for example, or for the mouth to refuse to pass along that food to the stomach. "Self-interest" was like that. If left uncontrolled, it could result only in the failure of the community and of every person within it.

From infancy, a Puritan was raised to distrust his private will, to perceive it as the "old Adam" which, above all, constituted original sin. It was this innate self-interest—more than sexual lust, more than any of the "sins" we commonly (and mistakenly) think of as particularly repugnant to the Puritans—that had to be tamed if it could not be eradicated.

Thus, Winthrop's insistence that the men and women aboard the *Arabella* were "members of the same body" was no casual figure of speech or sentimental paean to a vague commonality of feeling. It was, for Winthrop, a statement of certain very specific social and economic policies—policies which he enunciated again and again in his lecture: "We must be willing to abridge ourselves of our superfluities, for the supply of others' necessities"; "The care of the public must oversway all private respects"; "We must not look only on our own things, but also on the things of our brethren." [35] And Winthrop's scheme contained an enforcement procedure as well: the constant scrutiny and regulation of all facets of individual

34. John Winthrop, "A Modell of Christian Charity," *Winthrop Papers*, 4 vols. (Boston, Massachusetts Historical Society, 1929–1944), II, 294.
35. *Ibid.*, 293–294.

behavior in order to nip in the bud deviations that threatened the interests of the community as a whole.

The important thing is not whether very many people actually behaved in this fashion (almost certainly most of them did not), but rather the fact that when they did not act in this way—when they pursued their self-interest at the expense of the greater good of the whole—they felt that they were not behaving properly.

By the end of the seventeenth century, however, this sense that there was a dangerous conflict between private will and public good had become seriously eroded in many quarters by two generations of population growth, geographic dispersal, and economic opportunity: the emergence of pre-industrial capitalism. By the next century all that would remain would be a general sense that there were *some* limits beyond which an individual might not venture in pursuing his private interests. This qualification aside, however, New England towns of the 1700's conceded that they were made up of a diverse mixture of imperfect and self-seeking human beings, and they largely abandoned the effort to be anything more.

To be sure, factional conflicts, intra-town fights, and rural-urban struggles continued to be bitter enough in the eighteenth century, but they no longer involved the conviction that the fate of the community itself was hanging in the balance. Factions might temporarily fall from power, but that was all. Whatever their rhetoric, all sides recognized at heart that the stakes for which they played, while vital to their immediate interests, were nevertheless limited. The crucial change in the eighteenth century, then, was not in the frequency of conflicts, or in the objective issues that produced them, but in their diminished moral resonance. By mid-century, certainly, the fundamental questions as to the nature and structure of the social order had been resolved—and resolved on the side of individual freedom.

But in the 1690's, it was still possible for the farmers of the pro-Parris faction to believe that the outcome of this shadowy struggle remained very much in question. Thus, for them, Salem Town was not suspect just because of its vaguely hostile political climate, or because it was following a different line of economic development, but because the total thrust of that commercial development represented a looming *moral* threat with implications of the most fundamental sort.

As we have seen, Salem Village itself in the late seventeenth century was neither a haven of pastoral tranquility nor an embodiment of John Winthrop's public-mindedness. And yet, coupled with the inescapable realities of social turbulence and diminished opportunity was the sense that if any place *could* offer shelter against sweeping social change and provide a setting where the Puritan social vision might yet be realized, it would likely be an agricultural, essentially noncommercial settlement such as Salem Village. The very nature of farm life, with its settled routines and seasonal rhythms, offered at least the illusion of social stability and continuity—and perhaps, in comparison to what was happening in Salem Town, it was more than illusion.

Thus the merchant capitalists who controlled the Town—and to an extent the Village, too—were not merely outsiders; they were outsiders whose careers could be seen as a violation of much that is contained in the word "Puritan." As Bernard Bailyn has put it, commenting on Massachusetts commercial development in these very decades:

> In the larger port towns of provincial New England, particularly those in continuous touch with Europe, the business community represented the spirit of a new age. Its guiding principles were not social stability, order, and the discipline of the senses, but mobility, growth, and the enjoyment of life. Citizens of an international trading world as well as of New England colonies, the merchants took the pattern for their conduct not from the Bible or from parental teachings but from their picture of life in Restoration England.[36]

It may not be necessary to go quite this far in describing the merchant elite of Salem; and, in any case, Bailyn's description would apply to only a handful of the anti-Parris Villagers, since they were not themselves merchants, but mainly farmers who to a degree identified their interests with those of the Town's commercial element. Still, under the circumstances, it was only too easy for Parris's supporters to see the minister's opponents in terms like these. The anti-Parris leaders may have lived *in* the Village, but they were not *of* the Village.

It is tempting simply to label the pro-Parris faction as "Puritans," their opponents as "capitalists," and let it go at that. But we know from experience that human beings rarely fit quite so neatly into such categorical boxes. And as the work of several generations of scholars has made clear, the relationship between Puritanism and

36. Bernard Bailyn, *The New England Merchants in the Seventeenth Century* (Cambridge, Mass., Harvard University Press, 1955), p. 139.

capitalism is itself deeply ambiguous. In any case, the pro-Parris Villagers were certainly no more a group of Winthrop's self-denying communitarians than their opponents were the materialistic individualists we commonly associate with nineteenth-century entrepreneurship. The similarities between our two little microcosmic groups would probably, to most modern eyes, have seemed far more noticeable than the subtle differences of emphasis and priority which set them apart.

And, still further, at a time when one world view was imperceptibly yielding to another, each faction must have shared enough of the other's outlook to feel its power and be drawn to it. The anti-Parris men must at times have sensed with a pang what they were giving up in turning toward the burgeoning Town and away from the Village. And the pro-Parris Villagers, for their part, must have felt deeply the lure of the forces which were transforming the Town: the very forces they feared and despised. This, too, helps us understand the intensity of the conflict. For the Villagers were not only at war with each other; they were also at war with themselves.

Why Salem Village?

But many New Englanders must have been at war with themselves at the end of the seventeenth century, and for these very reasons. And many communities were undergoing factional struggles in this period when such conflicts were often invested with a particular freight of moral significance. Yet none experienced the kind of convulsion which prostrated Salem Village. Nowhere else did members of one faction willingly connive in the prosecution and, in certain cases, the deaths, of scores of persons they in some way identified with the other side. What was it that reduced the Salem Village struggle ultimately to a kind of total war?

The answer, obvious perhaps, seems to lie in the convergence of a specific and unlikely combination of historical circumstances at this particular time and place.

To begin with, *physical setting*. If the Village had been an isolated agricultural community, off in the back country, then Salem Town would hardly have loomed so large in its consciousness. A dissident group might still have arisen, but its presence, lacking any nearby source of real or symbolic support, would not have seemed so acutely threatening to the Village's stability.

Lack of autonomy. But whatever its physical proximity to the Town, if Salem Village had been granted full political and ecclesiastical independence in 1672 (or even, conceivably, in 1689) it might have been able to develop strong institutions of its own—institutions which would have given it the political strength to resolve its factional problems.

But a *taste of independence.* If, alternatively, "Salem Farms" had remained completely a part of the Town, the region would not have developed any institutions at all—meetinghouse, legal meetings, Committee, or minister—and so would have had no peg on which to hang its separatist impulses. Even though serious problems would certainly have persisted after 1672, a single town, physically and institutionally undivided, might have been able to contain those problems within tolerable limits.

Coupled with a *lack of power in Town politics.* The Villagers were, after all, still able to vote in Town elections and eligible to hold Town offices. If they had enjoyed anything like political parity with the Town, their political impulses might have found meaningful expression, and their grievances at least partial resolution. But as matters turned out, their numerical weakness was such that only on rare occasions were they able to use the Town's political apparatus as a weapon in Village conflicts. (The contrast here between Salem and other towns which experienced similar separatist conflicts in these years is striking. In Dedham, Massachusetts, for example, no fewer than five distinct outlying communities managed early in the eighteenth century to form ad hoc political alliances with each other which enabled them to maneuver very effectively in the arena of Dedham politics.)[37]

Finally, *a weak stick in Boston.* If authorities at the provincial (not to say the imperial) level had exerted a stronger and more consistent hand in settling matters, Salem Village factionalism would certainly never have flowered as luxuriantly as it did. But like vacillating or argumentative parents, the provincial authorities evoked neither affection nor deference from either Village faction. Those authorities had to be reckoned with at every point, to be sure, but more as an unpredictable and capricious obstacle than as a firm source of policy.

If any one of these circumstances had been significantly different, it is possible that Salem would be remembered today simply as the

37. Kenneth A. Lockridge, *A New England Town: The First Hundred Years* (New York, W. W. Norton and Co., 1970), pp. 97–101.

oldest town in the colony, and as the home of Nathaniel Haw-thorne—not as the site of one of the most notorious events in New England history.

But the trials came. Unable to relieve their frustrations politi-cally, the members of the pro-Parris faction unconsciously fell back on a different and more archaic strategy: they treated those who threatened them not as a political opposition but as an aggregate of morally defective individuals. Given the social assumptions which prevailed in seventeenth-century New England, it was a perfectly normal procedure for a town to rid itself of deviant or threatening individuals—by changing them if possible, by exile or execution if necessary. A long succession of people, including a number of isolated "witches," had learned that fact in the most vivid way possible. But what confronted Salem Village, as seems clear in retrospect, was not a handful (even a large handful) of "deviants." It was a group of people who were on the advancing edge of profound historical change. If from one angle they were diverging from an accepted norm of behavior, from another angle their values represented the "norm" of the future. In an age about to pass, the assertion of *private will* posed the direst possible threat to the stability of the community; in the age about to arrive, it would form a central pillar on which that stability rested. By treat-ing their "enemies" as deviants, the pro-Parris Villagers of the 1690's chose to proceed as if nothing fundamental had changed in New England society—another attempt, perhaps, to convince them-selves that nothing really had.

5 Two Families: The Porters and the Putnams

In July 1644 the Salem Town meeting chose a small group of men to perambulate the town each Sunday morning, two-by-two, reporting to the authorities any Sabbath breakers they might find— "such as either lie about the meetinghouse without attending to the word or ordinances, or that lie at home or in the fields." Among the men who joined forces for this duty were John Putnam, sixty-five years old at the time, and John Porter, who was forty-eight.[1]

The choice of Putnam and Porter was a natural one, for both were substantial farmers and respected members of the Salem Town church. Although separated in age by the better part of a generation, the two men had followed a similar path in life. Both had arrived in Salem in the early 1640's: Putnam from the English county of Berkshire, near London; Porter from the Channel county of Dorset, some sixty miles southwest of Putnam's English home. (Porter had emigrated first to Hingham, Massachusetts, where he lived for about five years before coming to Salem.) From the first, to be sure, there were significant differences in their situations— all but one of Porter's children were still very young when he reached Salem, for example, while Putnam's were nearly grown— but, still, they had even more in common.[2]

Both men settled in what would become Salem Village, and both men prospered. Beginning with an initial 100-acre grant in 1641,

1. Sidney Perley, *The History of Salem, Mass.*, 3 vols. (Salem, 1924–28), II, 165.
2. *Ibid.*, II, 109 (Putnams); *History of the Town of Hingham, Mass.*, 3 vols. (Published by the town, 1893), III, 115 (John Porter).

John Putnam gradually built up holdings which, by the time of his death in 1662, totaled nearly 800 acres. Porter's achievement was more impressive still. The extensive lands he had acquired and then sold during his years in Hingham gave him a head-start, and within a few years of his arrival he was the largest landholder in Salem. When Porter died in 1676, fourteen years after John Putnam, he had amassed holdings of nearly 2,000 acres. His estate was assessed at £2,753, and included four servants, two of them English and the other two black.[3]

The similarity of the two men's careers is heightened by the coincidence that each sired five sons, of whom three survived to adulthood and lived out their lives in Salem Village or its immediate vicinity. The three Putnam men of the second generation were Thomas (born in 1615), Nathaniel (born in 1619), and John (born in 1627), usually called "Captain John" in recognition of his rank in the local militia. The three Porter brothers to figure in Salem Village history were Joseph, born in 1638, Benjamin (1639), and Israel (1644).[4] (See Putnam and Porter Family Genealogies.)

Building on the solid foundation put down by their respective fathers, all six of these men were extremely well off by the standards of the day. By 1681, the first year for which Salem Village tax lists are available, the three Putnam brothers paid the largest taxes in the Village by a considerable margin. The average tax that year was just over forty-two shillings; the Putnam average was 105 shillings—two-and-one-half times greater. Though the three brothers and their adult sons made up only 7 percent of the 1681 taxpaying group, their taxes were just over 18 percent of the total. As for Joseph, Benjamin, and Israel Porter, although their wealth is not accurately revealed in the Village tax lists (since their lands lay outside the Village bounds as well as within it), it is clear that they were, in fact, even richer than the Putnams.[5]

In many ways, then, the Putnams and the Porters seem nearly indistinguishable: both immigrants from the same part of England; both living in the same village; both prosperous and pious farmers.

3. Perley, *History of Salem*, II, 109 (Putnam's 1641 land grant); 162 (reference to John Porter as Salem's largest landholder); 3 *PR,* 114–116 (John Porter will and estate inventory). On the land holdings of these two men see also Sidney Perley, "Hathorne: Part of Salem in 1700," 53 *EIHC* (1917), 334, 341–342; "The Plains: Part of Salem in 1700," 54 *EIHC* (1918), 298, 308; and "Hathorne: Part of Salem in 1700" [part II], *ibid.*, 122.

4. Perley, *History of Salem*, II, 109–111 (Putnam genealogy), 161–162 (Porter genealogy).

5. Tax list, Village Records, Dec. 27, 1681.

The Putnam Family

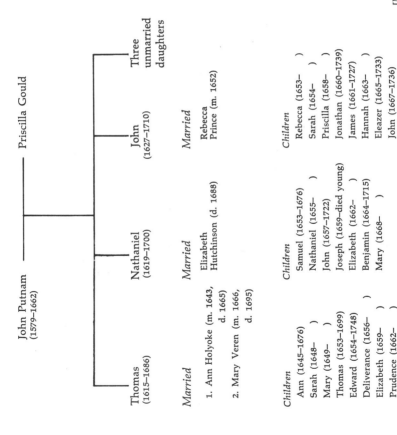

John Putnam
(1579–1662) ———— Priscilla Gould

Thomas
(1615–1686)

John
(1627–1710)

Nathaniel
(1619–1700)

Three
unmarried
daughters

Married

1. Ann Holyoke (m. 1643,
   d. 1665)
2. Mary Veren (m. 1666,
   d. 1695)

Married

Elizabeth
Hutchinson (d. 1688)

Married

Rebecca
Prince (m. 1652)

Children

Ann (1645–1676)
Sarah (1648–   )
Mary (1649–   )
Thomas (1653–1699)
Edward (1654–1748)
Deliverance (1656–   )
Elizabeth (1659–   )
Prudence (1662–   )
Joseph (1669–1725)

Children

Samuel (1653–1676)
Nathaniel (1655–   )
John (1657–1722)
Joseph (1659–died young)
Elizabeth (1662–   )
Benjamin (1664–1715)
Mary (1668–   )

Children

Rebecca (1653–   )
Sarah (1654–   )
Priscilla (1658–   )
Jonathan (1660–1739)
James (1661–1727)
Hannah (1663–   )
Eleazer (1665–1733)
John (1667–1736)
Susanna (1670–   )
Ruth (1673–   )

[*Note:* See also the
more detailed Thomas
Putnam genealogy in
Chapter 6.]

Sources: Sidney Perley, *The History of Salem, Mass.*, 3 vols. (Salem, 1924–
28), II, 109–111.

The Porter Family

John Porter
(ca. 1595–1676)

1. [ ]
2. [Mary d. 1683]

| JOHN (ca. 1618–1684) | SAMUEL (?–1660) | JOSEPH (1638–1714) | BENJAMIN (1639–1723) | ISRAEL (1644–1706) | MARY (1645–   ) | JONATHAN (1648–   ) Died as a young man. | SARAH (1649–   ) |

(Mariner; never married)

(Mariner)

Married
Anne Hathorne

(Never married)

Married
Elizabeth Hathorne

Married
Thomas Gardner

Married
Daniel Andrew

Children
Joseph (1665–   )
  Died young
Ann (1667–   )
Samuel (<669–   )
Nathaniel (1671–1758)
Mary (1672–   )
William (1674–1732)
Eliazer (1676–died young)
Abigail (1676–   )
Hepzibah (1678–   )
Joseph (1681–   )
Ruth (1682–   )
Mehitable (1682–   )

Children
Elizabeth
  (1673–   )
  m. Joseph
    Putnam
Sarah (1675–   )
  m. Abel Gardner
John (1677–1715)
  Mariner
Ginger (1679–   )
Israel (1683–   )
Anne (1687–   )
William (1689–   )
Benjamin (1693–   )

Children
Daniel (1677–
  d. young)
Thomas (1678–1702)
Samuel (1683–1702)
Daniel (bap. 1686–   )
Israel (1689–   )
Sarah
Mehitable

Source: Sidney Perley, *History of Salem, Mass.,* 3 vols. (Salem, 1924–28), II, 161-162; III, 42.

What a shock it is, then, to find these two families in absolute opposition in the 1690's—to find them providing both strength of numbers and recognized leadership to the two factions which were almost literally at each other's throats through much of the decade.

A glance at the church membership lists provides the first hint that the two families were following divergent paths. Eight of the ten Putnam men in the Village, and seven of their wives, joined the Village church during Samuel Parris's ministry. (The Putnam surname, indeed, comprised almost one-fourth of the total church membership in these years, and close to 30 percent of the male membership.) In stark contrast, not a single Porter or Porter in-law took this step.

Even more revealing of the breach which had opened between the Putnams and the Porters are the pro-Parris and anti-Parris petitions of 1695. No fewer than twenty-one Putnams signed their names in support of the Village minister—twenty-five, if we include the four Village men who had married Putnam girls of the third generation.[6] (There were two Putnams who opposed Parris —Joseph and his wife Elizabeth—but these two are a very special case whose story will be told in the next chapter.) Even in 1696, when Parris's enemies were mounting their most determined offensive, the minister could still count upon almost an embarrassment of support from this quarter: "At a Church-meeting at Brother Thomas Putnam's house . . . , [it was] voted that our Brethren John Putnam, Senior, and Nathaniel Putnam and Deacon [Edward] Putnam and John Putnam, Junior, be appointed to meet . . . the dissenters . . . to treat in order to an amicable issue."[7] The "amicable issue" remained a chimera, but through the long ordeal, the Putnams stood loyal.

The Porter commitment was just as strong—on the other side. Not a single Porter or Porter in-law supported Samuel Parris, while a total of eleven, including five unmarried young men of the third generation (one of them scarcely fourteen years old), proclaimed their opposition to the embattled clergyman.[8] From another angle, members of the Porter family comprised 13 percent of the anti-

6. Pro-Parris petition—Church Records, following entry for April 4, 1695. The four Village men who had married into the family were Jonathan Walcott, John Hutchinson, Henry Brown, and Edward Bishop. Two other Putnam girls had married and moved from the Village—Putnam genealogy, Perley, *History of Salem*, II, 109.

7. Church Records, April 9, 1696.

8. Anti-Parris petition—Church Records, following entry for April 4, 1695.

Parris faction, while Putnams represented 24 percent of the pro-Parris strength.

The very quality of the leadership which each family provided its respective faction offers a clue to the deeper differences we shall be considering in a moment. The Putnam approach was bluff, direct, and obvious. They worked for their man through the established channels: as Village Committeemen, as deacons, as church elders. They went to the courts and they went to Boston when they believed it would do some good.

The Porters, by contrast, were behind-the-scenes men. Except when their enemies flushed them into the open, they left few marks. (This is one of the reasons the Putnams figure so prominently in the popular histories of Salem witchcraft, and the Porters hardly at all.) They were flushed out in the petition war of 1695, to be sure, but more typical of their method of operation was the maneuvering in these years of the leader of the family, Israel Porter. Israel plays a crucial but shadowy role in Parris's account of the machinations of the dissenters, always hovering in the background, whispering advice, devising strategy, but never giving vent to passion, never backed into any corners.[9]

In 1692, as well, the Porters and the Putnams played diametrically opposite parts, and they played those parts in characteristic fashion. The intense, almost passionate, involvement of the Putnams in pushing the trials forward is all too well known; as early as 1700 Robert Calef, the first historian of the event, referred contemptuously to "that family of the Putnams, who were the chief prosecutors in this business"—and chroniclers of the event ever since have not failed to notice the almost monotonous frequency with which the Putnam name occurs on complaints, warrants, and accusatory testimony. Ann Putnam, the twelve-year-old daughter of Thomas Putnam, Jr., was by far the most active of the afflicted girls, and a total of eight members of the family, drawn from all three of its branches, were involved in the prosecution of no fewer than forty-six accused witches.[10]

9. See, e.g., Church Records, Oct. 23, 1693; Nov. 26, 1694; Nov. 30, 1694.

10. Robert Calef, *More Wonders of the Invisible World: or, The Wonders of the Invisible World Display'd in Five Parts* (London, 1700), excerpted in George Lincoln Burr, ed., *Narratives of the Witchcraft Cases, 1648–1706* (New York, Charles Scribner's Sons, 1914; reissued, New York, Barnes and Noble, 1968), p. 370. Our data on the Putnam role in 1692 is extracted from W. Elliot Woodward, *Records of Salem Witchcraft, Copied from the Original Documents*, 2 vols. (Roxbury, Mass., Privately printed, 1864; reissued in one volume, New York, Da Capo Press, 1969).

The Porters, that spring, threw their influence unmistakably against those who were promoting the witchcraft trials—but they did so in the Porter style, cautiously and by indirection. Israel himself had good reason to oppose and even fear the trials—accusations of witchcraft, as we shall see, came precariously close to his immediate family—but he chose his ground carefully. His son John, for example, offered testimony designed to cast doubt on the credibility of the most unsavory (and least respectable) of all the "afflicted girls," one Sarah Bibber—who was, in fact, a married woman in her mid-thirties from the neighboring town of Wenham. (John Porter described Goody Bibber as a person of "unruly, turbulent spirit, and double-tongued.")[11]

Israel Porter himself offered public support for only one accused witch. But significantly, the one he selected was Rebecca Nurse, a matriarchal woman who (probably alone among the accused) was on good terms with a number of people in the pro-Parris faction, including several Putnams. Israel at once saw in these circumstances an opportunity to mobilize Village opposition to the trials, and even to drive a wedge into the ranks of those Villagers who, with greater or lesser enthusiasm, were supporting the trials. He composed and circulated on Rebecca's behalf a carefully phrased document, difficult for anyone even vaguely in the middle not to sign; indeed, among its thirty-nine subscribers in the Village were eight Putnams.[12] Besides the petition, Porter and his wife Elizabeth offered in Goodwife Nurse's defense a piece of testimony that was perhaps as affecting as any document to emerge from the entire period. In a sworn deposition, the Porters described how they had visited Rebecca a few days before her arrest and found her in a "weak and low condition in body," but affirming (with Saint Paul) her determination to "press forward to the mark," and quoting "many other places of Scripture to the like purpose." The Porters' testimony went on to report her loving solicitude for the afflicted girls—"she pitied them with all her heart, and went to God for them"—and then her shock and pious resignation when they told her that she, too, was among those suspected of witchcraft. " 'I am

11. Woodward, *Records of Salem Witchcraft*, II, 203–204.

12. Nurse petition: Charles W. Upham, *Salem Witchcraft*, 2 vols. (Boston, 1867), II, 272. Israel Porter's name appears first on the petition. As for the Putnam support of Rebecca Nurse, it is significant that the four *wealthiest* of the ten male Putnams on the 1695 tax rolls all signed the petition, and also that all eight Putnam signers of the Nurse petition lived on the easterly side of the Village, while those most active against Nurse—notably Thomas and Edward Putnam—lived in the more distant western part of the Village.

as innocent as the child unborn. But surely,' she said, 'what sin hath God found out in me unrepented of, that he should lay such an affliction upon me in my old age?' "[13]

It is a moving document to read today, and—though it ultimately failed to save Rebecca's life—it must have been at least as moving in 1692. It is also true that every phrase of this seemingly artless composition is precisely chosen to convey—not in so many words, but in the careful shadings of a narrative account—that this woman was not only innocent of any crime but was a very model of Christian piety. Israel Porter's testimony for Rebecca Nurse, in short, is not the rough-hewn prose of a sturdy peasant; it is the studied product of a sophisticated and urbane intelligence.

This matter of contrasting styles poses directly the central question: what in the experience of these two families, seemingly so much alike, had driven them, by the 1690's, in such totally different directions?

First, let us take a further look at the Porters. As Map 6 shows, the Porter lands lay on the Town side of the Village—indeed, the holdings of this family extended well beyond the eastern boundary of the Village, into the Town proper.[14] They had easy access to the roadways and water routes which connected Town and Village, and in some instances they actually controlled these arteries. (The Putnam lands, by contrast, generally lay further to the west, with large tracts in the northwestern part of Salem Village.) It may have been this geographic advantage alone which accounts for the increasingly diversified nature of the Porter family's economic activities. For although John Porter farmed his Village lands intensively (with the help of his four servants), there is a good deal of evidence that his economic interests and aspirations were considerably more wide-ranging—certainly more so than those of his fellow-farmer John Putnam. In 1658 he turned up in the Carribean island of Barbados, as witness to a sugar contract involving the Salem merchant John Rucke. (Two years later his son Samuel died en route to Barbados.) In the early 1660's, John Porter's name appeared with those of the leading Salem merchants of the day in a list of men granted a tract of waterfront land by the Town, evidently for the construction of a new wharf and warehouse facility.

13. Upham, *Salem Witchcraft*, II, 58–59.
14. Data on Porter land holdings from "Map of Salem Village, 1692," *ibid.*, I, following p. xvii, and Sidney Perley, "The Plains: Part of Salem in 1700," pp. 289–316.

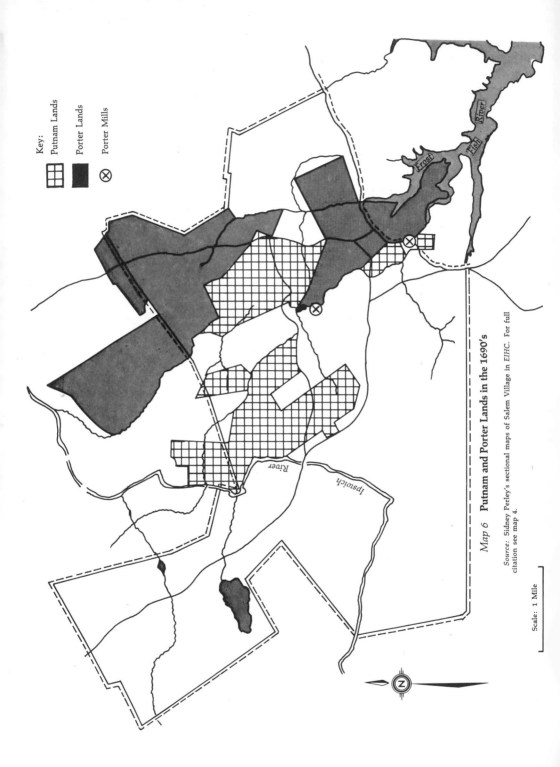

Map 6 **Putnam and Porter Lands in the 1690's**

Source: Sidney Perley's sectional maps of Salem Village in *EIHC*. For full citation see map 4.

Scale: 1 Mile

Key:

Putnam Lands

Porter Lands

Porter Mills

In 1670 he contracted with two Salem Village brothers, Joseph and John Hutchinson, to operate a sawmill on a stream which traversed his Village lands. (This dam and sawmill proved a great annoyance to the elder Thomas Putnam, who in 1672 brought suit in county court, arguing that the dam had been flooding the single access road to his farm for months at a time: "To be this long kept prisoner," Putnam testified, "will be the way to ruin me and mine forever." Prior to 1673, too, in partnership with a member of the Endicott family, John Porter built a dam and sawmill of his own on Frost Fish River in the Village, at the Ipswich Road crossing.[15]

In a variety of ways, John Porter's actions bespoke his fundamental orientation toward Salem Town. When he built his house at the head of the Frost Fish River, he faced it southward toward the Town, rather than westward toward the Ipswich Road, Salem Village, and the frontier beyond.[16] Living several miles closer to the center of Town affairs, from the first he figured more prominently than John Putnam in both Town government and church affairs. In 1647 he was foreman of the Essex County Grand Jury. In 1646 he was elected to the first of many terms as a Salem Town selectman, and in 1668 he served a term as deputy in the General Court.[17] In the Salem Town church, where he became a deacon in 1661, his seat was in the second row, directly behind the "Magistrates' Bench" where sat such powerful merchants as William Brown, George Corwin, and William Hathorne. (His wife Mary occupied a corresponding position on the women's side.) At his death in 1676 he left a bequest to the minister of the Salem church, John Higginson—but nothing at all to the Village congregation or its minister James Bayley.[18]

John Porter's rapid assimilation into the top echelon of the Town hierarchy suggests that he was already a figure of some note at the time of his arrival. (His first service in the General Court had come in 1644, while he was still living in Hingham.)[19] But it was also rooted in the fact that the emerging merchant group early recognized him as, in spirit, one of their own.

15. 3 *EQC*, 369 (Barbados); 5 *EQC*, 25–26 (Hutchinson contract and Putnam protest); 88 *New England Historical and Genealogical Register* (1934), 391 (Samuel Porter); Perley, *History of Salem*, II, 353 (the 1662 waterfront grant) and III, 63; 3 *PR*, 113 (the Porter dam and sawmill).

16. Perley, *History of Salem*, II, 164.

17. *Ibid.*, II, 5; 1 *EQC*, 129; James Duncan Phillips, *Salem in the Seventeenth Century* (Boston, Houghton Mifflin Co., 1933), p. 361.

18. *Ibid.*, 194; Perley, *History of Salem*, II, 221; 3 *PR*, 113 (will).

19. *History of the Town of Hingham*, III, 115.

The second generation of Porters strengthened the links to the Town which their father had already so strongly established. Both Joseph and Israel Porter married daughters of Major William Hathorne, a leader in the political and commercial life of the Town. (The third surviving brother, Benjamin Porter, remained a bachelor to his death.)[20] The most prominent of this second generation was Israel Porter, who inherited the family homestead in Salem Village, as well as his father's half-interest in the Ipswich Road sawmill. (By the mid-1690's, in fact, Israel Porter owned two of the four mills in Salem Village, and his son-in-law, Abel Gardner, owned a third.)[21] Israel was a member in full communion of the Salem Town church, and unlike the Putnams he did not transfer his membership to the Salem Village church in 1689. From 1679 through the rest of the century Israel Porter served almost uninterruptedly as a Salem Town selectman—the only farmer to maintain political power in the Town during these years of increasing merchant domination.[22]

John Porter's daughters, too, formed matrimonial alliances which strengthened the family's ties to the commercial elements in Salem Town. (The three daughters of old John Putnam, by contrast, all died as spinsters.) One Porter daughter married Thomas Gardner, a prominent Salem merchant, wharf owner, and politician, while another married Daniel Andrew, who would be accused of witchcraft in 1692. Andrew's career reveals with particular vividness how skillfully the Porters managed to keep one leg in Salem Village and the other firmly planted in the Town.

Born and reared in Watertown, Massachusetts, Daniel Andrew moved in 1669, at the age of twenty-five, to Salem Town. Apparently possessed of some capital, he bought, over the next few years, two small but valuable house lots in the very heart of the Town. (One of them contained an apothecary shop which had

20. Another brother, Jonathan Porter, before his premature death in 1669, had formed a partnership with a man of Salem Town to engage in the timber and barrel stave business—Perley, *History of Salem*, II, 162; 4 *EQC*, 109–110.

21. 3 *PR*, 112–113 (John Porter's will); Perley, *History of Salem*, I, 69 (Abel Gardner's marriage into the Porter family); "Map of Salem Village, 1692," Upham, *Salem Witchcraft*, I, following p. xvii; Sidney Perley, "The Woods, Salem, in 1700," 51 *EIHC* (1915), map following p. 176 (on Abel Gardner's mill). The fourth Salem Village mill was owned by Joseph Pope, Jr., another member of the anti-Parris faction.

22. Perley, *History of Salem*, II, 401; III, 252 (lists of selectmen); Church Records, Oct. 23, 1693 (reference to Porter's membership in the Salem Town church).

come to dispense liquor along with medicines.)[23]

As his choice of residence suggests, Andrew's ambitions do not seem to have involved farming. For a time in 1671 he was paid by the Town to teach school in his home; but soon afterwards he settled into the line of employment which was to bring him wealth and standing: the construction of fine houses. Although he is usually designated "bricklayer" in legal documents (and had had his apprenticeship in masonry from his stepfather), it is plain that this was no mean occupation in seventeenth-century Salem. At the very least, Andrew was a highly skilled craftsman, and in any case his activities seem to have involved oversight and supervision as much as physical labor. Through his work he came in close contact with some of the wealthiest men in town; as early as 1675, for example, he supervised an extensive renovation and enlargement of the town house of Jonathan Corwin, son of Salem's most eminent merchant. Two years later, his skill (or his connections) won him the contract for the new meetinghouse which the prospering Town had decided to construct.[24]

At almost the same time, this aspiring gentleman married John Porter's daughter Sarah, whose newly gained inheritance—her father had recently died—included half-interest in a large tract of good Salem Village land. It was at this point that Daniel Andrew moved out from the Town to a house situated on the Village property he had just acquired—over by the Wenham line and close to his Porter brothers-in-law, Israel, Joseph, and Benjamin. A year after his marriage he purchased (for cash) the remaining half-interest in this Village farm from another brother-in-law, Thomas Gardner.[25]

With these two strokes, then, Daniel Andrew became a major landowner and a dominant presence in Salem Village. He continued over the years to increase his estate through the fees he earned from his construction business and through shrewd land acquisitions in the Village. Perhaps the most important of these occurred in February 1692, when he purchased (from a Salem

23. Perley, *History of Salem*, II, 307; III, 42; Essex Deeds, III, 73; IV, 61.

24. Perley, *History of Salem*, II, 93; III, 71; G. Andrews Moriarity, Jr., "The Apprenticeship of the First Daniel Andrew," Danvers Historical Society, *Historical Collections*, 17 (1929), 107–108; Salem Town records, Sept. 8, 1677, 48 *EIHC* (1912), p. 166 (the meetinghouse contract). The house Daniel Andrew built for Corwin is now a tourist attraction, the "witch house," because some of the examinations of the accused may have occurred in it.

25. Perley, *History of Salem*, III, 42; 3 PR, 111–114; Sidney Perley, "The Plains: Part of Salem in 1700," p. 312.

Town owner) a landing wharf strategically situated at the point where the Frost Fish Brook, flowing southward through the eastern part of Salem Village, traversed the Ipswich Road and widened into the navigable Frost Fish River.[26] From this dock, supplies could conveniently be transported into the Village and farm products or livestock (especially from the Andrew and Porter lands on that side of the Village) could be economically floated down to market or warehouses in Salem Town center, some five miles away.

By 1695 Andrew was the fourth wealthiest man in the Village, and at his death in 1702 he was able to leave cash bequests of £100 to each of his two daughters in addition to lands in Salem Village, Watertown, and Cambridge. But even though he had been living in Salem Village for twenty-five years by that time, it is clear that his loyalties and ambitions, and even his ordinary employment, remained firmly linked to the Town and its development. This fact was recognized by the Townsmen, too: on five occasions, beginning in 1685, he was chosen a Town selectman.[27] His lands in the Village may have been used for farming, but Andrew remained essentially an urbanite who had chosen to move out into the country after he had made good.

While Daniel Andrew was a Porter only by marriage, his career (and perhaps even his temper) was easily assimilated into the particular ambience of that family. The Porters were among the largest landowners and taxpayers in Salem Village, but they were all, by inclination and marital ties, Townsmen. Old John Porter, though a "yeoman," had from the first identified with the nascent commercialism of the town, and the second generation perpetuated this attachment.[28] Their names appear in the political records of the Village almost as rarely as they do on the church rolls. In the eighteen years from 1672 to 1690, Joseph and Israel Porter served

26. Sidney Perley, "Rial Side: Part of Salem in 1700," 55 *EIHC* (1919), p. 65. On his other land acquisitions: Essex Deeds, IX, 32, 300.

27. Perley, *History of Salem*, III, 252. Daniel Andrew's will, Sept. 4, 1702, Essex Prob., Packet No. 611.

28. It is true that in the 1660's, when the consciousness of a distinct Village identity was beginning to emerge, the Porters seemed to share at least some of that consciousness. Old John Porter and his son Joseph signed the 1667 petition complaining about the necessity of participating in the Town's military watch. And in 1670 John joined with those farmers from the western part of Salem who refused to contribute to the cost of building a new meetinghouse in the Town. But the Porter family's support for these early expressions of a separatist mood was never very strong, and when the full implications of that mood began to sink in, the family quickly drew back. Not a single Porter or

precisely one term each on the Village Committee and their brother Benjamin served none at all.[29]

In their ambiguous relationship with the Village, as in their receptive involvement with the Town, the Porters reveal how a combination of economic and social interests, rooted initially, perhaps, in an accident of geography, flowered into the distinctive political orientation (and even the distinctive pattern of life) we have summed up in the terse and opaque term "anti-Parris." John Porter and John Putnam may have trod the same path as they made their Sabbath Day rounds in 1644, but their footsteps soon diverged, and they were not again to be joined.

For all this while, the collective lives of the Putnam family had been veering into quite a different trajectory. As we have already seen, the elder John Putnam's original hundred-acre grant in Salem Village lay somewhat to the interior, beyond John Porter's land. As the Putnams increased their holdings over the years, they necessarily did so by purchasing lands which lay, on the whole, still further to the interior. In the process, the family became locked into an agrarian existence in a way the Porters were not. Not only was their land cut off from convenient access to markets by either land or water, but much of it (especially the northwestern sections, close to the Ipswich River) was also less arable, consisting in large part of hills and swampy meadows. The 1686 will of Thomas Putnam, Sr., for example, is studded with such terms as "Blind Hole" and "Bare Hill" and phrases like "across the swamp to the cartway" and "all the upland [that is, hilly land] and swamp."[30] As the years passed and further expansion in the area proved almost impossible, the steadily growing Putnam clan came more and more to feel the constrictions inherent in its situation.

The Putnams' only major effort to break free of their total dependence on farming was an attempt to turn into an asset one of their major liabilities: the poor quality of their northern land. A swamp might not produce much wheat or barley, but perhaps it could be made to yield another kind of wealth. From reflections

Porter in-law signed the key 1670 petition to the General Court requesting authorization to hire a minister and erect a separate meetinghouse for the Village. Nor did any member of this family join the Salem Village church when it was formed in 1689, or for years afterwards.

29. Village Records, Nov. 11, 1672; April 7, 1687; 5 *EQC*, 273 (the 1670 petition).

30. Eben Putnam, *A History of the Putnam Family* (Salem, 1891), pp. 11–21 (will of Thomas Putnam, Sr.).

such as this must have sprung the family's curious venture into the iron-smelting business. The results, to say the least, were not encouraging.

Sometime prior to 1673, the brothers John and Nathaniel Putnam each acquired an eighth interest in an ironworks on Putnam lands in the neighboring village of Rowley. Few aspiring Massachusetts capitalists in the 1670's were putting their money into ironworks. The high hopes of earlier years that the iron-rich bogs and swamps of the Massachusetts coast could make the colony self-sufficient in this essential metal had been pretty thoroughly dashed by the failure of the ambitious and well-capitalized Saugus ironworks in 1652.[31] Nevertheless, the Putnams and their fellow speculators entered hopefully upon their far more modest venture.

The precise sequence of the disasters which ensued is difficult to reconstruct from the later tangle of suits, testimonies, depositions, and judgments, but the main line of development is clear. It appears that sometime prior to 1672 the clerk of the ironworks, Thomas Baker, and one of its co-owners, John Gould, leased the works to one Henry Leonard, an elderly Welshman, for the sum of two hundred pounds per year. Leonard was also permitted to move his family into a house which stood on the lands of the ironworks. Gould and Baker could hardly have been faulted for reposing confidence in Leonard, for the family had been closely identified with several earlier iron-making ventures. "Where you find iron-works, there you will find a Leonard" was a saying of the day.[32]

But for all his experience, Henry Leonard failed to make a go of the Rowley operation, and by 1673 he was beseiged by lawsuits. The owners sued Leonard for nonpayment of rent. The men who were supplying charcoal for his furnace sued him for debt. And various Salem merchants to whom he had agreed to deliver iron bars and anchors sued him for breach of contract. In the face of all this, Henry Leonard simply disappeared. In April 1674, victorious in their suit, the owners seized several of Leonard's household possessions, including a cupboard, a chest, and a trunk. They also terminated their lease with Leonard and gave him and his

---

31. Bernard Bailyn, *The New England Merchants in the Seventeenth Century* (Cambridge, Mass., Harvard University Press, 1955), pp. 62–71. For a list of owners of the Rowley works, see 42 County Court Records, leaf 81.

32. 6 EQC, 1; William B. Weedon, *Economic and Social History of New England*, 2 vols. (New York, 1890; reissued, New York, Hillary House Pub., Ltd., 1963), I, 192 (the Leonard quote).

family two weeks to vacate. Most of the family departed, but Henry's son Nathaniel and Nathaniel's wife remained in the company house.[33]

As a crowning indignity, in June 1674 three of Henry Leonard's sons were brought to court on complaint of a servant girl for lewd and lascivious behavior. (They were apparently in the habit of disporting themselves naked along the Ipswich River in the presence of women and courting couples.) No fewer than twenty-two local people came forward to testify against the Leonard boys. The crimes with which they were charged included profanity, assault, fornication, attempted rape, and indecent exposure. Old Henry Leonard's wife Mary, while not formally accused, was castigated in some of the depositions for her habit of bringing a chair down to the river bank to watch the men and boys of the Village swim in the nude and shouting out bawdy comments to them.[34] The entire episode offered an immediate and dramatic evidence of the social disruption which this almost Elizabethan family (which was serving, ironically, as the agent of capitalist industry) had brought to Rowley. The ironworks in which the Putnams had reposed such hope was obviously in imminent danger not only of failing, but of becoming a public nuisance and a laughingstock.

Proud of its reputation, the Leonard family vowed vengeance for the indignities it had suffered. The high-spirited Mary Leonard seems to have taken a leading role in inciting her men to action. In a later court case it was testified that shortly after the family had been driven from the ironworks, Goody Leonard "made a sad complaint how the owners had abused them, and said she did not question but that God would right their case, for they had done no wrong. She said that it was never known that any workmen were turned out of the works but some sad thing did befall the works, and she did not question that the works would be ruined, either by fire or water."[35]

Sure enough, early one Sunday morning in July 1674 the Rowley ironworks was demolished by fire. Nathaniel Leonard, it was later testified, placidly watched the conflagration from his window, commenting only: "Come hither and see how the forge do burn." The courts later found "great ground of suspicion" that the fire had been set by Thomas Leonard (another of Henry's sons) and he was

33. 5 *EQC*, 130, 173, 219, 264–265, 271, 337, 396. See also an account of a meeting of the owners, in 42 County Court Records, leaf 81.
34. 5 *EQC*, 351–355.
35. 6 *EQC*, 34.

warned that his future appearance within seven miles of the ironworks would result in a whipping.[36]

For Nathaniel and John Putnam, the fire represented a bitter
blow. At a rueful meeting of the owners held soon after the disaster, it was clear that all the spirit had gone out of the venture.
Some were for disbanding on the spot, others wanted to resume
operations long enough to pay off the heavy debts the undertaking
had accumulated. When one owner, Daniel Denison, angrily rode
off on his horse, the meeting broke up in confusion. About all that
had been definitely decided was that John Putnam and two other
men should try to hire some workmen to repair the damage, and
that Nathaniel Putnam should sue John Gould, Thomas Baker, and
Nathaniel Leonard for negligence. The owners won this particular
suit (in a case which was appealed up to the Court of Assistants)
but this was bitter recompense.[37] Though litigation continued for
a decade more, the Rowley ironworks was dead.

The Putnam brothers' tentative and cautious venture into the
world of manufacturing and commerce had ended in ignominious
failure, and the family was forced back to its nearly total reliance
on agriculture—back to lands that were inadequate to support the
maturing flock of third-generation Putnams at the family's accus-
tomed level of wealth. In the Putnam family, as in other propertied
families in Salem Village, a son was generally given land of his own
at the time of his marriage or shortly afterwards. This resulted
in the continual fragmentation of what had originally been very
large tracts. By the mid-1690's, for example, almost fifteen years
before his death, Captain John Putnam had divided his entire holdings among his four sons.[38]

Thus, while the overall total of Putnam lands remained constant
or even increased a bit over the years (the family's share of the
total Village tax expanded slightly between 1681 and 1695, from
just under 20 percent to just over 21 percent), this land was increasingly being divided among a larger number of individuals.
By 1695 the land that years before had been owned by only three
male Putnams was now split up among eleven of them. (See
Map 7.)

36. 42 County Court Records, leaf 81; 6 EQC, 34, 54.
37. 5 EQC, 396; 6 EQC, 1–5, 34; Records of the Court of Assistants of the
Colony of the Massachusetts Bay, 1630–1692, 3 vols. (Boston, 1901–1928), I,
27. For later legal actions stemming from the iron works see 42 County Court
Records, leaf 79 ff.
38. Sidney Perley, "The Plains: Part of Salem in 1700," pp. 308–310.

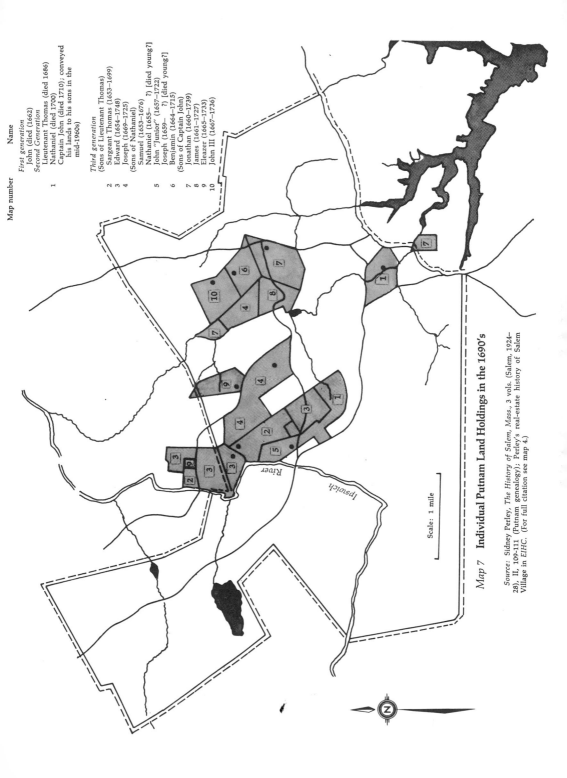

Map number   Name

First generation
     John (died 1662)
Second Generation
     Nathaniel (died 1700)
1   Lieutenant Thomas (died 1686)
     Captain John (died 1710); conveyed
     his lands to his sons in the
     mid-1960s)

Third generation
     (Sons of Lieutenant Thomas)
2   Sargeant Thomas (1653–1699)
3   Edward (1654–1748)
4   Joseph (1669–1725)
     (Sons of Nathaniel)
5   Samuel (1653–1676)
     Nathaniel (1655–   ?) [died young?]
     John "Junior" (1657–1722)
     Joseph (1659–   ?) [died young?]
6   Benjamin (1664–1715)
     (Sons of Captain John)
7   Jonathan (1660–1739)
8   James (1661–1727)
9   Eleazer (1665–1733)
10   John III (1667–1736)

Map 7   **Individual Putnam Land Holdings in the 1690's**

Scale: 1 mile

Source: Sidney Perley, *The History of Salem, Mass.,* 3 vols. (Salem, 1924–28), II, 109–111 (Putnam genealogy); Perley's real-estate history of Salem Village in *EIHC.* (For full citation see map 4.)

This dramatic diminution in individual wealth from one generation to another must have produced a large reserve of tension and anxiety, especially among members of the third generation. It may not be purely accidental that neither of the two surviving Putnam brothers of the second generation played a very active role in the witchcraft accusations, though both were still vigorous; it was the third (and even fourth) generation Putnams who took the lead in that enterprise.

The problem of crowding as successive generations came of age was one the Porter family did not, in fact, have to confront—not at this time, at least. The original John Porter was seventeen years younger than his counterpart John Putnam, and that difference loomed increasingly large as the third-generation Putnams came to adulthood in the 1670's and the '80's. (The third generation Porters, in contrast, were only being *born* in these decades; all of them, as it turned out, arrived between 1669 and 1693.) And the Porter situation was eased still further by the fact that one male of the second generation, Benjamin, never married, so that it was known that at his death approximately one-third of the land of the original Porter estate would revert to the total pool of acres available to the third generation.

The sense of claustrophobia the Putnams must have felt as they considered their economic situation extended to politics as well. They dominated the Village Committee most of the time, to be sure, but that was slim compensation for the fact that with the rise of Salem's merchant group, they were gradually frozen out of the larger (and in many respects more significant) arena of Town politics. Because of their geographic situation, and the outlook which it may have imposed, the Putnams—with one dramatic exception which will become the focus of our attention in the next chapter—formed neither marital nor commercial ties in Salem Town. Their steadily diminishing political role in the Town was ultimately a consequence of that fact.

As we have stressed, Salem Villagers in these years were still legally eligible (despite the partial separation of 1672) to attend Salem Town meetings, to participate in the choice of the Town selectmen and other officers, and even to serve in Town office themselves. Before the separation, the Putnams had been active in Town affairs in all these ways, and they remained so even after the creation of the Village parish. But the consolidation of power in the Town by a merchant class with which they had forged few connections severely reduced and finally almost silenced the Putnam voice in Town politics.

Nathaniel and Captain John, as the two Putnams who had been most actively engaged in the political life of the Town, were the principal victims of this change. In the eight years from 1665 to 1673, these two brothers served a total of seven terms as Town selectmen; but in the nineteen years from 1674 to 1692 they served only five widely spaced terms.[39] Nor were their sons, or any other third-generation Putnams, elected in their place. (See Chart 5.)

The Putnams' political displacement can be explained only in part by the voluntary redirection of their energies into Village affairs, for there is substantial evidence that they continued to seek power in the Town after 1672, albeit in a somewhat erratic, and at times quixotic, fashion. In June 1678, for example, John and Nathaniel Putnam took the lead in distributing about the streets of Salem a broadside which criticized the merchant-led selectmen for selling the common lands of the Town to newcomers and thereby depriving the original proprietors of their legal privileges. The broadside concluded by announcing a special meeting of the proprietors (or their heirs) to discuss these grievances.[40] A counter-blast from the selectmen denounced the proposed meeting as "very irregular and illegal" and a menace to "the peace and quiet of this town." In turn, the Putnams composed another petition, in which they repeated their earlier charges against the selectmen, and to which they secured the signatures of seventy-four men of the Town and Village in addition to their own. Brought into court by the selectmen for this act, the Putnam brothers, with several other men, were admonished and released. Their appeal to a higher court was rejected.[41] Increasingly cut off from power by the dominant merchant group, the Putnams seem by the late 1670's to have assumed at least sporadic leadership of an inchoate and largely ineffectual dissident faction in the Town.

While the Putnams were operating at the fringes of power in Salem Town by the 1680's, the Porters were increasingly moving to its political center by making common cause with the merchant

39. Perley, *History of Salem*, II, 401; III, 252 (lists of selectmen). What we are suggesting is diminished influence, not its total disappearance. For example, Captain John Putnam was sent as a deputy to the General Court for three one-year terms between 1677 and 1686—Perley, *History of Salem*, II, 5.
40. Phillips, *Salem in the Seventeenth Century*, p. 254; 7 EQC, 74–75.
41. *Ibid.*; *Records of the Court of Assistants*, I, 123.

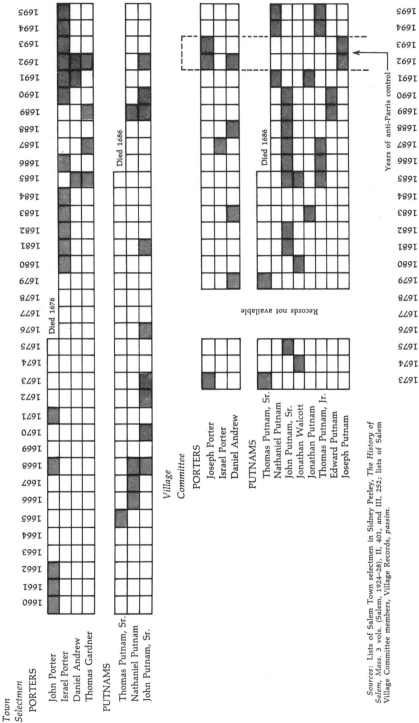

Chart 5. Putnams and Porters on Salem Town Board of Selectmen and Salem Village Committee

Sources: Lists of Salem Town selectmen in Sidney Perley, *The History of Salem, Mass.* 3 vols. (Salem, 1924–28), II, 401, and III, 252; lists of Salem Village Committee members, Village Records, *passim.*

group. As Chart 5 shows, Israel Porter served nine terms as Town selectman between 1680 and 1692, and in the same years his brother-in-law Daniel Andrew served three terms.

The economic and political divergence of these two families was revealed as open rivalry in the period immediately prior to the witchcraft outbreak. In July 1689, just as the separate Salem Village church was being established under Samuel Parris, those Villagers who wished to press on for a political as well as an ecclesiastical break with the Town, together with a dissident faction in the Town itself, succeeded (for the first time in years) in electing John and Nathaniel Putnam as selectmen. One week later, however, the four other newly chosen selectmen resigned in a body, apparently refusing to serve with the Putnams. The four included Israel Porter, Daniel Andrew, and Timothy Lindall, who was also connected to the Porters by marriage.[42]

But these obscure machinations did not signal the political defeat of the Porter clan in Salem Town: Israel Porter was returned to office in 1690, Daniel Andrew in 1691, and Timothy Lindall in 1692. And the seven selectmen picked in the annual election held in March 1692 included no fewer than four Porter kinsmen: Israel Porter, Daniel Andrew, Timothy Lindall, and the prominent merchant Thomas Gardner, husband of Israel's sister Mary.[43]

Another man chosen for the first time in this election was Phillip English, the largest shipowner in Salem and a political ally of the Porter clan. If one had to choose the single person most representative of the economic and social transformations which were overtaking Salem—and Massachusetts as a whole—in the late seventeenth century, Phillip English might well be that person. A native of the Channel Island of Jersey, Phillipe L'Anglois had come to Salem as a boy, anglicized his name, married into the Hollingsworth family of merchants, and proceeded to become one of the most successful entrepreneurs of his generation. By the 1690's he owned an imposing town house, fourteen lots in the Town, a wharf, and more than twenty sailing vessels. Building on his Gallic antecedents, he cultivated trading connections theretofore unknown to

42. Salem Town Records, July 5 and 11, 1689, 68 *EIHC* (1932), 214. Timothy Lindall was the husband of Mary Veren Putnam's child of her first marriage, Mary Veren, whose half-brother Joseph Putnam was married to Israel Porter's daughter Elizabeth—Lindall genealogy, Perley, *History of Salem*, II, 298.
43. Salem Town Records, March 8, 1692, 69 *EIHC* (April, 1933), 153; Perley, *History of Salem*, II, 161 (Porter genealogy); Phillips, *Salem in the Seventeenth Century*, p. 286 (on Thomas Gardner).

the merchants of seventeenth-century New England: connections in France, Spain, and Portugal, as well as more familiar ties with England and the West Indies.[44] The appearance of Phillip English for the first time as a selectman in March 1692, together with a group of Porters and Porter kin, was an event of considerable symbolic importance.

But at this point, in a dramatic and not wholly fortuitous convergence of events, normal politics in Salem Town was brought to a sudden halt by unexpected developments in Salem Village. Only a few weeks after the new selectmen had assumed office, warrants emanating from the Village were issued against two of them— Phillip English and Daniel Andrew—on charges of witchcraft.[45]

Both men were apparently warned in advance. Andrew escaped before he could be arrested, and went into hiding. English likewise escaped (along with his wife, who was accused with him), but the couple was found a few weeks later and kept in custody until they escaped once again.[46] While their status and connections saved the two men from the gallows, for the time being they had been effectively removed from power—and their allies in the Town momentarily placed on the defensive.

In July 1692, with the witchcraft furor at its height, a special election was held in the Town at which both Andrew and English, along with Timothy Lindall and two other selectmen, were voted out and five new men (four of whom had never before served in the office) chosen in their place. The revolution, though it would prove short-lived, was for the moment complete. Significantly, the moderator of this special election meeting was Captain John Putnam.[47]

In the strange summer of 1692, it seemed fleetingly possible that Salem might again become the kind of community which valued men like the Putnams and the things for which they stood.

44. On Phillip English: Bailyn, *New England Merchants in the Seventeenth Century*, pp. 144–145; Phillips, *Salem in the Seventeenth Century*, pp. 251, 284–285; Perley, *History of Salem*, II, 355; III, 70; Upham, *Salem Witchcraft*, II, 142.

45. Woodward, *Records of Salem Witchcraft*, I, 189–191; II, 23.

46. Upham, *Salem Witchcraft*, II, 142.

47. Salem Town Records, July 19, 1692, 83 *EIHC* (1947), 67.

6 Joseph and His Brothers: A Story of the Putnam Family

Few seventeenth-century Salem Villagers bore the name Joseph. It seems generally to have been reserved for certain special cases: for a son born to an older couple after a lapse of several years, or for the first son of a second marriage. Thus in 1690 Thomas Wilkins gave the name to his third son, born twelve years after his next older child. And Joseph Porter, the brother of Israel and Benjamin, was the eldest son of his father's second marriage. This interesting pattern was almost certainly linked to the fact that the Biblical Joseph, from whom the name derives, was the child of Jacob's old age and his first by Rachel, the favorite among his four wives and concubines.

It was probably by no mere whim, then, that in 1669 Thomas Putnam, Sr., a man of fifty-four with eight children by his first marriage, chose the name Joseph when his new wife bore their first (and only) child. The family into which Joseph Putnam was born was a dominant one in Salem Village, as we have seen, and the leader of that family, by any standard, was Joseph's father, Thomas Putnam, Sr. As the eldest son of the original John Putnam, Thomas had inherited a double portion of his father's Village land, and this legacy, augmented over the years by a series of purchases, eventually gave him a total of between 500 and 600 acres. His 1681 Village tax of over £10 placed him not only first among the Putnams, but well ahead of any other Salem Villager.[1]

1. Tax list, Village Records, Dec. 27, 1681. On Thomas Putnam's Village

The Family of Thomas Putnam, Sr.

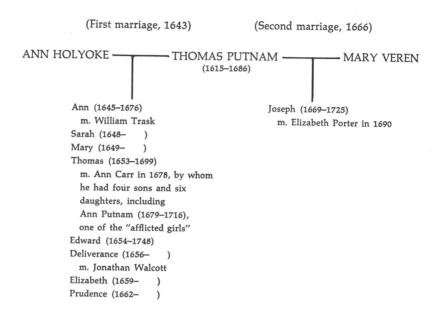

(First marriage, 1643)   (Second marriage, 1666)

ANN HOLYOKE ——————— THOMAS PUTNAM ——————— MARY VEREN
(1615–1686)

Ann (1645–1676)   Joseph (1669–1725)
  m. William Trask   m. Elizabeth Porter in 1690
Sarah (1648–   )
Mary (1649–   )
Thomas (1653–1699)
  m. Ann Carr in 1678, by whom
  he had four sons and six
  daughters, including
  Ann Putnam (1679–1716),
  one of the "afflicted girls"
Edward (1654–1748)
Deliverance (1656–   )
  m. Jonathan Walcott
Elizabeth (1659–   )
Prudence (1662–   )

Thomas Putnam married Ann Holyoke in 1643, when he was twenty-eight, and he sired eight children by her between 1645 and 1662. Only two of these, as it happened, were male: Thomas, Jr. (born in 1653) and Edward (1654).[2] As Thomas, Jr., came of age early in the 1670's and assumed his role as eldest son of the richest man in the Village, he could look forward eventually to occupying a similarly exalted position himself. This is not to say that his prospects were altogether untroubled. He knew that a part of his father's estate would probably have to go to provide dowries for his four sisters, and he knew, too, that he would have to divide the bulk of his father's acreage with his younger brother, Edward. And he must have recognized, like all the Putnams in these years, that the family's holdings were relatively isolated from the commercial center of Salem Town.

landholdings: Sidney Perley, "Hathorne: Part of Salem in 1700" [Part I], 53 *EIHC* (1917), 334, 336, 339, 341, 342; [Part II], 54 *EIHC* (1918), 122; Charles W. Upham, *Salem Witchcraft*, 2 vols. (Boston, 1867), I, 155 (the double portion).

2. Putnam genealogy: Sidney Perley, *The History of Salem*, 3 vols. (Salem, 1924–28), II, 109.

For young Thomas Putnam, Jr., then, the future may have been bright, but not quite so bright as the life he already knew. To live up to his father's station, and his own expectations, it would be necessary for him to take positive action. Accordingly, at about the time his uncles John and Nathaniel were beginning their ill-starred venture in the iron business, Thomas Putnam, Jr., too, attempted to diversify. He chose, however, another form of investment: matrimony. In 1678, at the age of twenty-five, young Thomas married Ann Carr, daughter of George Carr, one of the richest inhabitants of nearby Salisbury. Thomas had reason to expect that his marriage would bring him as a matter of course the economic diversification which his uncles had attempted so clumsily to achieve on their own. Not only was his father-in-law an extremely wealthy man, but his fortune was broadly based in a variety of economic activities: George Carr controlled some 400 acres of farm land in Salisbury, he owned a shipworks there, and he operated the ferry at a principal crossing point on the Merrimack River. At his death, Carr left an estate appraised (perhaps under-appraised) at more than £1,000.[3] Thomas Putnam must have had every hope, as he married into the Carr family, of making his way, in time, into that family's varied commercial activities.

But this was not to be. For when George Carr died in 1682 (four years after Thomas Putnam's marriage into the family), his widow and two of his sons moved decisively to hold the family enterprises under their own control. In a bitter protest filed with the courts in June 1682, several other members of the family (including Thomas Putnam, Jr.) charged that in settling the estate the widow Carr and her two sons, who had been appointed executors, were blatantly cheating the three Carr daughters, and their husbands, of their rightful portions.[4]

But this protest had little effect: about 60 percent of the Carr estate—including the shipyard and the ferry business—went, directly or indirectly, to the two Carr sons, with the remaining six children receiving comparatively modest cash bequests.[5] So vanished whatever hopes Thomas Putnam, Jr., may have entertained of using marriage as a vehicle to break out of his total economic dependence on the Salem Village lands he could expect to inherit from his father.

Still, those expectations were far from paltry. At the very least,

3. 8 *EQC*, 348–350 (George Carr's will and estate inventory).
4. 8 *EQC*, 354–355.
5. *Ibid.*, 348–349.

Thomas might have anticipated receiving from his father perhaps 300 acres, in addition to the family homestead, and—if his father followed the pattern of modified primogeniture by which he himself (as eldest son) had come into a double portion—perhaps considerably more.

But if Thomas Putnam, Jr., did entertain such prospects, he did not take into account the longevity and continued sexual vigor of his father. For in 1666, the year after his first wife died, the elder Thomas had taken for his second a widow by the name of Mary Veren. Second marriages were, of course, the rule for widowed persons in colonial New England, but this particular one had unexpected and far-reaching overtones. For Mary Veren was a woman of Salem Town, the widow of a Salem ship captain named Nathaniel Veren whose two brothers were among the more successful of the Town's emergent merchant class. Mary Veren herself was the owner of a house and lot in the Town, which she had purchased in her own name from one of her brothers-in-law. A daughter by her first marriage was to wed another Salem merchant and oft-time selectman, Timothy Lindall.[6]

The implications of his father's second marriage for Thomas Putnam, Jr., had deepened immeasurably in 1669 (although the sixteen-year-old youth may not have realized it at the time) with the arrival of Joseph Putnam. Perhaps Mary Veren had acquired some of the business acumen of the Salem circles in which she had moved, or perhaps her new husband had decided on his own to shift his deepest loyalties from the connections of his first marriage to those of his second. In any case, one or both of them began to promote the interests of their son Joseph at the expense of Thomas Putnam's other children, including Thomas, Jr., now on the threshold of manhood. When the elder Thomas Putnam died in 1686, he left a will which bequeathed to Mary *and to Joseph*—then sixteen years old—the best part of his estate, including the ample family homestead, the household furnishings, all the barns and outbuildings, and agricultural equipment (the "plow gear and cart and tackling of all sorts, with all my tools [and] implements of all sorts") and many of the most fertile acres that had been granted to old John Putnam forty years before.[7]

6. Perley, *History of Salem*, I, 303–304 (Veren genealogy); II, 109 (Putnam genealogy). See also 3 EQC, 264, for reference to Captain Nathaniel Veren.

7. Will in Eben Putnam, *History of the Putnam Family* (Salem, 1891), pp. 11–19. For a photograph of the Putnam homestead: Perley, *History of Salem*, III, 167.

Thomas Putnam, Jr., and his siblings were not left out altogether. Indeed, the old man may have died half-believing he had been scrupulously fair to all his children. He had already settled Thomas and Edward on farms of their own carved from his lands, and he confirmed those grants in his will. To his daughters he gave cash bequests.

But Thomas and Edward were convinced that they had been discriminated against, and their suspicions were deepened by certain rather unusual terms in their father's will. For example, the document specified that Joseph should come into his inheritance at the age of eighteen, rather than at the usual twenty-one. (This provision betrayed real concern that Joseph by some mischance or legal maneuver—set off, perhaps, by his mother's death—might be denied his full inheritance.) Even more important, Thomas named Mary and the lad Joseph as joint executors of his will and, in a surprising clause whose full significance would emerge only gradually, he appointed none other than Israel Porter (who also served as witness) as one of the overseers of the estate.

The depth of the grievance felt by the older children of Thomas Putnam, Sr., is revealed by the determination with which they tried to break the will. When the document was presented for probate, it was countered by a petition bearing the signatures of Thomas Putnam, Jr., his younger brother Edward, and their brothers-in-law Jonathan Walcott and William Trask. The four declared that they would be "extremely wronged" if their father's will were allowed to stand, and they pointed the finger at what they saw as the source of the wrong: the will, they said, "was occasioned to be made as it is by our mother-in-law" ("step-mother," by modern parlance). They asked the court to name Thomas Putnam, Jr., as executor, in place of Mary Veren Putnam and her son, in order for a "true inventory" to be taken "so that each of us may have that proportion of our deceased father's estate which by the law of God and man rightly belongs to us." But Mary hired a lawyer of Salem Town, and the challenge got nowhere.[8]

Thus it was that on September 14, 1687—his eighteenth birthday—Joseph Putnam became, overnight, one of the richest men in Salem Village. His 1690 tax was 40 percent higher than that of his older half-brothers; indeed, it was well above that of any of the third-generation Putnams, eight of whom had reached taxable status by that year. All the other members of the numerous family

8. Petition reprinted in Putnam, *History of the Putnam Family*, pp. 20–21.

—but especially Thomas Putnam, Jr.—watched impotently while Joseph, who could only have been seen as an interloper though he bore the family name, moved quickly and effortlessly into a privileged position in the Village.

But this was not to be all. In 1690, at the unusually youthful age of twenty, Joseph Putnam took a wife: she was none other than Elizabeth Porter, the sixteen-year-old daughter of Israel Porter.[9] The young man had managed to forge a formal alliance with the one family in the Village which rivaled and even surpassed the Putnams in wealth and prestige. This marriage confirmed for the other Putnams what was already only too clear: by joining the Porter clan Joseph Putnam had managed to break free of the narrow agrarian constraints which held the rest of the Putnams down, and to strengthen his links (already strong through his mother) to the social, commercial, and political life of Salem Town. And he had achieved all this—and here was the most galling part of the business—through no real effort of his own.

This is not to suggest that Thomas Putnam, Jr., or the other Putnams had meanwhile sunk into desperate poverty or been driven completely into the political wilderness. Thomas, like his brother, his brothers-in-law, and his Putnam cousins, still remained a fairly prosperous farmer and, in the local village sphere, an influential figure. But, in relative terms, these years of Joseph's dramatic rise saw the situation of the rest of the family remain more or less static. In the years from 1690 to 1695, while the total of Putnam taxes (excluding those paid by Joseph) rose by about 6 percent, Joseph's shot upward by about 50 percent. The tax rates of 1690 and 1695 indicate that, still in his twenties, he was the wealthiest Putnam and the second richest man in the Village. (The richest was his wife's uncle Joseph Porter, while the fourth richest was her uncle-by-marriage Daniel Andrew.) In that same five-year interval, the tax paid by Thomas Putnam, Jr., declined by about 10 percent, from £1 to eighteen shillings.[10] By 1695, this eldest son of the man who had been, by a wide margin, the wealthiest tax-

9. Perley, *History of Salem*, II, 109 (Putnam genealogy) and 162 (Porter genealogy).

10. Tax lists, Village Records, Dec. 30, 1690; Jan. 18, 1695. The comparative economic standing of the two men is also vividly revealed in the Salem Town tax rolls. In the Town tax of 1697, for example, the £1/9 paid by Joseph Putnam was more than double the fourteen shillings paid by his older half-brother. *Tax and Valuation Lists of Massachusetts Towns Before 1776*, microfilm edition compiled by Ruth Crandall (Harvard University Library), reel 8: "Salem, 1689–1773."

payer in Salem Village ranked only sixteenth among the 105 house-holders on the tax rolls.

Joseph Putnam's economic rise was paralleled by an increase in his political power. From the early years onward, the three Putnam brothers and, later, their sons had dominated Village affairs. Joseph's rise did not demolish this entrenched power, but it severely challenged it. As we have seen, the entirely new Village Committee elected by the dissident faction in October 1691 was made up of Joseph Putnam (still only twenty-two years old) and his newly acquired kinsmen Joseph Porter and Daniel Andrew, together with two other men of similar anti-Parris views. It was this Committee which so dramatically set itself against Samuel Parris and otherwise repudiated the policies of the group which had hitherto run the Village. The crucial meetings of late 1691, at which the Villagers voted to investigate the "fraudulent" conveyance of the parsonage to Samuel Parris in 1689, were called by Joseph Putnam. The political turbulence of this period is visually conveyed in the Village Book of Record, as the neat, methodical handwriting of Thomas Putnam, Jr. (who had served as Village clerk for years until 1691) gives way to someone else's hasty scrawl, probably that of Joseph Putnam himself. And, like his father-in-law Israel Porter, Joseph Putnam figures importantly as a behind-the-scenes figure in Parris's account of the factional maneuvering of 1693–95. Simultaneously, he won a place for himself in the politics of Salem Town, where he served seven terms as selectman.[11] Needless to say, alone among the Putnams, Joseph and his wife signed the anti-Parris petition of April 1695.

The final blow to the rest of the family came, as it happened, in that same month of April 1695, with the death of Mary Veren Putnam. The will which Mrs. Putnam left rubbed salt into her stepchildren's long-festering wounds. Not only did she leave to Joseph everything she had inherited from Thomas Putnam, Sr.—"without doors or within doors"—and make him her sole executor, but she cut off Thomas, Jr., Edward, and Deliverance (Putnam) Walcott with a contemptuous five shillings each, and two of the other sisters with ten. More would have gone to them, the will pointedly noted, had they not "brought upon me inconvenient and unnecessary charges and disbursements at several times."[12]

11. Perley, *History of Salem*, III, 252 (list of selectmen); Church Records, March 27, 1693.

12. Essex Prob., Docket 23077 (Mary Veren Putnam will and related documents). While it was not uncommon to leave such token sums to children

Goaded beyond bearing by both the substance and the tone of Mary's will, Thomas and Edward Putnam, along with their brother-in-law Jonathan Walcott (William Trask, their other brother-in-law, had died in 1691) now revived the court challenge which they had initiated, without success, nine years before. In two petitions filed in early June 1695, these three revealed how obsessive was the grievance which they—and especially Thomas—had built up since 1686. Their suspicion of wrong-doing had by now hardened into absolute conviction. For "several years," they charged, Mary and Joseph had "used and disposed" of the estate of Thomas Putnam, Sr., without ever opening it to a full and impartial inventory. In this way, they alleged, had they been cheated out of "three or four hundred pounds" of which they were the "right owners."[13]

The three petitioners went on to demand a full investigation of the circumstances surrounding the drawing up of Mary Putnam's will; such an inquiry, they declared, would reveal "great iniquity." Responding to this request, the probate court did, indeed, call several witnesses to testify as to Mary Putnam's mental condition in the final weeks of her life—and, implicitly, on whether the alleged will was, in fact, her own, or the work of someone else.

The testimony divided along predictable lines. William Griggs, the Village doctor who had first discerned the "Evil Hand" in the behavior of the Village girls three years earlier, now testified that Mary Putnam had not been of sound and disposing mind at the time the will was drawn up. But Timothy Lindall, Mary's son-in-law by her first husband, deposed that she had spoken "decently and rationally" up to the very end—"especially about her spiritual condition." Lindall's testimony was reenforced by that of Thomas Preston, a son-in-law of Rebecca Nurse (hanged as a witch in 1692 after having been accused by the wife and daughter of Thomas Putnam, Jr.).[14]

The most revealing and (to the modern reader) persuasive testimony was that offered by Abigail Darling, one of the servant girls who had attended Mrs. Putnam in her final days. Abigail gave a vivid picture of how close to death Mary had been for weeks—lapsing into unconsciousness, "dying away" for long periods—only to revive when everyone was convinced that the end had come;

who had already received their fair share of the parental estate, this was clearly not the case in the Putnam family.

13. Petitions of Thomas Putnam, Edward Putnam, and Jonathan Walcott, June 3 and June 10, 1695—*ibid.*

14. Testimony of William Griggs and Thomas Preston—*ibid.*

finally hardly stirring at all, but still staring intently into space. It was evidently while she was in such a condition that the events Abigail went on to describe took place. Her testimony made clear that throughout this protracted death watch, Israel Porter was often with Mrs. Putnam, tirelessly urging her to draw up a will. At last, one day near the end, after Mrs. Putnam had had a particularly bad spell, Abigail and another servant girl, Deborah Knight, were sent out to work in the malt house. (A curious thing: to send away persons who might at any moment be needed to minister to the needs of a dying woman.) But after a time the girls were "all of a sudden" called into the bed chamber again, and there was "Mr. Israel Porter" with a paper in his hand—the will—which he asked Mary Putnam to sign. With Israel guiding her hand, Mary did indeed put her mark to the document which left everything to her son (and Israel's son-in-law) Joseph Putnam—everything except for the few shillings reserved for "my husband Putnam's children." Israel specifically instructed the servant girls (who had been called in to sign as witnesses) to "take notice that our mistress was sensible." Abigail Darling, however, at that moment vowed to herself that she would never testify to any such thing.[15]

With Abigail's testimony on record, the full extent of the "great iniquity"—as it seemed from the Putnam perspective—was unfolded. From the moment the elder Thomas Putnam had turned to Salem Town to take a second wife, Israel Porter had sensed his opportunity and bided his time. He had been involved in the drawing up of old Thomas's will, he had probably brought Joseph Putnam and his daughter Elizabeth together, he had allowed Elizabeth to marry Joseph at the earliest possible moment (she was only sixteen), and finally he had lurked about the dying Mary Veren Putnam to make certain that no last moment slip-up would prevent the full estate from going to Joseph.

But in his own deposition, Israel Porter, cool as always, simply ignored all the implications and innuendoes in Abigail Darling's account, and offered his own terse version of the circumstances leading up to the signing of the will. The will was in his handwriting, to be sure (he could hardly deny it; the fact is plain to anyone who examines the document in the Essex County Registry of Probate), but only because he "was desired to write it for her." (Desired by whom? Mary herself? His son-in-law Joseph? Porter was always a master of the passive voice.) Only in response to

15. Testimony of Abigail Darling—*ibid.*

this request for his assistance did he "discourse" with the dying woman about how she wished to "dispose of what she had to dispose of and what she would give to her sons- and daughters-in-law." But, Israel reported, Mary had firmly rejected all suggestions that she make larger bequests to her stepchildren: "I don't know how Joseph can pay it. . . . [I]t is easy to write down a thousand, but where will it be had?" Israel had consulted also with Joseph Putnam, who for some reason stayed away from the sickroom while this was going on. All Joseph told his father-in-law was that "what his mother should do, he would be satisfied with." Only then, Israel testified, had he written out the document embodying Mary's wishes and guided her hand as she put her feeble mark to it: the entire estate to Joseph except for thirty-five shillings distributed in carefully calibrated gradations to five of her stepchildren.[16]

But all this testimony, revealing as it is, did little to help the cause of Thomas Putnam, Jr. Despite his protests, the will of Mary Veren Putnam stood in force, and Joseph Putnam—a "Putnam" in name only—was confirmed in his status as the family's preeminent figure in the third generation.

Joseph had achieved this position through his fortuitous access to channels of power, influence, and economic activity which remained closed to the other Putnams. The contrast between their situation and his is epitomized in the introduction to one of the 1695 court petitions of Thomas Putnam, Jr.: "I came this morning providentially to the Town of Salem, and accidentally heard that my brother Joseph Putnam doth intend this day to prosecute a confirmation of that instrument which is called his mother's last will."[17] "Providentially" and "accidentally" tell the story: Joseph Putnam might feel at home in Salem Town, but to Thomas it had become enemy territory, where one's only allies were Providence and luck.

What had occurred within the Putnam family is illustrated with particular poignancy if one follows into the eighteenth century the respective family histories of Thomas Putnam, Jr., and his half-brother Joseph Putnam. Thomas's middle years brought difficult times. In 1697 he sold the twenty acres of land on which his own homestead stood, evidently to raise cash, and built a small new house (out of second-hand lumber) elsewhere on his diminished

16. Testimony of Israel Porter—*ibid.*
17. Petition of Thomas Putnam, Jr., et al., June 10, 1695—*ibid.*

holdings. When he died intestate in 1699 at the age of forty-eight (and within two weeks of his wife), his estate of £437 was saddled with debts of nearly £200 which required his executors to sell off still more of his land. Of Thomas's four sons to reach maturity, one went to sea and two others moved away from the area; of his five daughters, three remained spinsters while the others married outsiders and moved away.[18]

Joseph Putnam, by contrast, remained prosperous throughout his life. He provided lands for his sons during his lifetime, and at his death in 1723 he distributed an additional 300 acres among his sons and gave cash bequests to his daughters. Not surprisingly, two of his three sons married local girls and remained in the area, and all eight of his daughters became the wives of local men. (The one son who did move away was Israel Putnam—"Old Put," as he became known, a highly successful land speculator and military man who made his mark on American history in 1775 at Bunker Hill.)[19]

Young Thomas Putnam, in fighting for the land which he believed his by "the law of God and man," had been struggling to preserve living space in Salem Village for himself and his children. He lost, and his family vanished from the Village. It was as simple, and as harsh, as that.

Stepmothers and Witches

By 1692 the children of the first Thomas Putnam—and especially his eldest son's family—were prepared to believe that witchcraft lay at the root of their troubles. They were hardly the first, under similar circumstances, to reach such a conclusion. Indeed, this episode in the history of the Putnam family, as well as its tragic denouement, is echoed in what might at first seem the least likely of sources: the folk-literature of medieval Europe, in which the evil

18. Perley, *History of Salem*, II, 109–110 (Putnam genealogy); Sidney Perley, "Hathorne: Part of Salem in 1700" [Part I], p. 342; Essex Prob., VIII, 74.

19. Joseph Putnam will: Eben Putnam, *History of the Putnam Family*, pp. 52–55. On Israel Putnam: *Dictionary of American Biography*, XV, 281; Perley, *History of Salem*, II, 110. It was Israel Putnam who is traditionally credited with having contributed to the American heritage the line, "Don't shoot until you see the whites of their eyes." He appears in the Jonathan Trumbull painting of the Bunker Hill battle, the only Salem Villager of these years for whom a likeness is known to exist—Theodore Sizer, *The Works of Colonel John Trumbull: Artist of the American Revolution* (rev. ed., New Haven, Yale University Press, 1967), figure 145.

stepmother and avaricious half-sibling frequently play central roles. The father of Cinderella, for example, takes as his second wife a widow associated with high society who, with the two daughters of her previous marriage, quickly comes to "govern him entirely" (as Mary Veren was accused of doing with her husband Putnam) and to relegate Cinderella, the child of his first marriage, to the role of a menial.[20]

The parallels are even closer in *Hansel and Gretel*, even though in this most famous witch story of all, the central family (unlike the Putnams) is poor and the stepmother brings no children of her own into the household. But like Cinderella—and the older children of Thomas Putnam, Sr.—Hansel and Gretel find themselves victimized and exploited by their father's selfish second wife, who ultimately persuades her somewhat reluctant husband to abandon them to certain death in the forest. But a magical bird leads them to a cottage made of bread, cake, and sugar—an impoverished child's image of prosperity. The old witch who lives in the place captures them and treats them precisely as their stepmother had done, exploiting their labor and even plotting their murder. ("Get up, you lazybones," she orders Gretel, "fetch water and cook something for your brother. When he's fat I'll eat him up.") But instead, it is the children who kill the witch, using the method often employed in European witch trials: fire. They return home—no trouble finding their way this time—laden with the "pearls and precious stones" they have discovered hidden in the witch's house. These they show to their overjoyed father, who "had not passed a single happy hour since he left them in the wood" and who informs them that their stepmother has died in their absence. Only the original family is left to share the witch's wealth.[21]

Both structurally and psychologically, the "witch" in *Hansel and Gretel* is a symbolic projection of the stepmother herself. Each of these women exploits the brother and sister and actually tries to kill them, and after the children execute the witch, the stepmother turns out, in a most improbable coincidence, to have died at about the same time. It is tempting to speculate about what actual event may have given rise to the tale of *Hansel and Gretel*. Perhaps there existed a real stepmother who was killed by her husband's children —children who then excused their deed by calling the selfish

20. Andrew Lang, ed., *The Blue Fairy Book* (Looking Glass Library, distributed by Random House, New York, 1959), pp. 96–97.
21. *Ibid.*, pp. 331–341; quoted passages on pp. 338, 340, and 341.

woman a witch. Or perhaps the historical prototypes of "Hansel" and "Gretel" merely made the initial accusation of witchcraft, leaving it to the authorities to burn the hated stepmother at the stake.

If, like the real Hansel and Gretel, the Putnams had expressed their frustration and rage in one terrible act of violence directed against a solitary individual, they would probably be remembered, if at all, not as historical villains but as folk figures—again like Hansel and Gretel, or (to take a more recent example) Lizzie Borden. But as even a summary of their role in 1692 makes clear, the Putnam response, if no less deadly, was far more diffuse and indirect. In that year Thomas Putnam, Jr., testified against twelve persons and signed complaints against twenty-four. His wife, Ann; his twelve-year-old daughter, Ann, Jr.; and a servant girl in his house named Mercy Lewis were all counted among the afflicted. Indeed, the younger Ann Putnam, who testified against at least twenty-one persons, has remained the most infamous of the band of "afflicted girls." Thomas's brother Edward participated in thirteen cases; his brother-in-law Jonathan Walcott in seven; and Walcott's daughter Mary (who lived in Thomas Putnam's house) was not far behind her cousin Ann in attracting spectral torturers, sixteen of whom assaulted her in 1692.[22]

Strangely enough, the younger Thomas Putnam and his siblings never directly attacked the two persons most obviously responsible for their difficulties: their stepmother and their half-brother. Neither Mary Veren Putnam nor Joseph Putnam was named as a witch in 1692—though family tradition long held that Joseph kept a horse saddled day and night during that summer, and never ventured forth without a gun.[23] But, in the end, his precautions proved unnecessary. Was this because Mary and her son (unlike wealthy persons living outside the Village) were simply too powerful and too immediate a presence to be challenged directly? Or would accusations against them—since they were, in spite of everything, still part of the family—have involved psychic strains too intense to be borne? Whatever the reason, it seems clear that the Putnams in 1692 (like Hansel and Gretel in the folk tale) projected their bitterness onto persons who were, politically or psychologically, less threatening targets: notably older women of Mary Veren Put-

22. W. Elliot Woodward, *Records of Salem Witchcraft, Copied From the Original Documents*, 2 vols. (Roxbury, Mass., Privately printed, 1864; reissued in one volume, New York, Da Capo Press, 1969), index.

23. Upham, *Salem Witchcraft*, II, 457.

nam's generation. Against such persons they vented the rage and bitterness which they were forced to deny (or to channel through such stylized outlets as legal petitions) in their relations with Mary and Joseph.

The original "afflictions," though evidently beginning in the Parris household, quickly spread from there to the three girls who lived in the household of Thomas Putnam, Jr.: Ann, Mary, and Mercy. But the imprisonment of the first three accused witches on March 1, Sarah Good, Sarah Osborne, and Tituba, did not cause the symptoms to abate. Indeed, they now spread to Thomas's wife, Ann Putnam, Sr. By the second week in March, both mother and daughter were complaining that they were being tortured by another woman, Martha Cory. The sufferings of the elder Ann Putnam became especially acute on the afternoon of the eighteenth: already "wearied out in helping to tend my poor afflicted child and maid," Mrs. Putnam was just lying down in bed "to take a little rest" when Goody Cory's apparition appeared and "torture[d] me so as I cannot express, ready to tear me all to pieces." [24]

Like the three women already in prison, there was a taint about Martha Cory: she had given birth, years earlier, to an illegitimate mulatto son, and the young man was still living in the Cory household, just over the Village line in Salem Town, with Martha and her second husband, Giles Cory. (Martha's first husband had been a Salem Townsman named Rich—like Mary Veren she had come as a mature woman to Salem Village after having been long identified with Salem Town.) But Goody Cory was not simply another Village outcast like Sarah Good or Tituba, for her husband was a prospering though somewhat obstreperous farmer and landowner, and—a fact of considerable importance—Martha herself was a covenanting member of the Salem Village church.[25]

The accusation of such a person as Martha Cory was a key point along the psychological progression which the Thomas Putnam family, and the entire witchcraft episode, followed in 1692. For in turning on her they betrayed the fact that witchcraft accusations against the powerless, the outcast, or the already victimized were not sufficiently cathartic for them. They were driven to lash out at persons of real respectability—persons, in short, who reminded

24. Deposition of Ann Putnam, Sr., quoted *ibid.*, II, 278.

25. On Martha Cory, see Perley, *History of Salem*, I, 193; III, 292; on Giles Cory: 1 *EQC*, 152, 172; 4 *EQC*, 275; 6 *EQC*, 191; 7 *EQC*, 89–91, 123–124, 147–149; 10 *New England Historical and Genealogical Register* (1856), 32 (will); Sidney Perley, "The Woods: Part of Salem in 1700," 51 *EIHC*, 195.

them of the individuals actually responsible (so they believed) for their own reduced fortunes and prospects. Martha Cory was the ideal transition figure: she combined respectability with a touch of deviance. If the Putnams could bring her down, they would be free, not only politically, but psychologically as well, to play out their compulsions on a still larger scale.

And they brought her down in less than two weeks. On March 19, on the strength of Edward Putnam's complaint that she had afflicted Thomas Putnam's wife and daughter, Martha Cory was arrested.[26] Others would subsequently testify against her, but initially—unlike the first three accused women—she was a Putnam family witch pure and simple.

For their next play in this deadly game of psychological projection, the Putnams moved further up the social and economic ladder —and thus, in a sense, that much closer to Mary Veren Putnam. It was as early as March 13 that the younger Ann Putnam first saw the new and strange female apparition. "I did not know what her name was then," she later testified, "though I knew where she used to sit in our meetinghouse." On the fifteenth, Samuel Parris's niece saw the same specter, and four days later, it appeared to Ann Putnam, Sr. By this time its identity had somehow been ascertained: it was Rebecca Nurse, a respected older woman of Salem Village, and the wife of Francis Nurse, a once-obscure artisan who in 1678 had established himself as a substantial figure in the Village by purchasing, on credit, a rich, 300-acre farm near the Ipswich Road.[27]

Rebecca was convicted largely on the basis of spectral afflictions which befell the elder Ann Putnam between March 19 and 24, 1692. At first, until Martha Cory was imprisoned, Rebecca was distinctly a secondary figure in Ann Putnam's roster of spectral visitors. But after the twenty-first, with Cory safely in prison, Goody Nurse became the dominant presence in Ann's life. On Tuesday March 22, as Mrs. Putnam would later testify, her apparition "set upon me in a most dreadful manner, very early in the morning, as soon as it was well light." The struggle which ensued, and which was to continue almost without respite for three days, was at once physical and spiritual. Dressed at first "only in her shift," Nurse carried in her hand the morning of her first visitation to the Putnam household a "little red book" which she "vehe-

---

26. Woodward, *Records of Salem Witchcraft*, I, 50.
27. *Ibid.*, I, 88–89. For more on the Nurses, see pp. 199–200 below.

mently" urged Mistress Ann to sign (to sign away what? her soul? her estate?). When Ann refused, the specter (as she put it) "threatened to tear my soul out of my body," and denied that God had any power to save her.[28] The ordeal lasted almost two hours, and it recurred intermittently for the rest of the day.

It was on the next day, Wednesday the twenty-third, that the Reverend Deodat Lawson, Parris's predecessor in the Village pulpit, visited the besieged household. When he arrived, Ann had just recovered from a "sore fit." At the Putnams' request, Lawson began to pray, but by the time he had finished, Mrs. Putnam "was so stiff she could not be bended." A little afterwards, she "began to strive violently with her arms and legs" and to shout at her tormenter: "Goodwife Nurse, be gone! be gone! be gone! Are you not ashamed, a woman of your profession, to afflict a poor creature so! What hurt did I ever do to you in my life? . . . [B]e gone, do not torment me!"[29]

The scene thereupon turned into an argument about what the future held in store for the two women. Mrs. Putnam, for her part, insisted that her spectral visitor had "but two years to live" and that then the Devil would carry her off to hell: "For this your name is blotted out of God's Book, and it shall never be put in God's Book again." But the specter of Rebecca Nurse, for its part, seems to have had the same plans in store for Ann Putnam herself: "I know what you would have . . . ," Ann told her, "but it is out of your reach; it is clothed with the white robes of Christ's righteousness."

The encounter between Ann Putnam, Sr., and "Rebecca Nurse" is the most vivid and intimate record we have of the actual process by which a "witch" was singled out for accusation, and of the degree to which the accusers felt palpably threatened by the specters which haunted them. In retrospect, perhaps, Rebecca Nurse appears the inevitable victim, since she was an ideal "substitute" for Mary Veren Putnam: both were women of advanced years, both were prosperous and respected, both were in failing health,

28. Deposition of Ann Putnam, Sr., quoted in Upham, *Salem Witchcraft*, II, 279.

29. Deodat Lawson, *A Brief and True Narrative of Some Remarkable Passages Relating to Sundry Persons Afflicted by Witchcraft, at Salem Village Which Happened from the Nineteenth of March to the Fifth of April, 1692* (Boston, 1692), in George Lincoln Burr, ed., *Narratives of the Witchcraft Cases, 1648–1706* (New York, Charles Scribner's Sons, 1914; reissued New York, Barnes and Noble, 1968), p. 157.

and both were members of the Salem Town church (though Rebecca occasionally worshiped in the Village).

To be sure, there were also a number of reasons, on the conscious and "rational" level, why Ann Putnam may have resented and even feared Rebecca Nurse. Rebecca was from Topsfield, whose town authorities had for years been harassing the Putnam family by claiming that parts of their lands actually lay in Topsfield rather than in Salem Village. And her husband Francis had been involved during the 1670's in a protracted dispute with Nathaniel Putnam over some mutually bounded acreage.[30] Furthermore, Francis Nurse, though not a real leader in Village politics, was clearly identified with the faction which the Putnams opposed. Along with Joseph Putnam, Daniel Andrew, and Joseph Porter, he had been elected to the anti-Parris Village Committee which took power at the end of 1691. And it was around the Rebecca Nurse case, as we have seen, that Israel Porter was soon to try to rally opposition to the trials. Finally, even more than Martha Cory, and through no doing of her own, Rebecca was particularly vulnerable in 1692: years earlier, her mother had been accused of witchcraft (though never arrested or brought to trial) and local gossip had it that the taint had been passed on to her daughters. (Indeed, probably because the accusations against Rebecca jogged memories about the earlier episode, her two sisters were later accused as well.)[31]

But while such circumstances made Rebecca Nurse an acceptable and even plausible "witch" once she had been accused, they did not themselves provide the emotional impetus which led to her being singled out in the first place. The source of that drive lay in the fact that Ann Putnam was unable or unwilling publicly to vent her terrible rage on its living source: her mother-in-law Mary Veren Putnam, and perhaps her own mother Elizabeth Carr—the two old women who had somehow managed over the years to deprive Ann and her family of the high station which, by birth, was rightfully theirs. Of this redirected rage, Rebecca Nurse, like Martha Cory before her, was the innocent victim.

Once Rebecca *had* been singled out, and Ann Putnam's spectral struggle with her had begun, Ann's frantic monologues reveal a

---

30. 7 *EQC,* 10–21; 8 *EQC,* 116–121, 319–323 (Topsfield dispute). For a timber dispute which pitted the Putnams against Rebecca's family in the 1680's, see 47 County Court Records, 42–43.

31. The earlier charge against Rebecca Nurse's mother is mentioned in the testimony of Ann Putnam, Sr.—Woodward, *Records of Salem Witchcraft,* I, 95.

great deal about the nature of her obsession: "I know what you would have . . . , but it is out of your reach," she insists. "[W]e judged she meant her soul," interpolated Deodat Lawson (a little defensively?) at this point in his published report of the interview; but Ann's own words remain laden with unconscious ambiguity. Indeed, it is surprising how little energy Ann devoted during these hours of her travail to accusing Rebecca of witchcraft: it is "Rebecca's" death (or, more specifically, the obliteration of her psychological presence) which obsessed her. "Be gone! Be gone! Be gone!" she cries; "Be gone, do not torment me." She insists that Rebecca's name has been "blotted out" of God's mind forever. She even ventures a prediction: her spectral visitor has "about two years to live." [32] (In fact the guess was only a little optimistic: Mary Veren Putnam survived for almost exactly three years.)

But there is guilt as well as rage in all of this: for when the family of Thomas Putnam was deprived of its birthright, first by Elizabeth Carr and then by Mary Veren Putnam, it was forced openly and perhaps even consciously to confront the fact that it cared, and cared profoundly, about money and status. The apparition which for six days urged Ann Putnam to "yield to her hellish temptations," and which denied, as Ann put it, "the power of the Lord Jesus to save my soul," was, after all, in the mind of Mrs. Putnam herself. Did she fear that, covenanting church member or no, she had indeed lost her soul?—that it was she and her husband, with their open and drawn-out pursuit of money through the county courts, who were the real witches?

Might any of the other Putnams—or Lawson himself—have sensed danger here? In any case, by this time, the family had seen (and heard) enough. Later that same day, March 23, Edward and Jonathan Putnam went to the officials to swear out a complaint against Goody Nurse, and a warrant for her arrest was issued on the spot.[33] Rebecca's public examination was held the next day. But although the scene had shifted from Ann Putnam's bedroom to the Village meetinghouse, Ann still dominated it. She called out to Rebecca (in what must have been their first non-spectral encounter in some time): "Did you not bring the Black Man with you? Did you not bid me tempt God and die? How often have you eat and drunk your own damnation?"

At this, the exhausted Mrs. Putnam fell into still another fit;

32. Lawson, *Brief and True Narrative*, in Burr, *Narratives*, p. 157.
33. Woodward, *Records of Salem Witchcraft*, I, 76–77.

with the permission of the presiding magistrates her husband Thomas carried her home.[34] Almost as soon as Rebecca was imprisoned, the elder Ann Putnam's afflictions ceased—and they would not return for over two months. For a while, at least, the obsessive presence of Mary Veren, and all she represented in the life of Thomas Putnam, Jr., and his family, had been exorcised.

To understand Thomas Putnam, Jr., and his family is to begin to understand Salem Village. For in Puritan New England, the line between public and private concerns was a thin one. Since individual behavior was scrutinized by the full community just as closely as it was by a person's own family, it is hardly surprising that public issues should so often have been approached from the perspective of family relationships. It was, for example, altogether natural (and not in mere rhetorical hyperbole) that a Connecticut legislator of the 1690's, while denouncing an outlying section of his town for seeking autonomy, lamented to his fellow lawmakers that "one of your first born, a lovely, beautiful child, should be disinherited, and lose its birthright to an inferior brat." [35]

Similarly, the family of Thomas Putnam, Jr., readily wove its personal grievances into a comprehensive vision of conspiracy against Salem Village as a whole. In this way, the "pro-Parris" Villagers (who might otherwise have remained a disorganized collection of farmers ultimately to vanish from the historical record without a trace) attracted a powerful and determined leadership. Most Salem Village farmers must have found the forces which threatened them amorphous and difficult to pin down; for the Putnams, however, that task was all too easy: it was Mary Veren and her son Joseph who were the serpents in Eden, and if they, or their psychological equivalents, could only be eliminated, all might again be well.

34. Lawson, *Brief and True Narrative*, in Burr, *Narratives*, p. 159; Woodward, *Records of Salem Witchcraft*, I, 82–87, quoted passage on pp. 83–84. If Rebecca Nurse was a substitute for Mary Veren Putnam, then John Willard, against whom Ann Putnam also testified, may have been a substitute for Joseph Putnam. For more on Willard, a young, upwardly mobile outsider who had married into an established Salem Village family, see Chapter 8 below.

35. Richard L. Bushman, *From Puritan to Yankee: Character and the Social Order in Connecticut, 1690–1765* (Cambridge, Mass., Harvard University Press, 1967), p. 66.

Epilogue — Genesis 37: 3-8

Now Israel loved Joseph more than all his children, because he was the son of his old age: and he made him a coat of many colours.

And when his brethren saw that their father loved him more than all his brethren, they hated him, and could not speak peaceably unto him.

And Joseph dreamed a dream, and he told it [to] his brethren: and they hated him yet the more.

And he said unto them, Hear, I pray you, this dream which I have dreamed:

For, behold, we were binding sheaves in the field, and, lo, my sheaf arose, and also stood upright; and, behold, your sheaves stood round about, and made obeisance to my sheaf.

And his brethren said to him, Shalt thou indeed reign over us? or shalt thou indeed have dominion over us? And they hated him yet the more for his dreams, and for his words.

7 Samuel Parris: A Pilgrim in Bethlehem

It was cold and blustery in Salem Village on November 19, 1689—the day of Samuel Parris's ordination—and bec se of the "sharpness" of the weather, Parris delivered only an abbreviated version of the sermon he had prepared. Nevertheless, he said enough to reveal a good deal—not only about himself, but also about his perceptions of the community to which he had come as pastor.

For example, he referred openly to the political turmoil which had been generated by the campaign for an independent Salem Village church. He acknowledged, too, that some Villagers were "grieved" by the "disquietness" and "restlessness" which his supporters had displayed in their drive for ordination. But he had a ready explanation for this "restlessness"—an explanation implicit in the very text he chose for his ordination sermon. That text, drawn from the Book of Joshua, was God's message to the Israelites after they had crossed the Jordan River: "This day have I rolled away the reproach of Egypt from off you."

Parris's point was that Salem Village, too, had long lain under such a "reproach"—a curse almost—for its failure to establish a full-fledged church: "[W]hat an Egyptian-like disgrace and reproach was it for such a number of people (so well able to maintain the Lord's ordinances) in such a land as New England, so long to continue, unlike their professing neighbors, without the signs and seals of the blessed Covenant of Grace."

It was the oppressive consciousness of this divine reproach, contended Parris, that had driven his supporters to such relentless efforts. Whatever excessive zealousness they had displayed had merely reflected their longing for "the seals of the covenant to be brought home to their own doors." They had thrown themselves into a cause with which no other earthly effort can compare: the creation of a church. "The very seals of the Covenant, whereby we are initiated into, and confirmed in an interest in Christ . . . is (as holy Calvin says) worth an hundred lives." This lofty motivation, Parris insisted, should be more than enough to "vindicate and justify" the measures of the advocates of ordination and prevent any Villager from being "offended at the work of this day."

Even as he explained and justified the conflicts of the past, Parris held out the prospect that a new era was dawning for the Village. For the "reproach" had now been "rolled away"; those who had been "groaning" under its weight were now at ease. Whatever the divisions of former times, Parris implied, the community could now look forward to a future of tranquility and unity. Though it must have seemed somehow inappropriate on that raw November day, Parris tried to impart a message of new hope and fresh beginnings. "Hence learn, ye of this place (this Village), that God hath graciously brought you to a good day this day."[1]

What the men and women of Salem Village perhaps did not fully realize, as they saw Samuel Parris ordained to the Christian ministry by the Reverend Nicholas Noyes, and as they watched him kneel to receive the benediction of the Reverend John Hale and the Reverend Samuel Phillips, was the extent to which this occasion also represented the opportunity of a fresh beginning for Parris himself—perhaps the last he could reasonably expect to be granted. For Parris was thirty-six years old in 1689, and his life up to that point had been marked by economic setbacks, career frustrations, and mounting anxiety about what the future might hold.

Samuel Parris was born in 1653, a younger son of Thomas Parris, a London cloth merchant with peripheral interests in commerce and real-estate on the island colonies of Ireland and Barbados. When Thomas died in 1673 he left all his land and personal estate in England and Ireland to his eldest son, and made extensive cash bequests to the children of this eldest son as well as to a smattering of other relatives and friends. To twenty-year-old Samuel he left only his Barbados property: a twenty-acre section of a cotton

1. Sermon Book, Nov. 19, 1689, pp. 1, 12, 13.

plantation which had been tied up some years before in a long-term lease. Even on the intensively cultivated island of Barbados, this represented a relatively small tract; it may also have been affected by the disastrous hurricane of 1675, which struck with particular ferocity the northern part of the island, where Parris's twenty acres were situated. ("[H]e who was heir of all things," Parris was later to observe in a sermon on Christ, "sometimes was scarce owner of anything.")[2]

With so limited a foothold in Barbados, and no prospects at all in England, Parris decided upon Massachusetts. Arriving in Boston by the early 1680's, he was admitted as a freeman in 1683, at the age of thirty, and the following year chosen by the Court of Assistants as foreman of the Jury of Attaints and Appeals. (One of the cases he heard involved a successful appeal by Captain John Putnam of an adverse judgment in a county court case. This chance encounter may have been the beginning of a connection which was eventually to bring Parris to Salem Village.)[3]

But commerce, not the ministry, was Parris's first choice. In March 1682, signaling his intention of engaging in trade, he purchased a wharf and warehouse in Boston. In making this move, he may have been seeking to emulate an uncle, John Parris, who a generation before had used an interval of mercantile activity in Boston as a stepping-stone to a highly successful career as a Barbados planter.[4]

But as a businessman Parris did not meet with "any great encouragement or advantage" (as another Boston merchant, Robert Calef, later rather drily put it),[5] and it was at this point that he

2. *Ibid.*, May 25, 1690, p. 64. On Parris: G. Andrews Moriarity, "Genealogical Notes on the Rev. Samuel Parris of Salem Village," 49 *EIHC* (1913), 354–355; Middlesex County Probate Records, Courthouse, Cambridge, Mass., Docket 16951 (will and estate inventory); Richard S. Dunn, "The Barbados Census of 1680: Profile of the Richest Colony in English America," 26 *William and Mary Quarterly* (1969), 4.

3. Records of the First Church of Boston, Feb. 7, 1683; 3 *New England Historical and Genealogical Register* (1849), 345; *Records of the Court of Assistants of the Colony of the Massachusetts Bay, 1630–1692*, 3 vols. (Boston, 1901–1928), I, 255–256.

4. Richard Harris, *et ux.* to Samuel Parris, March 20, 1682, Suffolk County Registry of Deeds, Courthouse, Boston, XII, 285; Bernard Bailyn, *The New England Merchants in the Seventeenth Century* (Cambridge, Mass., Harvard University Press, 1955), p. 88 (on John Parris).

5. Robert Calef, *More Wonders of the Invisible World: Or, the Wonders of the Invisible World Display'd in Five Parts* (London, 1700), in George Lincoln Burr, ed., *Narratives of the Witchcraft Cases, 1648–1706* (New York, Charles Scribner's Sons, 1914; reissued, New York, Barnes and Noble, 1968), p. 341.

decided to abandon the frustrating world of commerce and enter the ministry—the vocation, as it happened, of the older brother who had been so favored by the terms of his father's will. Thus it was, in 1688, that Salem Village learned that Parris might be available to fill the Village pulpit.

At the time of his ordination, few Salem Villagers, in all likelihood, were familiar with the full story of Parris's commercial activities. But all of them must have been only too familiar with the full year of hard and divisive negotiations to which he had subjected the Village between its initial approach to him and his final decision to accept. It is a story worth recounting at length, not only because it so clearly exposes the process by which Parris came to the Village, but also because it provides the only detailed example we have of Parris as businessman—a *persona* he had brought to a high degree of development through fifteen or sixteen years of trying, with no great success, to live by his wits.

The Village's first official approach to Parris had taken place on November 15, 1688, when the "inhabitants" selected a three-man committee to negotiate with him "about taking ministerial office." Ten days later, after Parris had preached a sample sermon for them, the congregation remained in the meetinghouse and (as Parris himself later reported) requested him, "by a general vote," to "take office" as their minister. But Parris failed to respond, at least for the record, and on December 10, the Village appointed a new committee to find out "whether Mr. Parris would accept of office." To this delegation Parris replied only that "the work was weighty; they should know in due time." [6]

Parris kept his silence for nearly five months (though the terms of employment continued to be discussed informally during this time). In the interval, as he became increasingly aware that Salem Village was not the tranquil rural settlement he had perhaps originally envisioned, he may well have been honestly pondering whether this, indeed, was a place to which he wished to commit himself permanently. Again the Village took the initiative in late April 1689, by appointing still another committee to reactivate the stalled negotiations. Seemingly more eager to "finish the thing up" than either of its predecessors, this third committee approached Parris with a firm offer: an annual salary of sixty pounds—one-

6. 1697 deposition of Samuel Parris quoted in Charles W. Upham, *Salem Witchcraft*, 2 vols. (Boston, 1867), I, 287–288.

third in money, the rest in corn and other provisions at specified rates.[7]

While accepting the proposed salary, Parris responded with his own counter-offer, in the form of a detailed and carefully drawn up eight-point document:

First, when money shall be more plenteous, the money part to be paid me shall accordingly be increased.

Second, though corn or like provisions should arise to a higher price than you have set, yet, for my own family use, I shall have what is needful at the price now stated, and so if it fall lower. [This was Parris's hedge against inflation.]

Third, the whole sixty pounds to be only from our inhabitants that are dwelling in our bounds, proportionable to what lands they have within the same.

Fourth, no provision to be brought in without first asking whether needed, and myself to make choice of what, unless the person is unable to pay in any sort but one.

Fifth, firewood to be given in yearly, freely.

Sixth, two men to be chosen yearly to see that due payments be made.

Seventh, contributions each sabbath in papers [that is, envelopes, with the names of the donors written on them]; and only such as are in papers, and dwelling within our bounds, to be accounted a part of the sixty pounds [that is, contributions from visitors would be considered a bonus].

Eighth, as God shall please to bless the place so as to be able to rise higher than the sixty pounds, that then a proportionable increase be made. If God shall please, for our sins, to diminish the substance of said place, I will endeavor accordingly to bear such losses, by proportionable abatements of such as shall reasonably desire it.[8]

If the Salem Village representatives were taken aback by the niggling detail of this proposal, they did not reveal it. Eager to conclude a settlement, the Village spokesmen accepted all eight points without qualification, and assured Parris that the Village as

7. *Ibid.*, I, 289; Samuel P. Fowler, "An Account of the Life and Character of the Rev. Samuel Parris, of Salem Village, and of his Connection with the Witchcraft Delusion of 1692," in Samuel G. Drake, *The Witchcraft Delusion in New England, Its Rise, Progress and Termination*, 3 vols. (Boston, 1866), III, 199.

8. Upham, *Salem Witchcraft*, I, 289–290.

a whole would go along with the arrangements. But as word of Parris's demands filtered through the community, resentment and opposition seem to have developed, and on May 17, 1689, a full-scale negotiating session was held between the would-be minister and his future parishioners.

The only available record of this meeting is that set down by Parris himself eight years later, in a 1697 court deposition.[9] According to Parris's later account, discussion at this May meeting focused on two of his eight demands. On the issue of firewood, it was pointed out that unlike most New England communities (again the frustrations of its anomalous situation!) Salem Village lacked the common lands from which a minister's fuel needs could easily be supplied; for the individual Villagers to provide Parris with firewood, a complex arrangement would be needed for determining each parishioner's appropriate share. To avoid such complications, the Villagers offered simply to add £6 to Parris's salary as a firewood allowance, figuring on thirty cords of wood per year at the current rate of four shillings a cord. But it was now Parris who balked: what if the price of wood went up, and £6 proved inadequate to his needs? In reply, there was "a general answering from many," assuring Parris that they would continue to sell him wood at the current rate, no matter how high the market price might go. Finally, after "much urging," Parris reluctantly agreed to this plan —on a one-year trial basis.

Discussion next turned to the troublesome question of the outsiders who worshiped in the Village (some of them quite regularly) but who could not legally be included in the tax rolls: should their technically voluntary contributions count toward Parris's basic salary? The Villagers plausibly contended that the contributions of all who attended the Village services, wherever their residence, should help defray the minister's salary. But Parris would not yield. Finally, amidst "much agitation," the parties settled on a compromise (or so Parris recalled in 1697): the "out-persons" would be asked to decide individually whether they wished their payments to count as part of the £66, or as private contributions that would, in effect, constitute a bonus for Parris.

After what must have been several fairly rigorous hours of bargaining, the meeting came to an end. Oddly, however, it was not

9. This deposition is summarized and in part quoted in Fowler, "Account of the Life and Character of the Rev. Samuel Parris . . . ," in Drake, *Witchcraft Delusion in New England*, III, 200–201. It is from the deposition that the following narrative is derived.

until a month later, on June 18, and in Parris's absence, that a contract was actually written down in the Village Book of Record. This contract either ignored or left vague certain points which Parris believed had been definitely settled: the terms upon which provisions in lieu of cash would be acceptable; the procedures by which abatements would be granted in times of recession; and, most important, the status of contributions from non-Villagers.

The better part of a year went by before Parris, to his intense and lasting anger, learned of these discrepancies. It is difficult to be certain today precisely what had gone awry. The written version of the contract in the Book of Record may represent an honest effort to reproduce the conclusions of the May meeting—a meeting perhaps more confused and inconclusive than Parris later remembered.

But what *is* clear is that Parris allowed that May bargaining session to end without insisting that its conclusions be set down in black and white in his presence. Having launched these abrasive negotiations, and having suffered the erosion of goodwill which they entailed, he neglected at the crucial moment to secure a binding written agreement! The lapse is revealing, and may go a long way toward explaining not only Parris's difficulties in Salem Village but those earlier failures in the world of commerce which had driven him in the first place to seek the apparent security of a New England pulpit.

But in the summer of 1689, before he learned of the misunderstanding, Parris still had reason to feel sanguine about the results of his hard and canny bargaining, and even to believe that he might successfully try for still more. Thus he directed his attention to the matter of his long-range property interests. As a matter of course, Parris had been offered, free of rent, the use of the Village's ministry house and the two acres of land which went with it. But now, sometime during the summer, he proceeded (though not in writing) to make his most far-reaching demand: that the Village deed this property outright to himself and his heirs! On October 10, 1689 (as we have seen in Chapter 3), the "inhabitants" all-but-unanimously voted to accept this final demand, even though it directly violated the conditions under which the land had been given to the Village eighteen years before.

From this point, things at last moved swiftly. On October 22 the Village chose two men (as Parris had proposed in May) to assess the estate of every Salem Village property owner so that Parris might receive in advance—retroactive to the previous July 1

—his first year's salary.[10] Sometime before or on November 19, the list of assessments was completed and turned in by the two Villagers to whom the task had been assigned, Benjamin Putnam and John Tarbell. Samuel Parris and Salem Village had come to terms.

In his ordination sermon, Parris somehow contrived to relegate this recent sequence of events to another era. For just as he envisioned a new beginning for the Village in that sermon, so, too, he clearly wanted to believe that his new vocation would bring about dramatic changes in his own style of life. He was now spiritual leader of a little body of believers, and he could at last, perhaps, put hard bargaining over money behind him. It was now perfectly appropriate for him to exhort his congregation openly (as, in fact, he did in his ordination sermon) to "communicate" to him their "carnal good things"—"not as a piece of alms or charity, but of justice and duty."[11] From now on, economic security would be his by right, dependent on neither his own shrewdness nor the goodwill of others.

Having marshaled all his commercial acumen for a kind of final orgy of negotiation and bargaining over the terms of his appointment (and having thereby become party to maneuvers which had deepened existing cleavages in the Village), Parris now publicly dedicated himself to a new social role—a role which would release him from the nagging and demeaning concerns which had made such a shambles of the first half of his life. "Much work is laid, or like to be laid, upon my weak shoulders. . . . I am to carry it not as a Lord but as a servant. . . . I am, in all godliness, to labor to be exemplary."[12]

Thus the ordination sermon had a double dimension: it was both public and intensely personal. November 19, 1689, would be the day when both he and the Village, through a collective act of will, aided by the power of Christ, could make a clean break with the past.

But, as we know, Parris's hopes for a new beginning turned to ashes. This man who had sought to escape from the humiliation of money-grubbing found himself utterly enslaved by it during his years in Salem Village. This man who longed to be accepted as the "exemplary" leader of a united church and community saw that

10. Village Records, Oct. 22, 1689.
11. Sermon Book, Nov. 19, 1689, p. 15.
12. *Ibid.*, p. 14.

community sink into conflicts more bitter than any it had ever known.

Part of the reason for Parris's resounding failure, of course, lay in the very dynamics of Salem Village factionalism. His hope that the Villagers would let bygones be bygones simply could not be realized. The community's endemic divisions—rooted as they were in real economic, geographic, and social differences—far from diminishing, only intensified in the 1690's. And furthermore, the minister himself became a kind of reference point by which the two groups identified themselves. When his salary was withheld, first by individuals and then as a matter of official Village policy, Parris was driven to desperate lengths to try to extract from the Village what he had expected would come to him as a matter of "justice and duty." His efforts, which first took the form of urgent appeals and political maneuverings within the Village, eventually escalated into protracted and bitter suits and counter-suits wending their way from court to court. At one point—according to testimony offered by Joseph Porter, Daniel Andrew, and Joseph Putnam—he went so far as to denounce all who opposed him as "knaves and cheaters." [13]

Once it had become clear to Parris that his parishioners' sense of "justice and duty" offered no guarantee of his material well-being, the minister reverted to engrained modes of behavior dating from his pre-1689 days. Not only did he fight with increasing ruthlessness those who appeared responsible for his economic embarrassment, but in 1692 and 1693 he began to speculate on Village lands, acquiring a succession of small tracts (he could hardly afford larger ones) scattered throughout the Village.[14]

But the source of Parris's inability to make a fresh beginning lay within himself as well as in the objective circumstances around him. Over the years, the disappointments and setbacks he had encountered had arranged themselves in a pattern in his mind and had given rise to a characteristic set of concerns—obsessions, really—which continued to dominate his thinking even after he started to clothe his body in the garb of a Puritan clergyman.

His sermons, though in form typical Puritan exercises in Biblical exegesis, nevertheless include passages that are revealingly idiosyncratic. As he carefully wrote out these exhortations in his me-

13. Testimony of Joseph Porter, Daniel Andrew, and Joseph Putnam, April 13, 1697, quoted in Upham, *Salem Witchcraft*, I, 295–296.

14. John and Hannah Shephard to Parris, Feb. 15, 1692; John Bullock to Parris et al., Aug. 13, 1693; Thomas and Sarah Haines to Parris, Dec. 5, 1693 —Essex Deeds, IX, 70, 71; X, 35.

ticulous hand—there are fifty-two of them, spanning the years 1689 to 1694—Parris occasionally lingered over a point slightly longer than his didactic purpose required, pursued a thought to lengths hardly warranted by the text under consideration, or introduced ideas which superficially seem to have little bearing on his text of the day. Such personal touches, while hardly an overwhelming part of the total bulk of his sermons, nevertheless offer us revealing glimpses into the deeper recesses of the man's mind.

Essentially, these obsessions were rooted in his complex fascination with the forces which had shaped his life—money, trade, and commerce, and the kinds of social attitudes they engendered. The very stridency with which he denounced the worldly life attests to the allure it still held for him. In a most revealing sermon preached only a week after his ordination, Parris declared:

> When a man undertakes that great and dreadful work (which I have so lately undertaken among you) of ministerial office, merely as a trade—to pick a living out of it—quite contrary to the design of God in this most holy service . . . , he converts God's service to his own service; and that which God hath designed for his own glory, to his own private profit. Everyone will readily acknowledge such a one to be (as indeed he is) a deceitful worker: for he works for himself, and yet pretends he works for God. As if an ambassador, entrusted by his prince to do him special service, should under pretence of serving his master do indeed somewhat for him, but yet chiefly and principally aim at himself. And so it is here. It is very true, as one wittily says, the ministry is a most noble calling; aye, but it is a bad trade—a pernicious trade indeed.[15]

"Trade," "picking out a living," "private profit," "pretence," "deceit"—coupled with a profound longing for the unselfish dedication of a "noble calling": these were the subjects which preoccupied Samuel Parris.

The attraction which the mercantile world still held for him is revealed by the frequency with which he introduced commercial images into his sermons. Spiritual concerns, he argues, should rank before "our worldly business, our carnal interests." People should pay attention to their eternal welfare as closely as "the shop-keeper, the merchant, the trader" pay attention to their ledgers.[16]

15. Sermon Book, Nov. 24, 1689, p. 19.
16. *Ibid.*, July 2, 1693, p. 206; Feb. 4, 1694, p. 261.

The Biblical event which inspired Parris's most passionate denunciation, and to which he returned again and again in his sermons, was Judas's betrayal of his Master for money.

> Judas betrayed him and sold him to the Chief Priests . . . for thirty pieces of silver. A small, poor, and mean price, to be sure. There are different apprehensions about the sum: the most that is made of it that I know of is £3/15 in English money. But to be sure, it was but a poor and mean price. For it was the common and known set price of a base slave . . . , a female slave.[17]

While Parris denounced the chief priests who made this bargain ("spiritual merchants," he called them), it was for Iscariot himself that he reserved his bitterest words. But it may be a measure of Parris's ambivalence toward mercantile activity that one can hardly tell from such passages whether his loathing of Judas for having sold Christ outweighed his contempt toward him for having failed to get a better price.

Out of the depths of Parris's resentment against a way of life which attracted him but at which he had failed, this erstwhile merchant developed an exaggerated concern for honor, dignity, and respect: those badges of status and deference which were most likely to be absent in a commercial environment. It was vitally important to him to believe that every variety of social encounter was, or ought to be, governed by certain fixed, mutually recognized, and punctiliously observed proprieties: "To every thing, work, or person, both in civil and also sacred matters, there is a meetness, rightness, and decency belonging unto it, according unto which, he that rightly behaves himself may be said to do it worthily, i.e., suitably, conveniently, fitly, agreeably, and becomingly."[18] The Church Record entries in which Parris gave a blow-by-blow account of the Village's factional fight make clear that what most deeply offended him about his opponents was their failure to observe such proprieties, their lack of decorum and respect. Repeatedly he complains of their "rough" and "irreverend" behavior, of their "scoffing" and "contemptuous" tone in addressing him.[19]

From this perspective, the drawn-out "firewood dispute" which so preoccupied Parris takes on a new interest. Initially, as we have

17. *Ibid.*, Jan. 12, 1690, p. 38.
18. *Ibid.*, Nov. 5, 1693, p. 240.
19. Church Records, May 18, 1693; Feb. 7, 1695.

noted, Parris had proposed that the Villagers freely supply him with firewood. For practical reasons, however, they had induced him to accept a straightforward market arrangement: they would increase his salary sufficiently to allow him to buy his own wood. But Parris soon gave up this extra allowance and resumed his efforts to impose the more complicated system of individual firewood contributions. "I told them I had scarce wood enough to burn till tomorrow, and prayed that some care might be taken," he noted in the Church Record as winter came on at the end of 1691.[20] In economic terms, this dispute seems petty enough—firewood, after all, was in abundant supply, and cost only four shillings a cord—but its social and psychological overtones were more complex. In his insistence that each Village householder personally deposit wood at his door, Parris was clearly striving for a symbolic acknowledgment of the deference to which he felt entitled. He was attempting to demonstrate to himself, as well as to his parishioners, that in his new role as minister he had at last been liberated from the sordid world of the marketplace.

This obsessive dwelling on the *tone* of social encounters, on the precise arrangements by which the perquisites of his office were to be supplied, were not simply petty digressions from what was "really" bothering Parris. In a very real way, these *were* the issues. Indeed, Parris's very decision to come to Salem Village may have sprung from the hope that in this rural setting, so unlike any he had ever known, he would be respected for his station rather than for his skill at the kind of day-to-day maneuvering he had been forced to employ as a petty merchant in Boston. Yet it was precisely this expectation that the dissenters, with their fast-moving and unsparing stratagems, most thoroughly undermined, by forcing Parris to rely on the very talents he despised in himself.

In his sermons as well as in the Church Records, Parris dwelled tirelessly on questions of dignity and status—often in the most unexpected and unlikely contexts. Indeed, in the ordination sermon itself he did not defend the divine ordinances on theological grounds but rather on the grounds that failure to observe them exposed a person or a community to deep humiliations: to what Parris called, in a characteristic litany, "reproach, contempt, dis-

---

20. *Ibid.*, Nov. 18, 1691. For similar pleas see *ibid.*, Oct. 8 and Nov. 2, 1691. On Parris's decision to forego the £6 firewood allowance, see Village Records, October 28, 1690: "[A]greed and voted . . . that our Committee shall make a rate of sixty pounds for Mr. Parris's salary . . . , Mr. Parris have [*sic*] relinquished the six pounds voted . . . for firewood."

grace . . . , shame and dishonor." Conversely, by joining or forming a church and sharing in its rituals, a people might "exalt, promote, and dignify" themselves. Here, as always, Parris was not
nearly so concerned about the morality of an act as he was about
its social consequences: whether it brings honor or shame to those
who commit it.[21]

A series of sermons in 1690 and 1691 on the life of Christ seemed
to arouse Parris to a particularly elaborate development of these
obsessions. His emphasis was almost exclusively on the low points
of Jesus's career—the humble birth, the persecutions, the temptations, the revilings, the betrayal, and the crucifixion; and he repeatedly emphasized the personal indignity to Jesus—the Son of God!
—which such experiences entailed. Though set apart from the
"vulgar and common people by a special vocation," yet He was
"humbled and abased" and subjected to "revilings and reproach-
ings" and "all manner of disgraces." And this treatment came not
from people of whom it might have been expected, the "mean,
beggerly, and unlearned," but from the "great and famous," from
men like the chief priests in Jerusalem who spent their time "studying, plotting, and contriving" His downfall. The very legal system
was used against Him: "Our Lord Jesus was most injuriously dealt
with in their courts, their corrupt courts of judicature, both ecclesiastical and political." In an oddly anachronistic interpretation,
Parris declared that Jesus's arrest and trial seriously damaged his
"credit and reputation," so that His subsequent resurrection and
ascension were necessary vindications of "the dignity of his person." [22]

As the references to the chief priests and the courts suggest,
Parris introduced a geographic dimension into his preoccupation
with status, dignity, and respect: it was the chief priests of *Jerusalem* who were against him. On a number of occasions he conveyed to his hearers his own rankling sense of the sharp, even
humiliating, contrast between small, backwater communities and
their larger, richer neighbors. He quite explicitly developed the
idea that the obscure inhabitants of obscure villages are at the

21. Sermon Book, Nov. 19, 1689, pp. 6, 8, 7. While Parris's fascination
with honor and shame may have been particularly keen, we are not suggesting
that it was unique except in degree, for these were matters of common concern
in seventeenth century New England. For this reason, his constant and un-
abashed discussion of such matters would not have seemed outlandish or
unacceptable to his Salem Village audience.
22. *Ibid.*, March 5, 1693, p. 174; May 25, 1690, p. 64; Jan. 12, 1690, p. 39;
Aug. 17, 1690, p. 71; Jan. 12, 1690, p. 40.

mercy of more cosmopolitan institutions and authorities who do not have their interests at heart.

Once again, the life of Christ provided the imagery. Jesus was not born in Jerusalem "or any other famous, opulent, or wealthy city," but in little Bethlehem, "a poor, mean, and contemptible town or village"; not in an inn "full of rich folks," but in "an odd corner, a contemptible stable."[23] But again the ambivalence: Jerusalem may have been corrupt, but Bethlehem, and its holy stable, were *contemptible*.

Clearly what Parris found most disturbing as he surveyed the life of Christ was the social dislocation: the appalling disparity between Christ's divine status and the buffetings and low treatment he received from the unknowing. Did he discover in Christ's earthly sojourn resonant parallels to the experience of the London merchant's son, the nephew of a great Barbados planter, who had himself failed so miserably to make his mark in the world of commerce and who now found himself embroiled in a demeaning controversy in an obscure farm village on the outskirts of a thriving commercial center?

For at least the past 150 years, historians have treated Samuel Parris as a kind of Svengali who somewhat inexplicably gained brief power in a fundamentally healthy if "deluded" community, but who quickly became an outcast pariah as the good sense of the sturdy yeomen reasserted itself. The traditional view is summed up in the judgment of Sidney Perley, a local antiquarian whose three-volume chronicle of Salem's past was published in the 1920's. In Salem Village after 1692, wrote Perley, Parris was "disliked, probably hated for his part in the [witchcraft] prosecutions. He was not free to go among the people. He hardly knew who his friends were, if indeed he had any. . . . His preaching must have been to few persons, and his sermons without force. His influence was gone."[24]

In reality, Parris was not a petty ecclesiastical tyrant manipulating his congregation like passive clay, and he never (at least during his days in Salem Village) became the universally despised outcast conjured up by Perley. As late as 1695, as we have seen, he still commanded the support of a clear majority of the Villagers.

23. *Ibid.*, Feb. 23, 1690, pp. 50–51.
24. Sidney Perley, *The History of Salem, Mass.*, 3 vols. (Salem, 1924–1928), III, 359–360.

The emotional bond between Parris and the Village, which underlay this political support, was a profound and complex one. He was a driven man, to be sure, and his obsessions grew from a set of experiences quite different in detail from those of most Salem Villagers. But nevertheless, his compulsive reiteration of certain key themes struck a responsive chord in the minds of many of the men and women of Salem Village. For they, too, out of their own experience, felt deep uncertainty and ambivalence toward the economic and social changes which were sweeping the Anglo-American world.

On the positive side—though again as an outgrowth of his own psychological needs—Parris exalted the supposed virtues of a precapitalist society: a society whose central characteristic was the stability of its social relationships and institutions, a society in which honor and deference naturally flowed to those of high status or social position. The very shrillness with which Parris summoned up this vision reveals how alien it was to his own experience, how completely a construct of his imagination.

In a sense, Parris's appeal lay in his mastery of a pattern of behavior which one historian has described as characteristic of the Jacksonians of the 1830's:[25] he did his best to get ahead in a fluid and shifting economic situation, yet he even more strenuously repudiated such behavior, lashing out at those who were more successful at it than himself, reducing complex social struggles to the moral failings of individuals, and harking back to a mythic past when a man might look forward to a "noble calling," and not merely to "picking out a living."

But the relationship was reciprocal, for while Parris clearly had an impact on the Village, the Village had its impact on him as well. The alluring idea of a place like "Salem Village" must have figured prominently in his imaginative life in the years before 1689 —a stable, almost medieval community, where the deferential social structure he longed for might actually be experienced. But that was before he came to the place. For Salem Village embodied in its collective experience what Parris already knew only too well from his own career: the nagging annoyance of being somehow second-rate, of eddying in a backwater while the main current swept on.

25. Marvin Meyers, *The Jacksonian Persuasion: Politics and Belief* (Stanford, Calif., Stanford University Press, 1957).

Samuel Parris and the Witchcraft Episode:
From Eden to Gethsemane

But the tightly written pages of Samuel Parris's Sermon Book have still more to tell us. For not only do these pages provide a key to some of Parris's deepest preoccupations, they also contain Parris's extended commentary on the increasingly intense factional struggle in which the Village was embroiled. That commentary is rarely explicit, to be sure. Embedded in a sermon form based on typology and close textual exposition, it is often most pointed when it seems most abstractly Biblical and theological.

The prevailing motif of that commentary—from 1689 to 1692, at any rate—is one of encircling menace: a menace which thrusts closer and closer to the heart of the Village as it becomes increasingly cosmic in origin. In this quite specific sense, Parris unconsciously helped set the scene for the climax of 1692.

Fleetingly, at the very beginning, Parris offered a hopeful prospect of a united, peaceful community with the church at its center. Evil and menace remained real enough, but they could be held at bay if the Village would unite and bury past differences. The Biblical chapter from which Parris chose the text of his ordination sermon summed up his initial view. The Children of Israel faced profound dangers: Egypt lay to their rear, Jericho loomed before them. But these were external dangers. Within their own well-guarded encampment, Gilgal, they were united, secure, and certain in the knowledge of God's favor.

This ostensibly optimistic view of things hardly outlasted the ordination Sunday itself, however. As it became clear that the establishment of a church had not erased the political divisions within the Village—and that became clear very quickly indeed—Parris began to speak of infiltration and subversion; of betrayal from within as well as hostility from without. For the very first sermon he preached after his ordination, Parris chose the volatile text: "Cursed be he that doeth the work of the Lord deceitfully." [26]

Here and later, he emphasized that *no one* is above suspicion of deceit. Surface appearances, superficial evidences of goodwill—none of these can be taken at face value. The person one least suspects may, in fact, be concealing traitorous intent:

26. Sermon Book, Nov. 24, 1689, p. 16.

Hence learn [he said in January 1690] that there is no trust to a rotten-hearted person, whatever friendship may be pretended. There are too many in this guileful and deceitful age who live as if they had drunk in that heretical notion together with their mother's milk, *Qui nescit dissimulare, nescit vivere* [He who cannot manage to dissimulate cannot manage to live.] [27]

If only the "rotten-hearted" could be confined to separate enclaves (such as Salem Town?) where they would be operating "wholly among themselves," their menace might be minimized, even in a "guileful and deceitful age." But, no, they infiltrate even innocent communities. Parris found this point sufficiently crucial to justify one of his most explicit references to the immediate situation: "Oh that men would have a care of false words . . . ," he warned in February 1690; "I am afraid here is great guiltiness upon this account in this poor little village." Even individual families might be affected by the taint of subversion. "Not seldom," he observed at the beginning of 1692, "great hatred ariseth even from nearest relations." [28] It is easy to imagine the Putnams listening intently to words like these.

Here the psychological function of Parris's repeated references to Judas Iscariot begins to become clear. Judas, one of the Twelve, one of the inner circle, was the very man who betrayed Christ and broke up the little band of disciples. In February 1691, when some Villagers were beginning to withhold their payment of the ministry tax, Parris came as close as he ever did to identifying himself explicitly with Christ, and his opponents with Judas:

[I]f temptation and opportunity present, wicked men will be at more pains and cost to be rid of Christ than to entertain him. . . . [T]hey gave thirty pieces of silver to be rid of Christ. They would not give half so much for his gracious presence and holy sermons. For idolatry, men will lavish gold out of the bag. (*46 Isa. 6*). They will not do so very rarely for the maintenance of the pure religion.[29]

---

27. *Ibid.*, Jan. 12, 1690, p. 43.

28. *Ibid.*, Feb. 23, 1690, p. 52; Jan. 3, 1692, p. 138.

29. *Ibid.*, Feb. 1, 1691, p. 86. Parris's nerve failed him at the prospect of delivering so direct a thrust. A marginal note indicates that he silently passed over this passage when he actually delivered the sermon. (That he did so offers the strongest possible evidence that his words, here and elsewhere, were often intended to evoke in the minds of his congregation the contemporary situation within the Village.)

Intermingled with Parris's fear of internal subversion was his belief that this subversion was linked to outsiders who were controlling, or trying to control, the affairs of the Village. Parris bitterly criticized his opponents for "sending abroad" their petitions and statements of grievance and for "imposing upon the [Salem Village] Church others not of our Church society." The dissenters, he charged, should "first have spoken with the pastor himself before they went to consult with neighboring Elders." After one meeting between the leaders of the two factions in November 1694, he noted darkly that not only had his local Village opponents, "to suit their designs, placed themselves in a seat conveniently together," but also that "several strangers" had been present as well.[30] In this single scene (not conjured up in a sermon, but actually witnessed and recorded in the Church Records), Parris discovered what he felt to be vivid empirical evidence of his dual fear of internal betrayal and external subversion.

As to the source of such menaces, Parris traced them neither to excusable human frailty nor to the natural (and universal) depravity of man, but to actual, conscious collaboration between individual human beings and the powers of Satan; there existed, as he put it, "a lamentable harmony between wicked men and devils, in their opposition of God's kingdom and interests." As early as December 1689 Parris applied to such collaborators their proper name; the wrongdoings of King Saul, he noted, were rooted in the fact that he had become "haunted with an evil and wicked spirit," and had gone for advice "to the Devil, to a witch." [31]

Having so quickly given up the expectation—held out in his ordination sermon—that the entire Village could be preserved as a haven of righteousness and stability, Parris retreated to a far more limited, but also more defensible, bastion: the church. The church will be attacked and buffeted, to be sure, but the danger, unlike that in civil communities, is wholly external. To those Villagers who were dismayed by the conflicts rending their community, Parris declared that only the church could "gather together" isolated individuals into "one spiritual and mystical body." As for "other societies," Parris now conceded, "no such oneness and entireness" is possible. Individuals may attempt to "cleave together"

---

30. Church Records, Feb. 16, 1693; Nov. 26, 1694; Feb. 7, 1695 (Point 16 of Parris's statement of grievances).
31. Sermon Book, Jan. 12, 1690, p. 42; Dec. 1, 1689, p. 34.

through secular institutional forms, but outside the fellowship of Christ they can never achieve true unity.[32]

In articulating this model, Parris was hardly unique among early New England divines. What is striking about Parris's analysis, however, is his perception of the church itself: not so much a brotherhood of saints as a refuge against devils and their human cohorts—less a way of changing human society than a way of escaping from it. "The Church may meet with storms, but it shall never sink. For Christ sits not idle in the Heavens, but takes most faithful care of his little ship (the church) bound for the Port of Heaven, laden with many precious gems and jewels, a treasure purchased by his own inestimable blood."[33]

But with such dangers all about, the church members could hardly limit themselves simply to the passive enjoyment of Christian fellowship. They had to act far more aggressively in order to protect their sacred bond. From the very beginning, Parris had toyed with this idea as a kind of theoretical possibility. In the ordination sermon, quoting "holy Calvin," he had declared that the creation and preservation of a church was "worth an hundred lives," and in his very next sermon, in commenting on Jehovah's bloody command to Samuel utterly to destroy the Amalekites ("Cursed be he that keepeth his sword back from blood"), he had said: "A curse there is on such as shed not blood when they have a commission from God."[34]

By the summer of 1691, with the anti-Parris group emerging as an increasingly powerful and united force, the minister's imagery of the church took on a more and more martial cast. Finding his inspiration in the sixth chapter of Ephesians—"Put on the whole armour of God, that ye may be able to stand against the wiles of the devil"—Parris declared on July 19, 1691: "Christ furnisheth the believer with skill, strength, courage, weapons, and all military accomplishments for victory. They [sic] are well appointed for war. And the reason is because the Lord Jesus sets them forth, furnisheth them with all necessaries for battle. The Lord Jesus is the true believer's magazine."[35] On February 14, 1692, while lamenting "the present low condition of the church in the midst of its enemies," Parris added—in what, under the circumstances,

32. *Ibid.*, Nov. 9, 1690, p. 80.
33. *Ibid.*, Feb. 14, 1692, p. 146.
34. *Ibid.*, Nov. 19, 1689, p. 13; Nov. 24, 1689, p. 17.
35. *Ibid.*, July 19, 1691, p. 103.

amounted to a self-fulfilling prophecy: "Oh, shortly the case will be far otherwise."[36]

The arrest of the first of the accused witches two weeks later could have come as no surprise to those Salem Villagers who had been attentive to their minister in the preceding months and years. The outbreak merely signaled the open eruption of a Satanically inspired conspiracy which had long been festering in the Village. On March 27, 1692, now apparently confronted with the literal existence of a plot whose reality had hitherto been, at most, typological, Parris preached a sermon—"Christ Knows How Many Devils There Are"—in which the themes he had been developing for more than two years came finally together, at full volume. For this sermon, he chose as his text Jesus's public denunciation of his betrayer, Judas Iscariot: "Have not I chosen you twelve, and one of you is a Devil?"

Judas the betrayer, Judas the avaricious: these had now become Judas the "devil." In the character of Iscariot, and the vile transaction which had doomed him to eternal infamy, Parris found the perfect symbols for his conviction that the cash nexus was responsible for the destruction of trust and security in human relationships, and that Satanic influence was behind the whole process. To be sure, Parris treated the witchcraft outbreak as one evidence of Satan's growing power, but what is even more striking under the circumstances is the particular attention he devoted to the economic source of that power: the pervasiveness of lust. In Parris's usage, the term "lust" meant not sexual desire but greed: "Now, if we would not be devils, we must give ourselves wholly up to Christ, and not suffer the predominancy of one lust—and particularly that lust of *covetousness*, which is made so light of, and which so sorely prevails in these perilous times." Speaking even more bluntly, he declared: "Christ . . . knows who they are that have not chosen him, but prefer farms and merchandise above him and above his ordinances."[37]

References to commerce and land pervade the imagery as well as the central structure of this sermon; the church is compared to

---

36. *Ibid.*, Feb. 14, 1692, p. 144. The Reverend Deodat Lawson, catching the mood of the Village during his brief visit, struck a similar martial note in his sermon of March 20, 1692. After dwelling upon the horrors of a witchcraft outbreak in "this poor village," Lawson declared: "I am this day commanded to call and cry an alarm unto you: ARM, ARM, ARM! . . . [H]andle your arms, see that you are fixed and in a readiness. . . . Let us admit no parley, give no quarter."—quoted in Upham, *Salem Witchcraft*, II, 81, 85.

37. Sermon Book, March 27, 1692, pp. 147, 149, 151. Italics added.

a field that produces noisome weeds as well as useful crops; those who have transferred their loyalty to Satan are "the freeholders of hell, whereas other sinners are but tenants." [38] In Samuel Parris's formulation, witchcraft, deceit, and money hunger were but the varied manifestations of the single diabolical menace which now openly confronted Salem Village.

But there was one feature of the witchcraft outbreak for which Parris had not prepared his communicants and for which, it would seem, he himself was unprepared. In recording his March 27 discourse in his Sermon Book, Parris prefaced it with this remark: "Occasioned by dreadful witchcraft broke out here a few weeks past, and one member of this Church, and another of Salem [Town], upon public examination by civil authority vehemently suspected for she-witches, and upon it committed." [39] While the accusation of these two church members (Martha Cory and Rebecca Nurse) may have brought relief to Ann Putnam, Sr., they forced Samuel Parris to confront a central ambiguity in his thinking. For, while dwelling on the menace of betrayal from within, he had at the same time attempted to portray the church itself as a secure refuge from the "rotten-hearted." But now even *that* line of defense had been breached.

On March 27, in his attempt to deal with this problem, Parris did nothing less than redefine the character of the Puritan church. The church, no less than the world, he now concluded, was a promiscuous institution which embraced the "rotten-hearted" as well as the pure. "There are devils as well as saints . . . here in Christ's little Church."

> The Church consists of good and bad: as a garden that has weeds as well as flowers, and as a field that has wheat as well as tares . . . , a net that taketh good and bad. . . . Here are good men to be found—yea, the very best; and here are bad men to be found—yea, the very worst. Such as shall have the highest seat in glory, and such also as shall be cast into the lowest and fiercest flames of misery.[40]

For the church members of Salem Village who had accepted Parris's assurances that the church, alone, was inviolable, the arrest of one of their number for witchcraft was a most unsettling event, and in

38. *Ibid.*, p. 149.
39. *Ibid.*, p. 147.
40. *Ibid.*, pp. 148–149.

interpreting its meaning, Parris offered small consolation. For his message implied that, after all, the church no longer offered safe passage over the rough seas of human conflict; it had now itself become simply another arena of that conflict.

If by the spring of 1692 the threat was proving even more insidious than Parris had earlier suggested, it was proving even more terrifying as well. For while Parris had earlier seen wicked people as in *league* with the devil, his sermons during the witchcraft period blurred even this fragile distinction between the human and the supernatural. By 1692, for Parris, evil persons *were* devils. "By *devil*," he argued, "is ordinarily meant any wicked angel or spirit," but, he continued, it may also mean "vile and wicked persons— the worst of such, who for their villainy and impiety do most resemble devils and wicked spirits." Though perhaps not a devil in "nature," a person may nevertheless become, with Judas, a devil in "quality and disposition"—and "there are such devils in the Church."[41] With this subtle, but crucial, alteration, Parris was perhaps steeling himself, and his hearers, to accept without protest the punishment which he knew faced the accused witches—not really persons, but devils—when they were convicted.

The spring and summer months were hectic ones in Salem that year, and it is hardly surprising that during those months Parris did not write out his weekly discourses in his Sermon Book. Instead, he simply recorded the texts and noted: "See loose pages." But these loose pages have not survived. Only in September did he resume his practice of writing out his sermons in full. By that time the trials and executions were reaching a crescendo, and the proponents of the witch-hunt seemed in the ascendancy. And yet a strong reaction had clearly begun to set in, particularly beyond the confines of the Village. More serious still, the identification and elimination of those "devils" who had infested the Village had not perceptibly soothed either its physical or its political afflictions. Apparently sensing this ambiguous situation, Parris in a sermon preached on September 11—the first he had written out since March—struck a note of somewhat shrill confidence which served to mask his gathering despair. On the one hand, in commenting on the progress of "the war the devil has raised amongst us by wizards and witches," the minister appeared as intransigent as he

41. *Ibid.*, p. 148.

had in his most belligerent sermons of 1691: "Here are but two parties in the world: the Lamb and his followers, and the dragon and his followers. . . . Here are no neuters. Everyone is on one side or the other." And, in at least one part of this sermon, Parris professed utter confidence about the outcome of this party struggle: "Devils and idolators will make war with the Lamb and his followers. But who shall have the victory? Why, the Lamb (i.e., Christ) and his followers." To join Satan's faction, he continued, is "to take the weakest side": it is to "fight for him who will pay you no other wages than [that] of being your eternal torturer." [42] (Even in the most turbulent days of 1692 the question of wages was never far from Parris's mind.)

But even as Parris sought to rally and encourage his party (a party he could no longer treat as identical with his church), he also perceived that witchcraft trials could never halt the kind of "subversion" that had afflicted Salem Village, and that the battle to which he had so confidently summoned his supporters was turning into catastrophic defeat. From the depths of this realization, Parris made still another crucial change of emphasis. Shifting his hopes away from the natural world altogether, he now focused instead upon a final triumph lying entirely beyond this world: "After this life the saints shall no more be troubled with war from devils and their instruments. The city of heaven, provided for the saints, is well-walled and well-gated and well-guarded, so that no devils nor their instruments shall enter therein." [43] Parris's conception of the limits which could be set upon the incursions of "lust" and "deceit" and other evils had steadily narrowed during his years in Salem Village. At first seemingly confident that Salem Village itself might offer such a refuge, he soon shifted his expectations to the Village Church. But finally he was forced to abandon even this refuge and fell back on the prospect that only in a "well-walled and well-gated" heavenly city could the pure in heart enjoy that security against betrayal and subversion which neither Salem Village nor its church had ever achieved.

For Parris and his supporters, what the spring and summer of 1692 had finally demonstrated—though their recognition of it remained inchoate—was that the good society would not be achieved on this earth. When they at last came to recognize the significance of what had happened, they entered a new stage of religious and

42. *Ibid.*, Sept. 11, 1692, pp. 154, 155, 153, 156.
43. *Ibid.*, p. 154.

social development which, whatever it may have been, could no longer be called "Puritan."

By October 1692 the evidences that Parris himself was ready to abandon the struggle grew more pronounced. Abruptly dropping his martial imagery, Parris on October 23 almost unbelievably turned for his inspiration to the Song of Solomon and preached from the text: "Let him kiss me with the kisses of his mouth." In a sermon suffused with sensual imagery ("Let me see, let me feel, let me sense thy love"), Parris called emotionally for the transcendance of factionalism through love: "Oh, be reconciled to me, and give me a kiss of reconciliation. . . . [L]et me sense and feel thy love. . . . Kisses are very sweet among true friends after some jars and differences, whereby they testify true reconciliation."

But two decades of "jars and differences" were not to be overcome by a single gesture of reconciliation, however poignant or deeply felt. Indeed, even in this sermon can be found an implicit acknowledgment that formal legal encounters were increasingly coming to constitute Parris's only relationship with his opponents: "by virtue of covenant relation," he pleaded, "I may *sue* for kisses." Nor, even here, could he overcome that element of mistrust, that fear of betrayal, which his experiences had so ingrained in him: "We read of a kiss of treachery. . . . Thus . . . Judas kissed his Master, Christ. . . . There are the kisses of enemies, which are deceitful, says the Holy Ghost." [44]

By the summer of 1693, after the last accused witch had been released from prison, Parris recognized the full enormity of what had happened. On August 6, 1693, he preached a sermon on the death of Christ. "Come hither, then," he invited his congregation, "and see Him as in the most lively picture set forth as crucified before your eyes." But the minister must have been only too aware that he himself would be identified, under the circumstances, not with the crucified Christ but with those who had murdered Him. In a passage which must have been almost unbearable both for Parris to deliver and for his congregation to hear, he came as close as was possible for him, psychologically and politically, to a full and contrite confession:

> To see a dear friend torn, wounded, and the blood streaming down his face and body, will much affect the heart. But much more when those wounds we see, and that streaming blood we

---

44. *Ibid.*, Oct. 23, 1692, pp. 160, 161, 162, 159. Italics added.

behold, accuseth *us* as the vile actors. To see such a one gashed and gored, though it were done by some other hand, will affect our hearts, if they be not harder than the stones, and more flinty than the rocks. But much more when our consciences tell us that we, our cruel hands, have made those wounds, and the bloody instruments by which our dearest friend was gored, were of our own forging.[45]

But, for Samuel Parris, there was to be neither reconciliation nor expiation. As he realized this fact, his scorn and contempt for his enemies, which had from the beginning masked a deeper self-contempt, were resolved into a generalized conviction of the all-pervasive corruption inherent in the human condition. In a sermon of May 1694 he introduced a theme which, while standard enough in seventeenth-century Puritan writings, was nevertheless one which Parris, in all his attempts to come to terms with his experience, had heretofore managed completely to avoid: original sin. "[W]e are altogether filthy and polluted, conceived in sin. . . . The scripture assures us that from this our original filth, flows infinite pollutions. We go astray as soon as we are born. . . . As the fountain calls forth its waters, so do our filthy hearts their pollutions."[46]

After four and one-half years in the Puritan ministry, Parris had come to conclude what John Calvin could have told him all along: to commit evil, even on a monumental scale, man needs no special pacts with the devil—he is corrupt in his very heart. Idealist that he fundamentally was, Parris was brought by this insight to an impasse in his intellectual development. Though he would remain in Salem Village for well over two years, this discourse was the last he could bring himself to write out in his Sermon Book.

Samuel Parris did not deliberately provoke the Salem witchcraft episode. Nor, certainly, was he responsible for the factional conflict which underlay it. Nevertheless, his was a crucial role. He had a keen mind and a way with words, and Sunday after Sunday, in the little Village meetinghouse, by the alchemy of typology and allegory, he took the nagging fears and conflicting impulses of his hearers and wove them into a pattern overwhelming in its scope, a universal drama in which Christ and Satan, Heaven and Hell, struggled for supremacy.

Parris's cosmic translation of the Village's history carried such

45. *Ibid.*, Aug. 6, 1693, p. 215. Italics added.
46. *Ibid.*, May 6, 1694, pp. 289–290.

conviction because in making it he was apotheosizing his own experience as well. Bethlehem was a type of Salem Village, to be sure ("poor, mean, and contemptible"), but clearly the suffering Christ of his sermons was also, at some level of consciousness, Parris himself: blameless, yet doomed to betrayal. Israel Porter, Joseph Putnam, and all his other Village opponents—not to mention the first accused witch, the Indian Tituba, a member of his own household—were only the latest in a succession of Judases in Parris's life; all of them, perhaps, only reminders of the original betrayer: the cosmopolitan London merchant whose niggardly bequests to a younger son had forced him to eke out a precarious living in an obscure New England farm community.

But we are not dealing here simply with the psychopathology of a single eccentric individual. Parris was ultimately a representative man of his time, just as Salem Village was a representative community. All the elements of their respective histories were deeply rooted in the social realities of late-seventeenth-century western culture—a culture in which a subsistence, peasant-based economy was being subverted by mercantile capitalism. This process played itself out sometimes as a political struggle between vying groups of men, and sometimes as a psychological struggle within individual men. What is unique about our story is the lethal convergence of a man and a community in whom, and in which, these conflicts were already independently raging. Through Parris's sermons, many Salem Villagers discovered new and alarming dimensions in their chronic difficulties; at the same time, through his Salem Village experience, Parris found abundant nourishment for the obsessions which had long been gnawing at his soul.

8 Witchcraft and Social Identity

What we have been attempting through all the preceding chapters is to convey something of the deeper historical resonances of our story while still respecting its uniqueness. We see no real conflict between these two purposes. To be sure, no other community was precisely like Salem Village, and no other men were exactly like embittered Samuel Parris, cool and ambitious Israel Porter, or Thomas Putnam, Jr., grimly watching the steady diminution of his worldly estate.

This irreducible particularity, these intensely personal aspirations and private fears, fairly leap from the documents these Salem Villagers, and others, left behind them. And had we been able to learn to know them better—heard the timbre of their voices, watched the play of emotion across their faces, observed even a few of those countless moments in their lives which went unrecorded— we might have been able to apprehend with even greater force the pungent flavor of their individuality.

But the more we have come to know these men for something like what they really were, the more we have also come to realize how profoundly they were shaped by the times in which they lived. For if they were unlike any other men, so was their world unlike any other world before or since; and they shared that world with other people living in other places. Parris and Putnam and the rest were, after all, not only Salem Villagers: they were also men of the seventeenth century; they were New Englanders; and, finally, they were Puritans.

If the large concepts with which historians conventionally deal are to have any meaning, it is only as they can be made manifest in individual cases like these. The problems which confronted Salem Village in fact encompassed some of the central issues of New England society in the late seventeenth century: the resistance of back-country farmers to the pressures of commercial capitalism and the social style that accompanied it; the breaking away of outlying areas from parent towns; difficulties between ministers and their congregations; the crowding of third-generation sons from family lands; the shifting locus of authority within individual communities and society as a whole; the very quality of life in an unsettled age. But for men like Samuel Parris and Thomas Putnam, Jr., these issues were not abstractions. They emerged as upsetting personal encounters with people like Israel Porter and Daniel Andrew, and as unfavorable decisions handed down in places like Boston and Salem Town.

It was in 1692 that these men for the first time attempted (just as we are attempting in this book) to piece together the shards of their experience, to shape their malaise into some broader theoretical pattern, and to comprehend the full dimensions of those forces which they vaguely sensed were shaping their private destinies. Oddly enough, it has been through our sense of "collaborating" with Parris and the Putnams in their effort to delineate the larger contours of their world, and our sympathy, at least on the level of metaphor, with certain of their perceptions, that we have come to feel a curious bond with the "witch hunters" of 1692.

But one advantage we as outsiders have had over the people of Salem Village is that we can afford to recognize the degree to which the menace they were fighting off had taken root within each of them almost as deeply as it had in Salem Town or along the Ipswich Road. It is at this level, indeed, that we have most clearly come to recognize the implications of their travail for our understanding of what might be called the Puritan temper during that final, often intense, and occasionally lurid efflorescence which signaled the end of its century-long history. For Samuel Parris and Thomas Putnam, Jr., were part of a vast company, on both sides of the Atlantic, who were trying to expunge the lure of a new order from their own souls by doing battle with it in the real world. While this company of Puritans were not the purveyors of the spirit of capitalism that historians once made them out to be, neither were they simple peasants clinging blindly to the imagined security of a receding medieval culture. What seems above all to characterize them, and even to help define their identity as "Puritans," is the precarious way in which they managed to inhabit both these worlds at once.

The inner tensions that shaped the Puritan temper were inherent in it from the very start, but rarely did they emerge with such raw force as in 1692, in little Salem Village. For here was a community in which these tensions were exacerbated by a tangle of external circumstances: a community so situated geographically that its inhabitants experienced two different economic systems, two different ways of life, at unavoidably close range; and so structured politically that it was next to impossible to locate, either within the Village or outside it, a dependable and unambiguous center of authority which might hold in check the effects of these accidents of geography.

The spark which finally set off this volatile mix came with the unlikely convergence of a set of chance factors in the early 1690's: the arrival of a new minister who brought with him a slave acquainted with West Indian voodoo lore; the heightened interest throughout New England in fortune telling and the occult, taken up in Salem Village by an intense group of adolescent girls related by blood and faction to the master of that slave; the coming-of-age of Joseph Putnam, who bore the name of one of Salem Village's two controlling families while owing his allegience to the other; the political and legal developments in Boston and London which hamstrung provincial authorities for several crucial months early in 1692.

But beyond these proximate causes lie the deeper and more inexorable ones we have already discussed. For in the witchcraft outburst in Salem Village, perhaps the most exceptional event in American colonial history, certainly the most bizarre, one finds laid bare the central concerns of the era. And so once again, for a final time, we must return to the Village in the sorest year of its affliction.

Witchcraft and Factionalism

Predictably enough, the witchcraft accusations of 1692 moved in channels which were determined by years of factional strife in Salem Village. The charges against Daniel Andrew and Phillip English, for example, followed closely upon their election as Salem Town selectmen—in a vote which underscored the collapse of the

Putnam effort to stage a comeback in Town politics. And Francis Nurse, the husband of accused witch Rebecca Nurse, was a member of the anti-Parris Village Committee which took office in October 1691.[1]

Other accusations, less openly political, suggest a tentative probing around the fringes of the anti-Parris leadership. For example, George Jacobs, Jr.—accused with several members of his family— was a brother-in-law of Daniel Andrew, whose lands he helped farm. Jacobs was close to the Porter group in other ways as well. In 1695, for example, he was on hand as the will of the dying Mary Veren Putnam was drawn up, and his name appears with Israel Porter's as a witness to that controversial document. In May 1692 Daniel Andrew and George Jacobs, Jr., were named in the same arrest warrant, and they evidently went into hiding together.[2]

Another of Daniel Andrew's tenants was Peter Cloyce whose wife, Sarah (a sister of Rebecca Nurse) was among the accused in 1692. And Michael DeRich, whose wife Mary was also charged that year, seems at one time to have been a retainer or servant in the household of the elder John Porter, and his ties to the family may well have continued into the next generation. (Mary DeRich, in turn, was a close relative—perhaps even a sister—of Elizabeth Proctor, convicted of witchcraft along with her husband John.)[3]

Indeed, as the accused are examined from the perspective of Village factionalism, they begin to arrange themselves into a series of interconnected networks. These networks were not formally orga-

1. Village Records, Oct. 16, 1691; Chapter 5, notes 43 and 44 (election of Andrew and English as Town selectmen). Although the Nurses had been relatively inactive in Village politics up to 1692, their sympathies are suggested not only by Francis's willingness to join in the anti-Parris maneuver of 1691, but also by Rebecca's decision not to transfer her church membership from Salem Town to Salem Village in 1689.

2. Essex Probate, 23077 (Mary Veren Putnam will); Robert Calef, *More Wonders of the Invisible World: Or, The Wonders of the Invisible World, Display'd in Five Parts* (London, 1700), reprinted in part in George Lincoln Burr, ed.; *Narratives of the Witchcraft Cases, 1648–1706* (New York, Charles Scribner's Sons, 1914; reissued, New York, Barnes and Noble, 1968), p. 366; Sidney Perley, *The History of Salem, Mass.*, 3 vols. (Salem, 1924–28), III, 109– 110 (Jacobs genealogy); W. Elliot Woodward, *Records of Salem Witchcraft, Copied from the Original Documents*, 2 vols. (Roxbury, Mass., Privately printed, 1864; reissued in one volume, New York, Da Capo Press, 1969), I, 254 (Andrew and Jacobs arrest warrant).

3. 5 *EQC*, 428 (DeRich/Porter connection); Warrant for Mary DeRich's arrest, May 23, 1692, WPA, I (identification of Mary as wife of Michael De-Rich); Catherine S. Chandler, *The Bassett Family—Lynn, Mass. to Salem County, N.J., 1624–1964* (Salem, N.J., 1964), pp. 2–3, 11.

nized or rigidly structured, but they were nonetheless real enough. The kinds of associations which underlay them were varied: kinship and marriage ties were crucial, but marriage, in all likelihood, was simply the final step, the institutionalization of less tangible bonds built up gradually over a period of time. The traces of such bonds lie buried in a wide variety of sources, including real-estate transactions, court testimony, genealogies, and lists of witnesses and executors in wills and estate settlements. Ultimately, the evidence for these relationships fades off into shadowy associations which are frustratingly difficult to document with precision—although they were certainly well known at the time.

One such network, illustrated in Chart 6, links Israel Porter with a startling number of "witch" families, most notably the Proctors and the Nurses.[4] Other anti-Parris networks (and, for that matter, pro-Parris networks) could be reconstructed.[5] Though this chart is hardly complete or definitive—it could certainly be elaborated with additional research, or even extended outward to encompass additional witches—it does show the various kinds of connections which could hold such a network together. Perhaps the nature of these ties provides a key to one of the ways in which political "factions" were established, cemented, and enlarged in Salem Village (and in other communities as well) during the last part of the seventeenth century. If so, the pattern of witchcraft accusations may itself be

4. These are our sources for the "anti-Parris" network shown in Chart 6: genealogies in Perley, *History of Salem*, II, 22–23 (Proctor), 143 (Nurse), 161–162 (Porter), 295 (Wilkins); III, 1 (Very), 5 (Towne), 109–110 (Jacobs); Chandler, *Bassett Family*, pp. 2–3, 11; Charles W. Upham, *Salem Witchcraft*, 2 vols. (Boston, 1867), I, frontispiece: "Map of Salem Village, 1692" (Peter Cloyce and George Jacobs, Jr., as tenants of Daniel Andrew); II, 58–59, 272 (petitions and depositions of Israel Porter and Daniel Andrew on behalf of Rebecca Nurse), 466 (marriage of John Willard's widow to William Towne); Woodward, *Rec. ords of Salem Witchcraft*, II, 23 (warrant for the arrest of Sarah Buckley "and Mary Withridge, the daughter of said Buckley"), 24 (constable's return indicating that Daniel Andrew and George Jacobs, Jr., fled together); 5 *EQC*, 346, 428 (evidence linking Michael DeRich to the Porter family); Essex Deeds, VIII, 123 (John Proctor appoints Israel Porter a trustee of his estate, Jan. 26, 1689); Essex Prob., Dockets No. 611 (Israel Porter and George Jacobs, Jr., witness Daniel Andrew's will, Sept. 4, 1702) and 19688 (Israel Porter witnesses Francis Nurse's estate settlement, Dec. 4, 1694).

5. While it might be objected that such a "network" could be constructed for any randomly chosen group of Salem Villagers, our own work suggests that this is not the case. On the contrary, we have concluded that social and economic alliances, from marriage on out to the most shadowy links, did not cross factional lines with any real frequency until sometime after 1700, when these particular factions had begun to dissipate—to be replaced, perhaps, by others which we have not begun to study.

Chart 6. An Anti-Parris "Network"

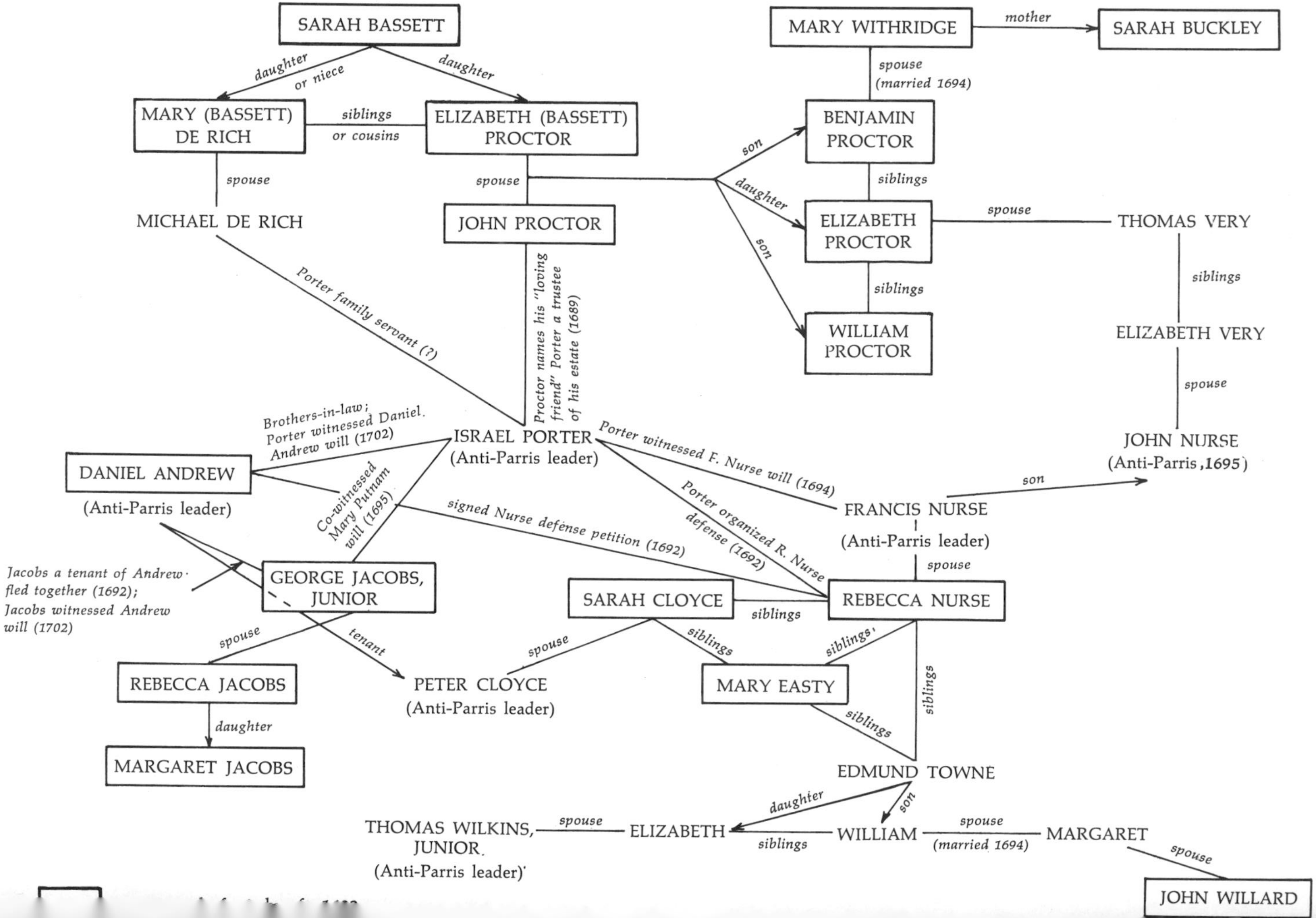

a more revealing guide than even the maps or tax lists to the origin of political divisions in the Village.

Given all this, it is not surprising to discover a high correlation between Salem Village factionalism and the way the Village divided in 1692 over the witchcraft outbreak. There are forty-seven Villagers whose position can be determined both in 1692 (by their testimonies or other involvement in the witchcraft trials) and in 1695 (by their signatures on one or the other of the two key petitions). Of the twenty-seven of those who supported the trials by testifying against one or more of the accused witches, twenty-one later signed the pro-Parris petition, and only six the anti-Parris document. Of the twenty who registered their opposition to the trials, either by defending an accused person or by casting doubt on the testimony of the afflicted girls, only one supported Parris in 1695, while nineteen opposed him.[6] In short, supporters of the trials generally belonged to the pro-Parris faction, and opponents of the trials were overwhelmingly anti-Parris.

Almost every indicator by which the two Village factions may be distinguished, in fact, also neatly separates the supporters and opponents of the witchcraft trials. Compare, for example, Map 1 showing the residences of accusers and defenders in 1692 with Map 3 locating Parris's supporters and opponents. The connection is clear: that part of Salem Village which was an anti-Parris stronghold in 1695 (the part nearest Salem Town) had also been a center of resistance to the witchcraft trials, while the more distant western part of the Village, where pro-Parris sentiment was dominant, contained an extremely high concentration of accusers in 1692.

Similarly with wealth: just as the average member of the anti-Parris faction paid about 40 percent more in Village taxes than his counterpart in the pro-Parris faction, so the average 1695–96 tax of the Villagers who publicly opposed the trials was 67 percent higher than that of those who pushed the trials forward—18.3 shillings as opposed to 11 shillings.[7]

6. Pro-Parris and anti-Parris petitions: Church Records, following entry for April 3, 1695; data on accusers and defenders from WPA and Woodward, *Records of Salem Witchcraft.* See Paul Boyer and Stephen Nissenbaum, eds., *Salem-Village Witchcraft: A Documentary Record of Local Conflict in Colonial New England* (Belmont, Calif., Wadsworth Publishing Co., 1972), pp. 379–382, for lists of accusers and defenders connected with Salem Village. In making this correlation, we have not included the nine petition signers who in 1692 were both accusers and defenders.

7. Tax list, Village Records, Dec. 13, 1695. Again, we have not included the eight taxpayers who appeared in both capacities—as accusers and defend-

But despite all the evidence suggesting that the accusations of 1692 represented a direct and conscious continuation of factional conflict, such an explanation is ultimately insufficient. In part, this is because of the sheer mechanical difficulties in reconstructing fully those linkages that do exist. The "networks" we have postulated are difficult to pin down, for instance, because they rested on the kinds of ties and associations often reflected only in the most fragmentary way, if at all, in the written records.

Furthermore, it is simply impossible to document the position of many Salem Villagers toward the witchcraft episode. While the data available on the Village's two factions is remarkably complete, a considerably smaller proportion of the Villagers openly committed themselves one way or the other on the witchcraft issue—fewer than one hundred, on the basis of surviving testimonies.[8] Of the somewhat larger number of Village men and women whose sympathies went unrecorded, some unquestionably did make their positions known at the time, since the issue was surely a matter of intense and incessant discussion in the community. But unless an individual actually committed himself on paper, by signing a complaint, a deposition, or a petition, and unless that paper was preserved in the archives, his opinions about what happened in 1692 are lost to history.

Other Villagers may have kept their silence throughout the episode and carried their opinions with them to the grave. Taking sides, after all, was a risky business. If a person seemed skeptical about the trials, he might find himself accused; if he joined in, on either side, he risked making some very powerful enemies. And nobody could be certain which side would come out on top. Samuel Parris recognized how tempting neutrality must have been for some, and he did his best to eliminate it as a viable alternative. "Here are no neuters," he insisted in September 1692; "Everyone is on one side or the other."[9] It was a theological point Parris was making, but (as was so often the case with him) the political implications were clear. Parris was attempting to compel commitment to his own faction by posing the alternatives so starkly: Will you

---

ers—at different stages of the witchcraft outbreak. If the taxes paid by these men are included in the averages, the disparity is naturally somewhat reduced, though by no means eliminated. The average tax of the supporters of the trials then becomes thirteen shillings, and that of the opponents 19.4 shillings.

8. Woodward, *Records of Salem Witchcraft*, index; WPA; Boyer and Nissenbaum, *Salem-Village Witchcraft*, pp. 379–382.

9. Sermon Book, September 11, 1692, p. 155.

be God's ally, or the Devil's? An accuser, or an accused? A saint . . . or a witch? There was no middle ground, he suggested. But, for all Parris's efforts, many Villagers refused to be pressured into a possibly dangerous affirmation of their loyalties, and simply lay low.

Another kind of difficulty is posed by those Villagers who did take sides in 1692—but involuntarily: the accused witches. With very few exceptions, these people were simply not around in 1695 to sign the anti-Parris petition, either because they had been executed or because they had left the area after 1692. For this reason, it is technically impossible to associate the great majority of the accused witches with the anti-Parris faction and thus all the more difficult to establish a neat correlation between the witchcraft outbreak and the broader pattern of political conflict.

A more significant difficulty in linking Salem Village witchcraft statistically to Salem Village factionalism is the fact that—for all the probing around the fringes of the anti-Parris group—the anti-Parris leadership generally escaped prosecution in 1692. Israel Porter, Joseph Porter, Joseph Hutchinson, Joseph Putnam: none was touched by accusation in 1692—at least by any accusation permitted to reach the court. This poses a touchy problem: it is obvious that the witchcraft outbreak was intimately connected with the factional conflicts which preceded it, and yet, with only one or two exceptions, the accusations did not fall on those men who were surely the most tempting targets. Why not?

One way to answer this question is to try to identify some of the ways by which the people who were accused may be distinguished from those who were not. For example, the matter of recognized Village status: it is revealing that the three Porter brothers, none of whom was accused, were all long-time Village residents who had been born to wealth and respectability, while the one member of the family who actually was accused, their brother-in-law Daniel Andrew, was a comparative newcomer to the Village who had been born in obscurity. Or again, it is noteworthy that of the anti-Parris Village Committee elected in 1691, the three who are consistently designated "Mr." in the records (Porter, Hutchinson, Putnam) were spared, while Francis Nurse, who never advanced beyond "Goodman," saw his wife hanged a year later. (Daniel Andrew, accused but able to escape, possibly with the connivance of the authorities, was sometimes "Mr. Daniel Andrew" and sometimes not: his precise status was apparently somewhat problematical.)

Powerful men *were* accused in 1692—men addressed as "Mr.," "Captain," "Honorable," and even "Reverend," but in every instance these men were remote from the immediate Salem Village scene. (Most of them were Bostonians.) They had never been to Salem Village, and few Villagers—certainly not the afflicted girls who first named them—could have known them except by reputation. The local anti-Parris leadership may have remained immune to attack, then, precisely because it was local. It was one thing for an afflicted girl to accuse some prominent individual in Boston (or even in Salem Town) of attacking her: men like John Alden or Nathaniel Cary would have been distant and essentially symbolic figures to her. But it was something else again to lash out at members of the Salem Village gentry like Israel Porter, men whom they encountered regularly and who held a recognized position on the day-to-day scale of social status. For all the depths of factional passion, habits of deference still ran deep in Salem Village—deep enough, at any rate, to save anyone who was by blood a Porter.

This is not to suggest that the pressures to accuse such men were not intense, even unbearably so. But yet they remained "off-limits," psychologically or politically. They could not be brought down in the Village meeting or in the courts, and neither could they be brought down as witches. The catharsis which might have come through an open assault on the anti-Parris leadership was not to be achieved.

Faced with this formidable psychological barrier, the witchcraft accusations soon began to generate a powerful dynamic of their own, a dynamic which rapidly heightened the sense of general conspiracy already pervading the Village by 1692. We have earlier suggested the kinds of "networks" that linked many of the accused witches to the anti-Parris leadership. Indeed, all it takes is a slight shift in our angle of vision to perceive the victims of the witch trials in 1692 the way they must have appeared to the pro-Parris people: as the well-organized minions of those immune figures who stood poised to take over and destroy Salem Village.

The preoccupation with conspiracy was encouraged not only by Parris's sermons, but also by a cumulative body of witchcraft testimony which focused on precisely this point. One confessing witch, for example, reported that a gathering of "about six score" witches in Salem Village had decided to "pull down the Kingdom of Christ and to set up the Devil's Kingdom." (Including their non-Village sympathizers, this figure of 120 would probably be a fairly accurate estimate of the strength of the anti-Parris faction.) Deliverance Hobbs revealed that at another large assemblage of Village witches—a kind of strategy session—George Burroughs had issued instructions "to bewitch all in the Village . . . gradually, and not all at once."[10] Most alarming of all was the detailed confession of William Barker of Andover, who reported a meeting of over 300 witches in Salem Village and revealed that Satan had singled out this obscure community for assault "by reason of the people's being divided and their differing with the ministers." Evidently sensing the interest which this particular theme had aroused, Barker elaborated in a further confession from behind prison walls: "[T]he design was to destroy Salem Village, and to begin at the minister's house, and to destroy the Church of God, and to set up Satan's Kingdom, and then all will be well."[11]

Unable to attack the men they saw as responsible for this subversion, some Villagers began to see witches everywhere. But although the accusations were diverted from their most obvious targets, they were not therefore aimless or random. We have already seen that a number of the accused were linked in one way or another to the anti-Parris group, and if we could fully reconstruct all the Village "networks" many more such links would certainly emerge. For example, one destitute accused witch, Sarah Good, was denied shelter by at least one pro-Parris Salem Village family in the years before 1692. Who eventually took her and her small children in? An anti-Parris household, perhaps? We simply cannot know.

But whether or not the accused witches were openly associated with the anti-Parris group, they represented—in their careers and even, perhaps, in their manner of life—precisely what many Villagers found so disturbing about the opposition to their minister: its lack of commitment to "Salem Village," its alien and unfamiliar quality. For the people who finally accused them, at least some of these witches may well have been substitutes for other persons who were less vulnerable to attack—just as Martha Cory and Rebecca Nurse substituted, in the mind of the senior Ann Putnam, for her husband's stepmother.

10. Woodward, *Records of Salem Witchcraft*, II, 191 (Deliverance Hobbs); 135 Mass. Arch. 33 (Elizabeth Johnson, Jr.).

11. 135 Mass. Arch., 30; John Hale, *A Modest Enquiry Into the Nature of Witchcraft, and How Persons Guilty of That Crime May be Convicted: and The Means Used for Their Discovery Discussed, Both Negatively and Affirmatively, According to Scripture and Experience* (Boston, 1702), reprinted in part in Burr, *Narratives of the Witchcraft Cases*, pp. 419–420.

The Village Witches: Toward a Collective Profile

Of the 142 persons named as witches in 1692, only twenty-five are described in the documents as living in Salem Village or its immediate environs. But although they were a minority of the total company of the accused, these Village "witches" were the ones most vividly present in the consciousness of the accusers, and thus it is they, of all the accused, whose lives are most likely to furnish clues toward our understanding of this event and its meaning.

Of these twenty-five, six are the subjects of biographical vignettes which follow. Six others are treated, at varying length, elsewhere in this chapter or at other points in this book. These are Daniel Andrew, Martha Cory, George Jacobs, Jr., Rebecca Nurse, the slave Tituba, and John Proctor's servant girl Mary Warren. Of the remaining thirteen, twelve—Edward Bishop, Sarah Bishop, Sarah Cloyce, Giles Cory, Mary DeRich, Dorcas Good, Rebecca Jacobs, Elizabeth Proctor, Benjamin Proctor, William Proctor, Sarah Proctor, and Mary Withridge—were the offspring, siblings, or spouses of accused persons with whom we do deal. (Once an individual had been named as a witch, the accusations often "spilled over" to take in other members of his or her immediate family.) The final accused witch in the Village was Nathaniel Putnam's slave Mary Black, about whom practically nothing is known.

As one examines the lives of these people, patterns begin to emerge: common characteristics which seem to have made them unusually vulnerable in 1692. What follows is an effort to identify some of these characteristics, and to describe how they manifested themselves in particular lives.

Outsiders . . .

In the most literal sense, of course, a large majority of the total group of accused witches would fall into the category "outsider," since about 82 percent of them lived beyond the bounds of Salem Village. Of these non-Village accused, seventeen, significantly, lived in Salem Town. Sixty-six lived in the other towns immediately bordering the Village (Andover, Rowley, Topsfield, Ipswich, Lynn, and Reading) and the remaining thirty were from fourteen other towns of northeastern Massachusetts—most of them in the second tier of towns encircling the Village.[12] A detailed explana-

---

12. Data from Woodward, *Records of Salem Witchcraft, passim,* supplemented by the WPA volumes. The arrest warrants usually included the place

tion of how and why each of these specific outsiders came to be singled out would require an examination of the immediate social context in each of these other towns, an examination at least as detailed as the one to which we have subjected Salem Village. The significant point, however, is the very willingness of the afflicted girls and the other Villagers who supported the trials to place in mortal jeopardy so many non-Villagers, many of them certainly known only hazily at best.

But even among those accusations directed against individuals who lived in the Village or its immediate environs, this obsession with "outsiders" is still visible. As we have already pointed out (see Map 1), geography played a large role in determining the pattern of Village accusations: of the twenty-five Village area witches, only three lived in the western part of the community, and another

of residence. For a full listing of all persons known to have been arrested in 1692, with their places of residence, see Boyer and Nissenbaum, *Salem-Village Witchcraft*, pp. 376–378. Of the accused from the immediately adjacent towns, a disproportionately large number came from Andover, Salem Village's neighbor to the west. While Andover accusations would be expected in terms of the geographic pattern we have described, chance seems to have played a part in focusing particular attention on this town. While the witchcraft episode was in progress, an Andover man named Joseph Ballard brought in two of the afflicted girls to see if they could tell him who was bewitching his ailing wife. They proceeded to name many residents of the town, including entire family groups. A confrontation between accused and accusers was held at the Andover meetinghouse, at the conclusion of which a large group of accused persons was arrested *en masse*.

While the flurry of witchcraft panic in Andover and other Essex County towns in 1692 clearly had its *origins* in the Salem Village outbreak, and while, so far as we have been able to ascertain, accused witches from outside Salem Village were in each instance *indicted* for the affliction of Village girls rather than their own townsfolk, it is true that once such outsiders had been arrested, their own neighbors frequently did come forward with hostile testimony. (See, e.g., Benjamin and Sarah Abbott of Andover *vs.* Martha Carrier of Andover, Woodward, *Records of Salem Witchcraft*, II, 59–61.) This is hardly surprising, since a central contention of this book has been that the circumstances which confronted Salem Village during these years were unique only in the intensity which, through a convergence of chance factors, they finally reached. With other communities enmeshed in so many of the same kinds of difficulties, it was easy for the spark of panic, once ignited in Salem Village, to spread through the volatile atmosphere of the province. Although Philip J. Greven, Jr., in his recent study of Andover, *Four Generations: Population, Land, and Family in Colonial Andover, Massachusetts* (Ithaca, Cornell University Press, 1970), does not discuss the witchcraft episode, he does suggest that problems of inheritance and land distribution were during these years producing severe strains among many Andover families—including (see p. 84) that of Joseph Ballard himself, the man principally responsible for the spread of ⸱⸱⸱ 1692 outbreak to that town. (Calef, *More Wonders*, in Burr, *Narratives*, pp. 371–372.)

four near the center. All the others lived on the eastern, or Salem Town, side—with a majority of these residing on or near the Ipswich Road or its spur, the Topsfield Road. (The accusers, by contrast, were heavily concentrated in the northwestern part of the Village.)

Viewed thus schematically, the residential profile of the accused offers a vivid geographic metaphor for the anxieties of the "pro-Parris" group: the regions beyond the Village bounds are dangerous "enemy territory," and even within the legal boundaries of the Village, the areas closest to Salem Town have already been tainted. The true "Salem Village" has been driven westward and confined to a small enclave from which, back to the wall (or, more literally, to the Ipswich River) it lashes out at the encircling enemy. The scenario is a lurid one; but no more lurid than, at some imaginative level, it seemed to some Salem Villagers in 1692.

But the lines that divided outsiders from the rest of the community were figurative as well as literal, and the way they were drawn often depended less upon where one happened to live in the Village than upon the depth of one's commitment to it. There was more than one kind of "outsider" in Salem Village. Particularly vulnerable on this score were those Villagers who had been living in the community for only a short time, or whose arrival had had a disruptive social impact. The pattern may be found over and over again among the accused of the Village—Daniel Andrew, for instance—but the variety of forms it could assume is revealed in the disparate careers of three witches we have not yet discussed: Bridget Bishop, Sarah Osborne, and John Willard.

Bridget Bishop (Hanged, June 10, 1692)

In 1685 Bridget Oliver of Salem Town married her third husband —old Edward Bishop, one of the founders of the Beverly Church— and moved from the center of town to his house on the Ipswich Road in Salem Village. (The Bishops retained title to Bridget's house in the town, however, and derived income from it as a rental property.) Having already built up a long reputation for aggressive behavior in petty commercial transactions, Bridget soon turned the Bishop house into a place of late-night conviviality where she sold cider manufactured from apples grown in her private orchard. As one witness put it, Bridget "did entertain people in her house at unseasonable hours in the night to keep drinking and playing at shuffle-board, whereby discord did arise in other families, and young people were in danger to be corrupted."[13] If John Proctor's licensed tavern was a rest-stop for wayfarers, Bridget Bishop's unlicensed one seems to have been a rendezvous for local youths.

Significantly, Bridget appears never to have ventured into Salem Village proper. "I never was in this place before," she claimed at her examination in the Village meetinghouse in 1692; "I know no man, woman, or child here."[14] None of the Villagers present challenged this statement, although on other occasions they freely accused persons under examination of lying. Though she had lived within the Village bounds for seven years, Bridget Bishop remained, in the most literal sense, an outsider—and one whose arrival had brought discord and family conflict in its wake.

Sarah Osborne (Died in Boston prison, May 10, 1692)

A native of Watertown, Massachusetts, Sarah Warren in 1662 married Robert Prince, a Salem Villager who some years before had purchased a 150-acre farm next to that of Captain John Putnam, his sister's husband. Robert Prince fully identified himself with the emerging movement for Village autonomy. He acquired additional land on the western edge of the Village, signed the 1667 petition against militia duty in the Town, and joined the other Villagers who in 1670 refused to help pay for a new Town meetinghouse.[15]

When he died in 1674, Prince left his land in trust to his wife, with the stipulation that it eventually be given to their two sons, six-year-old James and two-year-old Joseph, when the lads came of age. As executors he named his in-laws and neighbors, Thomas and John Putnam. But (as in the Putnam family itself) an outsider disrupted what would otherwise have been the uneventful transfer of land from one generation to the next. Soon after her bereavement, the widow Prince brought into the Village as her hired man

13. Testimony of the Reverend John Hale in Woodward, *Records of Salem Witchcraft*, I, 153–156, esp. p. 154; Perley, *History of Salem*, I, 443; II, 180–181; III, 149; Upham, *Salem Witchcraft*, II, 253 (Continued ownership of Salem Town house).

14. Woodward, *Records of Salem Witchcraft*, I, 140, 145.

15. Upham, *Salem Witchcraft*, II, 17–19; Sidney Perley, "The Plains: Part of Salem in 1700," 54 *EIHC* (1918), 304; Eben Putnam, "Some Materials for a History of the Prince Family of Danvers," 27 *EIHC* (1890), 171; 5 *EQC*, 26; Perley, *History of Salem*, II, 31–32 (Prince genealogy); 112 Mass. Arch., 175–177 (1667 petition); 5 *EQC*, 26, 273 (1670 petition).

one Alexander Osborne, a young Irish immigrant whose indenture she had purchased for £15. Alexander quickly advanced from Sarah's barn to her bed (later testimony hinted at the scandal), and eventually the two were married. They now began to maneuver to gain full and permanent legal control of the Prince lands, in direct defiance of Robert Prince's will.[16]

The resulting dispute was a protracted one. Only in 1696 were James and Joseph Prince confirmed in the possession of even part of their patrimony, and some of it remained under a legal cloud for a quarter of a century longer. The entire controversy was aired in a 1720 court case pitting the Princes against the Osborne heirs and featuring extensive testimony which revealed the depth of Village hostility toward the attempts of Alexander and Sarah Osborne to disinherit Sarah's sons.[17]

The meaning of Sarah Osborne's fate in 1692 becomes clearer as we begin to sense how she must have been viewed in the Village. The crucial issue, we would judge, was not the long-ago fornication with Alexander Osborne, though this certainly made her (like Martha Cory) more vulnerable, but rather the way she and her second husband had threatened established patterns of land tenure and inheritance. Significantly, too, it was not Alexander Osborne, the outsider, who was accused, but Sarah herself, the insider who had betrayed her own sons and, in the process, the structure of the Village itself.

In the petitions of 1695, the surviving members of this family aligned themselves as one would expect: Joseph and James Prince, the disinherited, supported Samuel Parris; Alexander Osborne, outsider and shrewd operator, opposed the Village minister.[18] So deep was their grievance, the two Prince brothers were thus willing publicly to endorse the leadership of a man who three years before had helped bring about their mother's death.

16. 5 *EQC*, 369–370 (Robert Prince will); Upham, *Salem Witchcraft*, II, 17–18 (on Alexander Osborne); Winfield S. Nevins, *Witchcraft in Salem Village in 1692* (fifth ed., Salem, 1916), p. 66; Perley, *History of Salem*, III, 260.

17. 38 Essex Deeds, 54; 39 *ibid.*, 122; Upham, *Salem Witchcraft*, II, 18. This hostility and suspicion had certainly not been reduced by the persistently tenuous nature of Alexander Osborne's connection with the Village. Although taxed as a Village resident, he was often abroad, perhaps in mercantile pursuits, and indeed his death (in about 1704) occurred in the midst of one such trip—Estate settlement, June 29, 1704, 108 Essex Prob., 228–229.

18. Pro-Parris and anti-Parris petitions, Church Records, following entry for April 3, 1695.

John Willard (Hanged, August 19, 1692)

It was sometime before 1690 that John Willard married Margaret Knight of Salem Village. Willard's origins, like those of most of the other witches we have investigated, are frustratingly obscure. Circumstantial evidence links him to Major Simon Willard, one of the most prominent Massachusetts land speculators, town founders, and politicians of the mid-seventeenth century: for a time during his youth John Willard lived in Lancaster, where Major Willard owned a trading post (indeed, it was to Lancaster that he fled when accused of witchcraft in 1692); in the 1680's, moreover, he resided with his wife in Groton, a town founded by Simon Willard; and he was frequently associated, in his land dealings in both communities, with men known to be Simon Willard's sons.[19] But published family histories have suppressed all reference to the man, and the best efforts of local historians and genealogists have failed to establish his precise connection with Simon Willard. If he was a relative—perhaps even a son?—of this rich and prominent man, he was an obscure and somehow ill-favored one.

Willard was not only an outsider to Salem Village but a newcomer to the Wilkins family, of which his wife was a third-generation member. This large and self-contained clan, including the seven children of old Bray Wilkins, together with numerous grandchildren, constituted almost a village unto itself on "Will's Hill" in the extreme western part of Salem Village.[20] (See Map 2.) The story of John Willard becomes comprehensible only when seen as a chapter in the story of the Wilkins family.

The Wilkinses, in their remote corner of Salem Village, had good reason to be chary of outsiders. Although they were devoting

19. H. S. Nourse, ed., *The Early Records of Lancaster* (Lancaster, Mass., 1884), p. 249 (John Willard's name appears as a land grantee after the founding of the town); p. 307 (John Willard's land granted to Benjamin Willard, a son of Simon Willard's, in February 1692); *The Early Records of Groton, Mass.*, ed. Samuel A. Greene (Groton, 1880), p. 66 ("John Wilerd" on a 1681 tax list); on Simon Willard: *Dictionary of American Biography*, XX, 240–241, and Ray A. Billington, *Westward Expansion: A History of the American Frontier* (third ed., New York, Macmillan, 1967), p. 65.

20. Perley, *History of Salem*, II, 294–295 (Wilkins genealogy); William C. Hill, *The Family of Bray Wilkins* (Milford, N.H., The Cabinet Press, 1943), pp. 25–26; WPA, III (1710 petition of Margaret Willard Towne). Margaret was the daughter of Bray Wilkins' daughter (also named Margaret) who had married Phillip Knight.

themselves exclusively to farming by the 1690's, there had been a time when Bray Wilkins and his sons, like John and Nathaniel Putnam, had entertained visions of profitable involvement in the commercial and mercantile life of Salem Town. But (in a fiasco similar to that of the abortive Putnam iron-works) those visions had proven illusory. In 1658 Bray Wilkins, then living in Lynn, had joined with a tailor named John Gingell to purchase, on credit, a 700-acre tract of land around Will's Hill. (The seller was Richard Bellingham, a Massachusetts politician and former governor who had received the land from the General Court in 1639 but never developed it.) Putting up houses and moving their families to this isolated region, Wilkins and Gingell soon began logging and timber-processing operations, converting the dense stands of oak and cedar into boards, shingles, marine supplies, and barrel staves. These they transported to Salem Town and sold to George Corwin, a leading merchant of the day. At first they prospered, with an annual production—as one of Bray Wilkins' sons boasted to a friend in town—as high as 20,000 barrel staves and 6,000 feet of boards. But in terms of profitability, the operation was from the first a marginal one. Indeed, in 1661, Bray Wilkins—otherwise a notably upright man—was forced to steal some hay to feed the oxen with which he transported his timber to Salem Town. When Bray was brought to court, his defense was that he had been "in great want of hay, and knew not what shift to make." His enterprise suffered a severe setback in the winter of 1664–65 when his house burned down.[21]

Under such circumstances, Wilkins and Gingell found themselves unable to keep up with their mortgage payments, and in 1664 they returned to Bellingham two-thirds of the land they had been attempting to purchase. But even a reduced mortgage burden proved too heavy, and in June 1666, after Bellingham (once again governor of the colony) won a foreclosure action in county court, his lawyers began to seize the stock of shingles and other goods belonging to the hapless entrepreneurs. Bray Wilkins ultimately managed to pay off the mortgage and to hang on to his land, but his commercial dream had proven to be just that and nothing more. By the 1680's Bray and his sons had lapsed into the prosaic role of subsistence farmers on marginal land. As a family, the Wilkinses ranked near

21. Perley, *History of Salem*, II, 294 and 394; *Dictionary of American Biography*, II, 166 (on Richard Bellingham); 3 *EQC*, 45–46 (quoted passage on the theft of hay) and 322–323 (the fire).

the bottom in the average per-capita Salem Village taxes assessed in the 1680's and 1690's.[22] While not precisely impoverished, the family which in mid-century had launched itself with such hope upon the commercial seas found itself a generation later in very modest circumstances indeed.

For the Wilkins family, as for the Putnams, only the land itself had proven trustworthy, and the survival of Salem Village as a stable agricultural community was particularly important to them. Not surprisingly, the Wilkinses were second only to the Putnams in the extent and intensity of their support for the Salem Village autonomy movement. Bray Wilkins signed the various petitions of the 1660's looking toward Village independence and (with Nathaniel Putnam) he led the 1679 effort to force the Reverend James Bayley from the Village.[23] Between 1689 and 1691, eight men and women of the Wilkins family joined the Salem Village church, and in 1695 no fewer than eleven Wilkins signatures, including those of the eighty-five-year-old Bray and his wife, appeared on the pro-Parris petition. Only three Wilkinses are to be found on the anti-Parris petition: one of Bray's younger sons, Thomas, together with Thomas's wife and daughter. For reasons we cannot now recover (but possibly connected with his marriage to a niece of Rebecca Nurse), Thomas Wilkins had not joined in the family's accusations against John Willard, and shortly after the witchcraft outbreak he had emerged as one of the four "dissenting brethren" who led the anti-Parris movement from within the church. Later, when Bray Wilkins died (having chosen his "loving friend" Thomas Putnam, Jr., as co-overseer of his estate) he virtually disinherited this turn-coat of a son.[24]

The decision of Bray's granddaughter Margaret Knight to take an outsider for a husband had profound psychological ramifications for this tight-knit and economically marginal family. The seventh member of the third-generation Wilkinses to marry, she was the first to choose a spouse who was not from Salem Village.

22. Tax lists, Village Records, Dec. 27, 1681, Jan. 18, 1695; 3 *EQC*, 322–323; 7 Essex Deeds, 35. Wilkins and Gingell had paid £25 down and agreed to pay an additional £225 over the term of the mortgage, with 8 percent annual interest on the unpaid balance—3 *EQC*, 322–323.

23. Chapter 2, notes 4, 5 and 6 (the petitions of 1666, 1667, and 1670) and 14 (Bayley dispute).

24. Hill, *Family of Bray Wilkins*, pp. 16–19 (the will of Bray Wilkins). Dividing his lands between his sons Henry and Benjamin, Bray stipulated that his "wearing apparrel" be divided among two of his grandsons—and his son Thomas.

Her kinfolks' uneasiness about John Willard must have been intensified when it became clear that he was interested in land speculation as well as in farming. In March 1690, with three partners, he purchased from the widow of George Corwin a large tract of land—"by estimation four or five hundred acres," as the deed rather vaguely has it, lying just north of the Salem Village line. In the succeeding months, at least two substantial portions of this tract were sold off to new purchasers.[25]

In 1692, the Wilkins family turned with particular ferocity against this outsider with his speculative bent. If Martha Cory and Rebecca Nurse were initially "family witches" in the household of Thomas Putnam, Jr., John Willard played a similar role for the Wilkins clan. The finger of witchcraft was pointed at him by no fewer than ten members of the family. In early May 1692, shortly after John Willard had been named by the afflicted girls, but before he was arrested, seventeen-year-old Daniel Wilkins was felled by a mysterious affliction from which he died the following week. At about the same time old Bray Wilkins was struck by a painful and alarming urinary difficulty. Both afflictions were blamed on John Willard. Not long afterwards, Ann Putnam, Sr., picked up the theme, accusing Willard of having murdered no fewer than thirteen Salem Villagers during his brief residence in the community.[26]

John Willard himself seems to have been genuinely mystified by the intensity of feeling against him. When first accused he came to Bray Wilkins "greatly troubled" and asked this respected church member and family patriarch to pray with him—but the old man refused, pleading a prior engagement. Bray Wilkins had learned, over the years, that you cannot be too cautious in dealing with outsiders.[27]

25. 9 Essex Deeds, 5; 13 ibid., 15. This latter deed refers to another, earlier sale for which the deed was evidently not recorded.

26. Testimony of Henry Wilkins, Bray Wilkins, and Ann Putnam, Sr.: Woodward, Record of Salem Witchcraft, I, 275–276; II, 7–10. For an account of Bray Wilkins' urinary problem, see Prologue, p. 14.

27. Ibid., II, 8. In 1656, two years before Richard Bellingham sold Will's Hill to Bray Wilkins, a woman thought by genealogists to have been the former governor's own sister, Mrs. Ann Hibbins, was executed for witchcraft. Was this connection somewhere in the back of Bray Wilkins' mind during his subsequent bitter dealings with Bellingham, and did it surface again, in some even more complex fashion, in 1692? Thomas Hutchinson, The History of the Colony and Province of Massachusetts-Bay, ed. Lawrence Shaw Mayo (Cambridge, Massachusetts, Harvard University Press, 1936), I, 160–161; William F. Poole, "Witchcraft in Boston," in Memorial History of Boston, ed. Justin Winsor (Boston, 1881), II, 130.

. . . who were mobile . . .

The experiences of Salem Village in the late seventeenth century had made one thing only too clear: no one could count on ending his career as he had begun it. Social flux of all kinds was a fact of life, and, as we have seen, it had its victims as well as its beneficiaries. It is no accident that the events of 1692 were set off when some young people became interested in fortune-telling: conjurations with various occult objects, including, at one point, a kind of crystal ball. And they had turned to these occult rituals for a single purpose: to predict the future course of their own lives, and particularly the identity and occupations of their future husbands. It is important to recognize that this kind of activity was not simply the romantic day-dreaming common to all cultures and all time periods; five of these girls, remember, lived in two Village households—those of Samuel Parris and Thomas Putnam, Jr.—that were experiencing with particular intensity the consequences of social dislocation. The girls' divinations were a specific reaction to urgent fears which obsessed their own families and which to a degree preoccupied the entire community. After all, the identity of their future husbands—"what trade their sweethearts should be of"—would determine their own future status. And the girls' only recorded vision in their crystal ball was not of bright promise . . . but of death: "a specter in the shape of a coffin."

Death and social status. As 1692 wore on, the strange blending of these two preoccupations moved beyond girlish divinations to a far more serious plane. It is striking how many of the accused witches from the Salem Village area had careers which testified to the power of unfamiliar economic forces to alter and reshape a life. The accused were, in many cases, people who had not been born to their 1692 standing, high or low, but who had reached it through force of circumstance, in the course of lives characterized by economic as well as geographic flux. John Willard, Alexander Osborne, Daniel Andrew, and Rebecca Nurse, for example, were all outsiders who had moved both *in* and *up*.[28]

The career of Goody Nurse (who figured so prominently in the imagination of Ann Putnam, Sr.) offers a particularly apt illustration of this pattern. One of the eight children of William Towne of Topsfield who died intestate in 1672 leaving a "small estate,"

---

28. In 1681, "John Wilerd," whom we believe to be our man, was assessed in Groton, Mass., at 10/10 shillings, which placed him below the town average for that year—Greene, ed., *Early Records of Groton*, p. 66.

Rebecca had married Francis Nurse, an obscure Salem Town tray-maker who in 1678 became at one stroke a major Salem Village landowner by purchasing, on credit, a rich 300-acre farm located near the Salem Town line. Unlike Bray Wilkins, Francis Nurse paid off his mortgage right on schedule. His economic rise after 1678 is documented in the Village tax lists; his 1690 tax went up 39 percent from that of 1681, and in 1695 it rose by another 16 percent. The Nurses' eight sons and sons-in-law, settling on lands surrounding the home farm, were in a similar flourishing condition.[29]

But the best example of all, perhaps, is John Proctor, the fictionalized hero of Arthur Miller's 1953 play about Salem witchcraft, *The Crucible.*

John Proctor (Hanged, August 19, 1692)

We have already encountered John Proctor as an Ipswich Road tavern keeper, but this was only one of his economic interests. In 1692, at sixty years of age, Proctor was coming to the conclusion of a successful career shrewdly built upon the varied economic opportunities available in the fluid Essex County situation. A native of Ipswich, Massachusetts, Proctor first came into the Salem Village orbit in 1666 when, as a young man in his mid-thirties, he leased one of the largest farms of the area, "Groton," a 700-acre spread lying immediately southeast of the Village line. This large farm had been put together in the 1630's, through purchase and town grants, by Emmanuel Downing, one of the leading original members of the Massachusetts Bay Company and a brother-in-law of Governor John Winthrop. Establishing himself on these ample acres, Proctor devoted himself to farming while his wife and daughter conducted the tavern business.[30]

His interests diversified still further upon the death of his father, when he inherited a one-third share in an estate of more than £1,200, about 60 percent of which was in the form of "houses and lands" in Ipswich. While continuing to live at Groton he retained ownership of the Ipswich property, which he seems to have man-

29. Perley, *History of Salem*, II, 143 (Nurse genealogy); 2 *PR*, 358 (William Towne estate); Nevins, *Witchcraft in Salem Village*, p. 111 (Francis Nurse's residence in Salem Town, 1638–1678); Upham, *Salem Witchcraft*, I, 79–83; 2 Essex Deeds, 189 (the purchase of the farm in 1678); tax lists, Village Records, Dec. 27, 1681; Dec. 30, 1690; Jan. 18, 1695.

30. Perley, *History of Salem*, II, 19–24 (genealogy and purchase of "Groton"); 7 *EQC*, 135 (tavern).

aged essentially as an absentee landlord. Through these varied enterprises, John Proctor attained a notable level of prosperity. In 1711, when the Massachusetts General Court paid compensation to the families of the condemned witches of 1692, the sum paid to the heirs of John Proctor was £150, while the average for all the others was only £21. The regular renewal of Proctor's tavern license is another gauge of his status, for in seventeenth-century Salem this economic activity tended to be reserved for the elite. When Proctor was first granted his license in 1668, for example, the Town's eight licensed tavern keepers included William Browne, Sr., George Corwin, Walter Price, Henry Bartholomew, and Edmund Batter—all men of considerable prominence in the political and economic life of the community.[31] Significantly, though, in the county-court listing of the licencees for that year, Proctor's is the only name not prefixed either by the sparingly used honorific "Mr." or the militia rank "Captain"—a fact which neatly suggests his status as a rising aspirant not yet fully accepted into the social elite of Salem Town.

As a flourishing man of affairs, Proctor was equally at home in Boston, Salem Town, and Ipswich. He attended church in the Town, and in 1667, when seats were being assigned in the new meetinghouse, he was placed in the fourth row. (On the women's side, his wife was seated next to Rebecca Nurse.) In a legal document of 1689 relating to the disposition of his estate, the four "trusty and well-beloved friends" he named as trustees included one man from Concord, two from Salem Town—and Israel Porter of Salem Village.[32]

Through frequent trips to Ipswich to see after his properties there, Proctor maintained close ties with the leadership circles of that town. After his imprisonment in 1692, thirty-two Ipswich men, headed by the minister, John Wise, signed a petition "on be-

31. 2 *PR*, 315–316 (father's will and estate inventory); 305 County Court Records, 100–101; Woodward, *Records of Salem Witchcraft*, II, 228–230 (1711 settlement); 4 *EQC*, 85 (1668 list of tavern licensees). Some evidence exists that in their commercial dealings the Proctors were given to sharp if not illegal practices. In 1678 John Proctor was fined for selling liquor to the Indians, and his wife sometimes demanded personal possessions in lieu of cash payment for drinks. In 1692 one of the afflicted girls testified that the spectors of two recently deceased men had appeared to her and blamed their deaths on Elizabeth Proctor, the one because "they had some difference in a reckoning" and the other "because he had a pot of cider of her which he had not paid for"— 7 *EQC*, 135; Woodward, *Records of Salem Witchcraft*, I, 111–112.

32. 8 *EQC*, 204 (Boston dealings); Perley, *History of Salem*, II, 433 (1667 church seating); 8 Essex Deeds, 123.

half of our neighbors John Proctor and his wife, now in trouble and under suspicion of witchcraft." [33] (The phrase "our neighbors" is revealing, for Proctor had not, in fact, actually resided in Ipswich for twenty-five years.) The one community with which he seems to have had least contact was the one which lay nearest to him: Salem Village.

But susceptibility to accusation in 1692 was not limited to people who had been the beneficiaries of a changing market. As the following two cases reveal, those whom it had claimed as its victims were equally vulnerable.

Sarah Buckley (Acquitted, 1693)

"Bred up by Christian parents" who brought her from England to Ipswich, Massachusetts, when she was still a child, Sarah joined the Ipswich church around 1650. At about the same time she married a local yeoman, William Buckley. The couple later moved to the Marblehead section of Salem, where Goodman Buckley acquired land and where they lived for "many years." At the time of this move, Sarah transferred her membership to the church in Salem Town.[34]

But in their middle years, things began to fall apart for the Buckleys. In 1675 William Buckley was sued for debt by Simon Bradstreet, the governor of Massachusetts and a prominent Salemite, and when he proved unable to pay, his house and lands were seized. Soon afterwards, he appeared with his family in Salem Village, where he pursued the shoemaking trade. But still the family fortunes declined. In 1680 Buckley was sued for debts contracted by a renegade son, and this time a table and a chest (which may have included his cobbler's tools) were seized. He sold his plot of Village land the following year, evidently to stave off utter destitution, and thereafter the Buckleys made shift in the Village without owning either a house or land of their own.[35]

33. Petition reprinted in Upham, *Salem Witchcraft*, II, 305–306.
34. 135 Mass. Arch., 29 (deposition of William Hubbard, minister at Ipswich, June 20, 1692, including "bred up by Christian parents" quote), *ibid.*, 99 (deposition of John Higginson, minister at Salem Town, including "many years" quote); Perley, *History of Salem*, III, 62 (land in Marblehead); Joseph B. Felt, *History of Ipswich, Essex and Hamilton* (Cambridge, Mass., 1834), p. 99 (reference to William Buckley as a cordwainer in Ipswich in 1664).
35. 6 EQC, 49, 114 (the 1675 suit); Woodward, *Records of Salem Witchcraft*, II, 23 (Sarah Buckley arrest warrant, identifying her husband as a shoemaker);

Both Sarah Buckley and her daughter Mary Withridge, a young widow who had come back to live with her parents after her husband's death, were accused of witchcraft in 1692, and the two women spent eight months in prison before their acquittal early in 1693. The fervent testimonials on Sarah's behalf which her husband secured from ministers in Ipswich, Marblehead, and Salem Town—testimonies which called to memory the earlier, stabler period of her life—may have saved her. One last hears of the family in 1702, when the new Village minister, the Reverend Joseph Green, recorded in his diary the death of old William Buckley, in utter poverty and completely alone.[36]

Although Sarah Buckley's career had moved in the opposite direction from John Proctor's, it offered an equally vivid illustration of the roller-coaster transformations of status which were all too easy to experience in late seventeenth-century Essex County. And probably because of these very experiences, the Buckleys never set down any roots, familial or institutional, in Salem Village—a situation underscored by Sarah's failure (like Rebecca Nurse's) to transfer her church membership from Salem Town to Salem Village, and also by the fact that all three of her defenders in 1692 were outside ministers who had known her years earlier, before her humiliating move into Salem Village.

Sarah Good (Hanged, July 19, 1692)

Even more than Goodwife Buckley, Sarah Good was a woman whose life had been little more than a steady downward slide. Sarah was the daughter of John Solart, a well-to-do Wenham innkeeper who drowned himself in 1672 leaving an estate of over £500, including seventy-seven acres of land. After her father's suicide, however, Sarah's fortunes declined steadily. Her mother quickly remarried, and with her new husband she attempted to deprive her seven children of their rightful share of John Solart's estate. In 1682 these children petitioned the General Court for redress, emphasizing that Sarah in particular had been offered, as her portion, only a small parcel of land worth far less than the share to which she was entitled.[37]

7 *EQC*, 427 (1680 suit); Sidney Perley, "Part of Salem Village in 1700," 52 *EIHC* (April 1916), 180.

36. 6 *EQC*, 192 (Mary Withridge); Joseph Green diary entry, Jan. 2, 1702, "Diary of Rev. Joseph Green of Salem Village, Communicated by Samuel P. Fowler," 8 *EIHC* (1868), 220–221.

37. 2 *PR*, 283–285; 5 *EQC*, 89–90; 8 *ibid.*, 432–433.

Meanwhile Sarah Solart had married a penniless indentured servant, Daniel Poole, who soon died, leaving her saddled with his funeral expenses and other debts. In 1686 one of Poole's creditors filed suit against Sarah and her second husband, William Good (who is described variously as "weaver" and "laborer"). When they were unable to pay the court judgment of some £9, a portion of the land Sarah had finally inherited from her father's estate was seized and sold by the authorities. A few months later, the Goods, evidently now in dire need, sold off another tract of this land. Shortly thereafter, homeless and utterly destitute, they began to appear in Salem Village, begging for shelter and provisions from the householders. When it was pointed out in 1692 that Sarah Good never attended religious services in the Village, she responded that she had stayed away "for want of clothes." [38]

. . . and lacking in deference.

What seems particularly to have disturbed people about Sarah Good was not the fact that she was forced to live by begging, but rather the unpleasant manner in which she engaged in this pursuit. By common agreement, Sarah was sullen and ungrateful. On one occasion she visited Samuel Parris to solicit charity for her young daughter; when the minister gave her something, Sarah's only response (as Parris later told the authorities) was to walk off "muttering." When confronted with this story at her examination, she denied having muttered at Parris, claiming instead that she had merely "thanked him" for his gift. But Parris was by no means alone in his judgment; it was commonly remarked in Salem Village that the unhappy woman went away "muttering from persons' houses" after she approached them for favors. At the end of 1689, for instance, she had begged for lodging in the house of one Sarah Gadge. When Goodwife Gadge turned her away, Sarah immediately "fell to muttering and scolding extremely." Denied the same favor by Henry Herrick several months later, Sarah again "went away grumbling." [39]

But it was not only when people refused to offer her charity that

38. 35 County Court Records, 70–71 (the 1686 suit and land seizure); 8 Essex Deeds, 441; testimony of Samuel Abbey and wife in Woodward, *Records of Salem Witchcraft*, I, 24–25; WPA, II (Sarah's "for want of clothes" comment).

39. Examination of Sarah Good in Woodward, *Records of Salem Witchcraft*, I, 18–19; testimony of Henry Herrick and Sarah Gadge, *ibid.*, I, 25–26, 29.

Sarah Good reacted with hostility: she could be just as sharp-tongued, it seems, when she did receive a gift or favor—when she "muttered" her thanks to Samuel Parris, for example. As early as mid-1689, when Sarah and her husband were already "destitute of an house to dwell in," a Salem Villager named Samuel Abbey and his wife Mary "out of charity, they being poor, let them live in theirs some time." But Sarah Good was of "so turbulent a spirit, spiteful, and so maliciously bent," that after some months the Abbeys "could not suffer her to live in their house any longer," and so turned the impoverished couple out "for quietness' sake." Sarah's own husband, William Good, referred to his wife's "bad carriage" toward him, claiming at her examination that he was "afraid that she either was a witch, or would be one very quickly." And he added (presumably intending no pun) "I may say with tears that she is an enemy to all good."[40]

With Sarah Good, perhaps more clearly than with any other accused witch, it is possible to see how an abstraction like "economic mobility" could take its toll in human personality. If the woman had been *born* to the poverty she was forced to endure in her adulthood, it is unlikely that she would have acted as she did. (Nobody complained about the behavior of her husband William Good, who was, in fact, born into a poor family, and who was unfailingly abject in all his recorded encounters with authority.) In all the testimony about Sarah's "spiteful" attitude, one gets an almost palpable sense of the woman's shame, her shattered pride: to have come so low, to be forced to live by the charity of those on whom she had once been able to look down! Each time Sarah Good scolded her way through another humiliating encounter, she must have reminded her would-be benefactors, by the manner and perhaps even the substance of her muttered remarks, that she had not always been dependent on the likes of them. (Perhaps Sarah resented her low-born husband for the same reason—and let him know as much!) Wandering as she did from house to house in Salem Village, Sarah Good served as a constant reminder that social and economic security were precarious commodities in a world where it took only the death of one parent, and the remarriage of another, to destroy the prospects of a defenseless child. And by her defiant lack of deference, Sarah served as an equally disturbing

40. Testimony of Samuel Abbey and wife, *ibid.*, I, 24–25; examination of Sarah Good, *ibid.*, I, 19 (William Good's comment).

reminder of how easily such experiences could lead to the spiteful bitterness of a "turbulent spirit."

Job Tookey (Acquitted, January 1693)

An even more direct exemplar of the way falling social status could lead to turbulence of spirit, less poignant only for the fact that he was not executed in 1692, is Job Tookey, a laborer and sea-hand who lived over the Salem Village line in the town of Beverly. In the only extended autobiographical statement known to exist for any of the accused witches, Tookey compared his present "sad, miserable, and deplorable condition" (he was writing this back in 1682) with the station to which he had been born:

> [M]y education and bringing up . . . was to learning: my great-grandfather was a Doctor of Divinity in London in Queen Elizabeth's time and deceased there. My grandfather was minister of St. Ives Covell—known by the honored Governor Bradstreet, as his honor told me himself. . . . My father . . . and Mr. William Bridge preached twelve years together in the new church of Great Yarmouth.
> I being his eldest son, he did intend I should have been a minister, and in my thirteenth year of age [he] sent me to Emmanuel College in Cambridge, it being the same College he himself was brought up in. But the providence of God ordered it so [that] the times altering, I had been there but a fortnight before my father sent for me home and asked me if I was willing to go to London to be an apprentice. My answer was that I was willing to submit to his pleasure; whereupon he sent me to London, and I was bound an apprentice to a wholesale grocer in Cheapside. But I had not been an apprentice much above a year before the chiefest part of the city was burnt; my master sustaining thereby so great a loss . . . [that he] was not able to set up his trade again. Whereupon I, being very young, desired my father, if he pleased, that he would give his consent that I might go to sea; which request of mine . . . he consented unto, and bound me an apprentice for three years to Capt. Samuel Scarlet of Boston, to serve to the sea.[41]

Tookey served his three years apprenticeship, but he continued to meet with a series of misfortunes, including an accident which severly injured his right hand and rendered him temporarily un-employable—"not being able to use one of my fingers in six months

41. Deposition of Job Tookey, June 1682, 8 *EQC*, 336–337.

time." At this point a Marblehead physician, merchant, and ship-owner named Richard Knott offered to pay the debts Tookey had accumulated during his convalescence in return for his services as deck-hand. Tookey accepted, and early in 1682 he worked briefly for Knott. But the two men took an intense dislike to each other—Knott accused his laborer of being lazy and defiant—and when Tookey refused to continue in Knott's employ, Knott had him jailed.[42]

During the three months of Tookey's imprisonment, from March through June, 1682, Knott engaged in a vindictive campaign to break his proud spirit and shame him into the deference he had refused to display. On periodic visits to the prison he rejected Tookey's emotional requests for his clothing and books, "reviled and railed" at him, and actually threatened to obtain the permission of the court to sell Tookey into slavery in Virginia or Barbados. On June 16, as Tookey reported, Knott approachd the prison "and called to me, saying 'Job, Job'; whereupon I looked out of the prison window and saw him scrape with his stick upon the ground. 'Job,' says he, 'do you know what this means?' I answered him 'No.' 'Oh,' says he, 'Sirrah, you are like to learn how to hoe in Virginia!'" Obviously aware of Tookey's pride in his family background, Knott tried yet another tack: insulting the prisoner's clergyman-father, "telling . . . me that he had better at home to wipe his shoes than ever my father was, for he said he was an anabaptistical quaking rogue that for his maintenance went up and down England to delude souls for the Devil." Cut to the quick, Tookey was prompted by this into an impassioned defense of his father, neither an anabaptist nor a Quaker, but "well known to be a religious Godly man by several good Godly people in New England . . . [including] a great many scholars of Cambridge, which bought several of the books pertaining to my father's library." Everywhere in these petitions it is plain that for Job Tookey, the discomfort and humiliation of imprisonment were intensified by the memory of those high expectations with which he had begun his career: "[C]onsider, I beseech you, my education and bringing-up, which never was in being used to a jail . . . [where I am] almost poisoned with the stink of my own dung. . . ."[43]

When the court actually met at the end of June 1682 Dr. Knott withdrew his charges and Job went free. But a decade later he was

43. *Ibid.*, 336, 334, 335.
42. *Ibid.*, 337, 330–331, 333.

still a poor laborer in Beverly, still antagonizing people by his manner, and still preoccupied by questions of status. All these elements converged in his dangerous boast, reported at his witch-craft examination in the summer of 1692, "that he was not the Devil's servant, but the Devil was his." [44] (Were memories of Dr. Knott, and perhaps others like him, still rankling?)

At Tookey's examination, Mary Warren, herself the servant of accused wizard John Proctor, saw eight of Tookey's murder victims —"three men, and three women, and two children . . . , all in their winding sheets." Said she: "[T]hey look pale upon us, but red upon Tookey—red as blood." Other specters, too, "rose from the dead," reported Ann Putnam, Jr., "and cried 'Vengeance! Vengeance!' " [45] Vengeance, of course, was precisely what must have been on Tookey's own mind—not to mention that of Ann Putnam and her family. Like Sarah Good's "turbulent spirit," vengeance was a volatile obsession in late-seventeenth-century Salem Village, and both Job Tookey and Sarah Good were its ironic victims.

As early as 1689, in his *Memorable Providences Relating to Witchcrafts and Possessions*, Cotton Mather had urged his readers to "shun a frame of discontent" if they wished to avoid becoming witches: "When persons through discontent at their *poverty*, or at their *misery*, shall be always murmuring and repining at the provi-dence of God, the Devils do then invite them to an agreement . . . , [and d]ownright *witchcraft* is the upshot of it." [46]

From the perspective of those who led the attack in 1692, such an analysis might have seemed to explain not only disruptive mal-contents at the lower end of the scale—people like Job Tookey and Sarah Good—but also prospering and upwardly mobile people like John Proctor, John Willard, and Rebecca Nurse. There were, after all, various ways to betray "discontent" with one's natural station: one could turn embittered and spiteful, to be sure; but on the other hand, like the young Proctor and Nurse, one might combine aggres-sive behavior with good fortune and improve one's status. From a seventeenth century viewpoint, swift economic rise was just as tangible an expression of "discontent" as was muttering or com-plaining.

44. Upham, *Salem Witchcraft*, II, 223.
45. *Ibid.*, II, 223–224.
46. Cotton Mather, "A Discourse on Witchcraft" in *Memorable Providences Relating to Witchcrafts and Possessions* (Boston, 1689), p. 23. Italics in original.

Everybody knew that by 1692 John Proctor was wealthier than any of his accusers, yet they also knew that he remained "Goodman" Proctor while Thomas Putnam, by virtue of his father's station, bore the more honorific designation "Mr. Putnam." As Abigail Williams cried out during a spectral visitation in mid-April, running down a list of newly accused witches: "Oh yonder is Goodman Proctor and his wife and Goody Nurse and Goody Cory and Goody Cloyse!" (Abigail's own uncle may not have been receiving his salary at the time, but he was nevertheless "Mr. Parris.") And at the witchcraft examination of Mary Clarke of Haverhill, young Ann Putnam commented sarcastically that even though the accused woman was now addressed as "Mistress Mary Clarke," Ann well knew "that people used to call her Goody Clarke." [47]

All of these people were on the move, socially and economically. Yet to many New Englanders of the seventeenth century, the stability of the social order rested on the willingness of everyone to accept his given station in life. Refusal to do so was more than a personal weakness; it represented a tangible threat to the social fabric itself. When Cotton Mather preached a sermon in 1689 in response to a Boston witchcraft case of that year, he chose a Biblical text which made this very point: *Rebellion is as the sin of witchcraft.* The rebellion Mather had in mind here was surely not the political sort—not in the very year that he had supported the successful overthrow of Governor Andros!—but the even more menacing variety implicit in both the spiteful turbulence of those who were sliding down the social ladder and the pushy restlessness of those who were climbing up. The feeling that Mather articulated in this 1689 sermon was one shared by many people in Salem Village three years later: the social order was being profoundly shaken by a superhuman force which had lured all too many into active complicity with it. We have chosen to construe this force as emergent mercantile capitalism. Mather, and Salem Village, called it witchcraft.

The Lure of Madame Bubble

But it was not only the accused witches who were tempted into complicity with the forces of change. We have over and over again

---

47. Woodward, *Records of Salem Witchcraft*, I, 65 (Abigail Williams); WPA, I (Examination of Mary Clarke, Aug. 4, 1692). Italics added.

stressed the conflicting emotions most Salem Villagers must have felt as they witnessed the transformation of Salem Town into a major commercial center, and as they saw an altered social and economic order beginning to take shape. The witchcraft testimony itself makes plain that even those who felt most uneasy about those developments were also deeply attracted by them. For one of Satan's most insidious guises in Salem Village during 1692 was that of thriving freeholder and prosperous merchant, and the afflicted girls of the Village acknowledged the persuasiveness of his blandishments by the very desperation with which they rebuffed him.

Often, to be sure, the strength of Satan's position in this bargaining lay solely in the threat of physical harm if the person he was recruiting refused to accept the contract he had to offer—usually, indeed, a literal contract, the parody of a church covenant. The Salem merchant Phillip English, for example, appeared spectrally to Susannah Sheldon, "and told me if I would touch his book, he would not bite me, but if I refused, then he did [sic] bite me." [48] The historian John Demos has recently emphasized the frequent references to such overtly aggressive behavior in the witchcraft testimony—the biting, choking, and pinching. But, as Demos also notes, there are other instances in which the aggression takes the more subtle form of wheedling through glittering promises of material gain and economic betterment. [49] The confessions which detailed these promises are at times poignant in their specificity: "new clothes," "a piece of money," "a pair of French fall shoes." Early in April, 1692, Satan appeared spectrally to Mercy Lewis, who worked in the household of Thomas Putnam, and offered her "gold and many fine things" if she would write in his book. A few weeks later Satan revisited young Mercy, this time in the form of Samuel Parris's unhappy predecessor in the Village pulpit, George Burroughs: "Mr. Burroughs carried me up to an exceeding high mountain and showed me all the kingdoms of the earth, and told me that he would give them all to me if I would write in his book." Parris's own servant girl, Abigail Williams, reported that she was "tempted by the offer of fine things." And his daughter Elizabeth Parris was promised by Satan that he would let her "go to a Golden City" if she would accept his rule. [50]

---

48. Woodward, *Records of Salem Witchcraft*, I, 169.
49. John Demos, "Underlying Themes in the Witchcraft of Seventeenth Century New England," 75 *American Historical Review* (1970), 1311–1326, esp. 1320–1322.
50. WPA, II (Examinations of Stephen Johnson—"French fall shoes") and

If "Satan," indeed, represented, at one level of consciousness, the forces of social change, it is appropriate that the afflicted girls should have found him simultaneously frightening and alluring; for that is also how they, and many of their elders, felt about the world they knew. This doubleness pervades the testimony of 1692 just as it pervades so much of the history of Salem Village. And it is precisely this doubleness which drove the witchcraft outbreak to its point of maximum psychological complexity.

For while the accusations thrust outward to draw in wealthy merchants and other ostentatious representatives of the new order —attempting thereby to affirm the externality of the menace—they simultaneously spiraled back toward the accusers themselves, until finally the distinction between accuser and accused, between afflicter and afflicted, threatened to vanish. Margaret Jacobs, an accuser of George Burroughs as well as of her own grandfather, George Jacobs, Sr., abjectly confessed to her own wickedness of heart after the two men had been executed. Deliverance Hobbs, a middle-aged woman who had for a time been afflicted, was herself on the examination stand by late April, accused of witchcraft: "Is it not a solemn thing, that last Lord's Day you were tormented, and now you are become a tormenter, so that you have changed sides? How comes this to pass?" When the tables were similarly turned upon Mary Warren, one of the principal afflicted girls, her examiner reiterated the same question: "You were a little while ago an afflicted person. Now you are an afflicter. How comes this to pass?" [51] One young woman charged with witchcraft, Sarah Cole of Lynn, was accused by the girls of the very act in which they themselves had engaged: fortune-telling.[52] Yet Sarah Cole was arrested as a witch, while Ann Putnam and Abigail Williams were called the innocent victims of her witchcraft.

Indeed, if Samuel Parris himself had not been so skilled in the

Richard Carrier ("new clothes"); Woodward, *Records of Salem Witchcraft*, I, 277 (Susannah Sheldon—"a piece of money"); *ibid.*, I, 264 and II, 118 (Mercy Lewis); *ibid.*, I, 106 (Abigail Williams); Deodat Lawson, *A Brief and True Narrative of Some Remarkable Passages Relating to Sundry Persons Afflicted by Witchcraft, at Salem Village Which Happened From the Nineteenth of March, to the Fifth of April, 1692* (Boston, 1692), in Burr, *Narratives*, p. 160 (Elizabeth Parris). See also examination of Abigail Hobbs, April 19, 1692, WPA, II.

51. Margaret Jacobs to George Jacobs, Jr., in Calef, *More Wonders of the Invisible World*, in Burr, *Narratives*, pp. 365–366; Woodward, *Records of Salem Witchcraft*, II, 188 (Deliverance Hobbs' examination); I, 120 (Mary Warren's examination).

52. Examination of Sarah Cole, WPA, I.

pulpit, it is not difficult to imagine that he, rather than George Burroughs, might have been the man finally pinpointed as the wizard masterminding the betrayal of the Village. Certainly Parris's behavior, far more than that of Burroughs, closely fit the pattern which Parris himself had described as clear proof of demonic possession. Burroughs may, in fact, have been a kind of surrogate for Parris: a substitute whose trial and execution helped Parris preserve both his ease of conscience and his continued immunity to accusation.[53]

How many other Salem Villagers had their own "George Burroughs"—a person they accused in an effort to expunge from their minds the suspicion that the real "guilt" was their own? A recent historian of sixteenth and seventeenth century witchcraft in Essex County, England, Alan Macfarlane, has concluded that some such process may have been what triggered many of the accusations there. Macfarlane notes how frequently the accused witch was a person whose neighbors had earlier denied him or her some requested favor or service, and he suggests that it was the accusers' sense of guilt over their own failures of neighborliness which underlay the accusations. He further hypothesizes that such outbreaks tended to occur (given a prevailing belief in witchcraft) when the evolution from a communal to an individualistic ethic reached a critical stage in a given locality. (Developments in the weaving industry had brought such a change early to this region of England.) Before the critical stage was reached, the peasant ethic of mutual interdependence remained strong: after it had been passed, erstwhile neighbors found themselves "far enough apart, so to speak, to be able to hate each other without repercussions on the mystical plane."[54]

For Salem Village (to apply Macfarlane's formula), the critical stage came in the 1690's, and the Villagers lashed out with accusations not only against those who seemed in one way or another to represent the new order, but also against those who reminded them how far they, themselves, had already been seduced from their

53. Indeed, the anti-Parris tract "handed about" the Village, apparently somewhat clandestinely, in the period just after the witchcraft episode (see chap. 3, note 30), actually did accuse Parris of having sought information from the devil through the intermediary of Abigail Williams. It concluded with a reminder that King Saul had been put to death for heeding the Witch of Endor.

54. Alan Macfarlane, *Witchcraft in Tudor and Stuart England* (New York, Harper and Row, 1970), pp. 158–164, 192–206, quoted passage on p. 202.

traditional moorings. In justifying their refusal to help the desperately poor Sarah Good, for instance, the people with whom she had sought shelter offered a variety of explanations. Samuel Abbey turned her out of his house in the winter of 1690 "for quietness' sake"; Sarah Gadge "was afraid she had been with them that had the smallpox"; Henry Herrick drove her from his place "lest she should lie in the barn, and by smoking of her pipe should fire the barn."[55] In their very profusion, such excuses reveal the guilt which these farmers—themselves not so very much more certain of their livelihood than Sarah Good—must have experienced at their failure to respond to the homeless woman's plight.

Ultimately, then, Salem witchcraft, by reducing real human beings to a single set of threatening impulses and temptations which they seemed to embody, was a kind of allegory-in-reverse. Self-purgation through allegorical projection: this was hardly a style of thinking alien to the late-seventeenth-century Puritan mind. Take, for instance, John Bunyan's classic account of one man's journey toward holiness, *The Pilgrim's Progress*. As Bunyan's Pilgrim (his name is "Christian") makes his precarious way from the City of Destruction to the Celestial City, he is beset by a whole bevy of inner temptations which take human form: "Mr. Worldly Wiseman," "Mr. Money-Love," and the like. (It is intriguing that many of these characters—but not Christian himself—are of high social station, as their honorific titles suggest.)

One of Bunyan's allegorical characters, as it turns out, is a witch: her name is "Madame Bubble," and Christian meets her in a mysterious, foggy region called the Enchanted Ground. She, too, is of high social station—a "gentlewoman," Bunyan insists. Her clothes are "very pleasant," she loves "banqueting and feasting," and she always speaks "smoothly" with "a smile at the end of a sentence." Madame Bubble is constantly fingering the gold in her "great purse" and is most at ease with those who are "cunning to get money." She is, in short, an especially seductive personification of the interwoven appeal of wealth, sensual pleasure, and worldly sophistication. Madame Bubble promises to make "great and happy" anyone who will follow her, and Christian—rough-hewn, earnest, and sturdy though he may be—is powerfully tempted to do so. Only his companion Great Heart is able to fortify him against her blandishments. Not only will Madame Bubble lead a man to eternal damnation, Great Heart warns the Pilgrim, but she

55. See above, notes 39 and 40.

will accomplish this by wreaking havoc with his social and psychological equilibrium on this earth:

> 'Twas she that set Absolom against his father, and Jereboam against his master. 'Twas she that persuaded Judas to sell his Lord . . . ; none can tell of the mischief that she doth. She makes variance betwixt rulers and subjects, betwixt parents and children, 'twixt neighbour and neighbour, 'twixt a man and his wife, 'twixt a man and himself, 'twixt the flesh and the heart.[56]

Underscoring the characterization with which Bunyan had introduced Madame Bubble, Great Heart sums up in a word the perpetrator of all these disorders: "This woman is a witch."[57]

Madame Bubble appears in the second part of *The Pilgrim's Progress*, published just eight years before the Salem witchcraft outbreak. In creating this character (and giving her a name which would soon be applied to any alluring but unsound speculative venture, such as the "South-Sea Bubble" of 1720), John Bunyan offered a vivid and somber warning against the commercial attractions which were enticing a great many Puritans—in Salem Village no less than in Restoration England—as the seventeenth century drew to a close.

As the witchcraft outbreak gained momentum, the accusers were thus compelled to face the possibility that they were themselves being transformed by the forces of change that were buffeting Salem Village. And so if the entire episode were not simply to result in a heightening of frustration and guilt, it had to include a mechanism for self-purgation as well as for self-definition. And, indeed, it did.

This mechanism was not, as one might expect, execution; it was *public confession*. Many of the accused witches acknowledged, under varying degrees of pressure, that they had joined the forces of the enemy. Indeed, they often added colorful bits of corroboratory detail. Nor should this fact seem strange to us, for public confession was a familiar, even routine, procedure in seventeenth-century New England. In many situations, indeed, it was not so much a prelude to further legal action as a social ritual which, at its

---

56. John Bunyan, *The Pilgrim's Progress From This World to That Which Is to Come* (Part II, London, 1684), ed. James Blanton Wharey; second edn. edited by Roger Sharrock (Oxford, Oxford University Press, 1960), pp. 300, 301, 302–303.

57. *Ibid.*, p. 301.

most effective, could by itself encompass what a later age would separate into three distinct steps: conviction, punishment, and rehabilitation. Public confession—the attendance of the community was crucial—was a ceremony through which a deviant individual might be transformed, forgiven, and reintegrated into the community.

The offense of witchcraft was certainly too serious to permit confession alone to stand for justice. Still, whenever it was possible in 1692—whenever an accused witch confessed in the course of the public examination—this ritual was attempted, and it seems to have had some temporary therapeutic value for everybody concerned. After Rebecca Eames confessed that she had been afflicting Mary Warren and Mary Lacey, for example, she "was bid to take [them] . . . by the hand and beg forgiveness, and did so, and they forgave her." [58]

In 1692, if we are correct, this familiar ritual would have taken on a particular resonance for the accusers and on-lookers, since the confession they had drawn from the mouths of the accused was surely one that on some level they themselves longed to make. By first projecting upon others the unacknowledged impulses which lay within themselves, and then absolving those they had accused, the accusers could bring such impulses into the open, gain at least temporary mastery over them, and thereby affirm their commitment to social values in which they very much wanted to believe. It is surely no coincidence that not one of the confessing witches was hanged.

If all or even most of the first group of accused "witches"—the first half-dozen, perhaps, or even the initial group of three—had played the roles required of them, it might have worked. If they had, indeed, confessed and taken upon themselves the collective guilt of the community, it is just possible that the outbreak would have come to a stop right there, fulfilled in its purpose.

This is very nearly what did happen more than a generation later in the episode which we introduced at the very beginning of our study to provide a new perspective on Salem witchcraft: the Great Awakening of the 1730's and 1740's. For in this massive outbreak of religious revivalism, the ambiguity which underlay the process of accusation in 1692 became open, even ritualized. In the Great Awakening, people accused *themselves* of corruption as

58. WPA, II. For other examples see *ibid.* (examination of Richard Carrier) and WPA, III (examination of Susannah Post).

passionately as they accused others, even including "worldly" ministers and secular leaders. Indeed, the accusations turned outward only against those who failed to accuse themselves first, so that public confession became a way of forestalling accusations by others. Perhaps because accusation and confession were so intimately linked, the Great Awakening generated neither trials nor executions—and occasionally it did succeed in reintegrating the afflicted communities which it touched.[59]

But in 1692, of course, events instead slipped downward into shuddering disaster. Some of the accused would not confess to deeds they knew they had not committed, and for their honesty, they died. The ironies are staggering. In this act of collective expiation aimed at affirming a social order based on stability and reciprocal loyalty, the only participants to suffer death were those who insisted on remaining faithful to the essential requirement for stable social relationships: simple honesty. And the event which might have brought a kind of peace to Salem Village brought instead a period of conflict so bitter that even the generation of struggle that had led up to 1692 paled by comparison. The pin that was to have pricked Madame Bubble had somehow turned into a flailing, bloody sword.

59. For an analysis of the liberating function of self-accusation in the Great Awakening, see Richard L. Bushman, From Puritan to Yankee: Character and the Social Order in Connecticut, 1690–1765 (Cambridge, Harvard University Press, 1967), pp. 187–195. In a provocative essay published just as this book went to press ("Social Change and the Meaning of the American Revolution," Journal of Social History, Summer 1973, pp. 403–439), Kenneth A. Lockridge, without specifically treating the Salem witch trials, does provide the basis for a connection between 1692 and the Great Awakening (as well as the American Revolution) similar to the one we have proposed. In the half century from 1720 to 1770, Lockridge conjectures, the kinds of social and economic changes we have discussed in this book—population and land pressures, concentrations of wealth, social differentiation, commercial dependence—increasingly impinged upon the consciousness of large numbers of Americans, creating "an agitated conviction that a good, simple, unified world was giving way to an evil, complex, selfish world under the impact of incomprehensible forces," and helping fuel large-scale efforts (such as the Awakening and the Revolution) to purge threatening forces and "restore the isolation, independence, and homogeneity of the real and imagined past" (p. 424). These changes were, of course, already astir in particular places by the late seventeenth century, and, if we are correct, nowhere more vigorously than in Salem Village.

Epilogue: To the Eighteenth Century

For years, Salem Village remained a little jumpy. On several occasions in the early 1700's the minister found it necessary to preach against divination. In 1702 the gruesome story went about that a young man (a Porter, as it happens) who had abandoned the Village to go to sea had been murdered and eaten by his shipmates. (The truth was less lurid: the unfortunate man had simply died and been buried at sea.) In March 1700 a rumor swept the Village that "a considerable quantity of something like brimstone" had fallen upon Salem Town.[1] Wishful thinking, perhaps.

But despite such evidence of continuing touchiness, these isolated flare-ups remained just that. Perhaps this descent from the emotional heights of the 1690's needs no more explanation than the return of normal weather after a hurricane, but one must nevertheless note the important role played by Parris's successor in helping the Village come to terms with itself. Fresh out of Harvard College, Joseph Green had just turned twenty-two when he arrived in Salem Village late in 1697. The Village was taking a chance on such a youth, of course, but more experienced ministers were not clamoring to move into the parsonage Samuel Parris had finally vacated.

1. The Reverend Joseph Green, diary entries, March 30, 1700, and June 12 and Nov. 7, 1702, in "Diary of Rev. Joseph Green of Salem Village, Communicated by Samuel P. Fowler," 8 *EIHC* (1866), 217, 221. Green's diary was printed in the following: 8 *EIHC* (1866), 215–224; 10 *EIHC* (1869), 73–104; and 36 *EIHC* (1900), 323–330.

As it turned out, Green proved a remarkably happy choice. By temperament and background he was ideally suited to help diffuse the factional divisions within the Village and to prepare the Villagers to accept those social and economic changes from which many of them had tried to turn away. Low-keyed, gregarious, and worldly, Green was not unduly preoccupied with religious or ideological issues. In his younger years it had been different; his early commonplace book and diary are filled with what his one biographer calls "agonized religious strivings."[2] A generation earlier, those strivings might have lasted till death; but for Green, as for other people of his time (even other ministers) they were now compressed into a relatively brief, intensive stage of personal development—a stage which in another two hundred years would be called "adolescence." (He had been sixteen in 1692, just about the age of the afflicted girls.) By the time Green arrived in Salem Village, he much preferred hunting and fishing with his small sons to religious introspection. "I killed eighteen pigeons at one shot," he boasted in his diary at one point.[3] Like so many other men of the eighteenth century, he was fascinated by the diversity and wonder of the natural world: rainbows, frogs, insects, bird songs—all find a place in his eclectic journal.

Unlike Samuel Parris, for whom disputation and controversy were meat and drink, Green hated a quarrel and knew how to sidestep one. On one occasion, when he felt that the inhabitants had dealt "unkindly" with him at the Village meeting, he simply decided to stay away from such events for a while.[4] (As a man of independent means, he could afford to be understanding in the matter of his salary.) Again in contrast to Parris, who used the church as a sounding board for his own resentments and obsessions, Green consciously separated his public and private roles—by keeping a personal diary distinct from the church records, for example. He was thus able to depersonalize political issues by depersonalizing his own involvement in them.

Joseph Green quickly made clear his belief that the witchcraft episode had been an unfortunate aberration, the sooner forgotten the better. Two weeks after his ordination he proposed that the

---

2. John Langdon Sibley, *Biographical Sketches of Graduates of Harvard University*, 4 vols. (Cambridge, Mass., 1873–1885), IV, 228–233, quoted passage on p. 232.

3. Diary entry, August 20, 1708, 10 *EIHC* (1869), 80.

4. *Ibid.*, March 11, 1703, 8 *EIHC* (1866), 222. See also Charles W. Upham, *Salem Witchcraft*, 2 vols. (Boston, 1867), II, 508.

church initiate steps of reconciliation toward the "dissenting brethren," and within a few months they were again taking communion. In 1699 he reseated the meetinghouse, systematically placing Putnams and Nurses on the same benches. By 1701 the Village felt strong enough to undertake the construction of a new and larger meetinghouse. Two years later, Green raised before the church the most sensitive issue imaginable: the excommunication of Martha Cory in 1692, shortly before her execution for witchcraft. His presentation was pure Green. He hadn't known the woman in question, he said, and he really didn't know much about the situation in those days, but people seemed generally agreed that "errors" had occurred, and perhaps the church would like to reconsider its action. A week later the church did, indeed, vote to rescind Goodwife Cory's excommunication, although with "six or seven" unnamed members dissenting.[5]

The reduction of factional conflict in the Village was also furthered by the emergence of two additional parishes—"Middle" (1710) and "Rial Side" (1713)—in the area between Salem Town and Salem Village.[6] These two new parishes not only created a buffer between Town and Village, but they incorporated within their bounds some of those eastern parts of the Village which had been such hotbeds of anti-Parris sentiment. The "reconciliation" of the Village was thus achieved, in part, simply by giving institutional expression to the fragmentation which had occurred. Joseph Green, valuing tranquility above all, actively supported the emergence of the two new parishes.

With the divisions of the 1690's safely buried, Green turned his attention to devising civic projects to which no reasonable person could well object. In March 1708, having first prepared the way informally, he proposed to the Village meeting the building of a school and the hiring of a person "to teach their children to read and write and cypher and everything that is good." "Many commended the design," Green noted, "and none objected against it."[7] Within three days the pastor himself was busy collecting timber for the new schoolhouse. Another of his projects had to do with the Village poor. Under his leadership, the Villagers began to collect an annual Thanksgiving offering for distribution to the needy.[8]

5. *Ibid.*, II, 506–507.
6. Sidney Perley, *The History of Salem, Mass.*, 3 vols. (Salem, 1924–1928), III, 388–390; 399–401.
7. Diary entry, March 22, 1708, 10 *EIHC* (1869), 78–79.
8. Diary entry, Dec. 29, 1707, 10 *EIHC* (1869), 77.

(Among the first beneficiaries was William Good, husband of Sarah Good, whose mean-spirited begging had so disturbed the Village fifteen years earlier.) With these two strokes—the founding of the school and the systematization of charity—Green had moved to bring under institutional control two social groups whose ill-defined status had contributed so significantly to the breakdown of 1692: young people and indigents.

Having learned all-too-vividly what could happen in a community whose minister overreached himself, Green gracefully adjusted to a far more circumscribed sphere. Indeed, by a series of seemingly small actions, he had sketched in the outlines of a somewhat new social role for the beleaguered New England cleric: not as an unquestioned authority to whom automatic obedience was due, not as the jealous protector of his community from ideological contamination, and not even as leader of a church faction in local squabbles, but rather as a "non-partisan" counterweight to the forces of factionalism and as the champion of unassailably beneficial (and noncontroversial) projects for the social good.

Joseph Green also played a strategic role in helping reshape the Village's response to the world beyond. The minister himself accepted wholeheartedly the emerging world of eighteenth-century Boston and Salem—urbane, commercial, secular—and he helped the farmers of Salem Village accept that world as well. While he obviously enjoyed at least gentleman farming—his diary is full of references to planting peas, making preserves, and brewing beer—he was also caught up in the broader social currents of the province. Unlike Samuel Parris, his roots lay deep in Massachusetts. He and his wife were constantly visiting, and being visited by, friends in Salem, Boston, and his native Cambridge. His diary enthusiastically records dinners with the governor, the president of Harvard College, the gentlemen of the Court of Assistants, college classmates, and fellow ministers from other towns; "the most genteel dinner and attendance that I ever saw," runs a typical entry.[9]

Green died in 1715, at forty. In the church record, the aging Deacon Edward Putnam entered a tribute to him, at once genuinely sorrowful and self-consciously "literary," as "the choicest flower

9. Diary entry, Sept. 30, 1700, 8 *EIHC* (1866), 219. Compare Perry Miller's discussion of Green's very close contemporary, the Boston minister Benjamin Colman, as a representative of the "enlarged catholic spirit" that was beginning to appear among the New England clergy at the turn of the eighteenth century. Perry Miller, *The New England Mind: From Colony to Province* (Cambridge, Harvard University Press, 1953), pp. 254, 269–274.

and greenest olive-tree in the garden of our Lord here cut down in its prime and flourishing estate." His widow soon married into the Brattle family of Cambridge, which included some of the leading merchants and political figures of the province.[10]

To be sure, Joseph Green had helped bring Salem Village back to "normal." During his years in the Village the fires which had flared up in the 1690's were safely banked; perhaps they had burned out altogether. But all this did not come about without a price. One senses in the Salem Villagers of the early eighteenth century—most vividly, of course, in the contrasting personalities of Parris and Green—a diminution of spirit, an abandonment of the effort to shape and control their world. "Salem Town" had emerged victorious in the shadowy struggle with "Salem Village." Only in a narrow political sense did the Village achieve its independence. In its larger effort, to stave off the powerful economic and social forces which were transforming New England in these years, Salem Village was defeated.

In 1702, ten years after the events which have mainly concerned us, Bray Wilkins died quietly at the age of ninety-two. The commercial dreams of his middle years had long since vanished; even the events of 1692, perhaps, had begun to fade. Recording the event in his diary, the Reverend Green struck an elegiac note: "He lived to a good old age, and saw his children's children, and their children, and peace upon our little Israel."[11]

From one angle, of course, these mellow words were accurate enough; but would Bray Wilkins himself have found them entirely fitting? It may be questioned whether Bray's old age was so very good; along with his health, it had drained him of his prosperity and the affection of at least one branch of his numerous family. It is true that he lived to see his children's children grow up and marry, but he also saw the husband of one of them hanged as a wizard—and at his own behest. And while peace may have descended at last on the "little Israel" of Salem Village, we can wonder how satisfying, for old Bray Wilkins, that peace could have tasted.

But, after all, it was Joseph Green who had the last word—and it was to him that the new century belonged.

10. Upham, *Salem Witchcraft*, II, 512; Perley, *History of Salem*, III, 361, 411–413.
11. Diary entry, Jan. 1, 1702, 8 *EIHC* (1866), 220.

Index

Abbreviations used in the Index:

Parris = Reverend Samuel Parris
S.T.   = Salem Town
S.V.   = Salem Village
w.   = witch, witches, wizard, or witchcraft

Abbey, Mary (wife of Samuel), 14 n.33, 15
Abbey, Samuel, 14 n.33, 15, 204, 205, 213
Afflicted girls, 1–5, 9, 15–16, 23–25, 27–30, 145, 218, 220; residence of, 35 n.26; accusations by, 33, 188, 191. *See also* Witchcraft, *in Salem Village*; Fortune telling; entries under individual girls' names
Alden, Capt. John (accused w.), 15 n.37, 32, 33
Allen, Rev. James, 72
Andover (Mass.), 33, 44, 91, 98 n.27, 190
Amherst (Mass.), 52 n.22
Amherst (N.H.), 91 n.21
Andrew, Daniel (accused w.), 57, 65, 95 (map), 120–122, 130 (chart), 131, 132, 138; marriage, 113, 121;

accused of w., 132, 181–182, 187; and anti-Parris faction, 139, 149, 184; testimony *vs.* Parris (1697), 161; uncertain social status, 187; as S.V. "outsider," 192; mentioned, 180, 190, 199
Andrew, Sarah (Porter), 113, 121
Andros, Sir Edmund, 61, 209
Anti-Parris faction. *See* Salem Village, factional divisions (narrative and analysis)

Bailyn, Bernard, 53 n.23, 106
Baker, Thomas, 124, 126
Balch, Elizabeth, 12 n.29
Ballard, Joseph, 190 n.12
Barker, William, 189
Barbados, 117, 154–155
Bartholomew, Henry, 201
Bartlet, Phebe, 28, 30
Bassett, Sarah (accused w.), 184
Batter, Edmund, 201
Bayley, Rev. James, 45–54, 79; mentioned, 119. *See also* Salem Village, factional divisions (narrative and analysis)
Bayley, Joseph, 102